AN
INNOCENT
ABROAD

Life-changing trips from 35 great writers

JAN   2015

Published by
Lonely Planet Publications

HEAD OFFICE
90 Maribyrnong Street, Footscray, Victoria, 3011, Australia
BRANCHES
150 Linden Street, Oakland CA 94607, USA
201 Wood Ln, London, W12 7TQ, United Kingdom
PUBLISHED 2014
Printed by Hang Tai Printing Company, Hong Kong
Printed in China

Edited by Don George & Samantha Forge
Project managed by Robin Barton
Cover design by Daniel Tucker
Design and layout by Daniel Tucker & Laura Jane

National Library of Australia Cataloguing-in-Publication entry
An Innocent Abroad: Life-changing Trips from 35 Great Writers
Edited by Don George
1st Editon
978 1 74360 360 4 (pbk.)

Cover photographs: Brandon Tabiolo/Design Pics/Corbis ©; Jane Sweeney/JAI/
Corbis ©; Barga, Tuscany, Italy, 2/Robert Harding/Ocean/Corbis ©;
David Noton ©; pkripper503/iStock ©; Pietro Canali/SOPA RF/SOPA/Corbis ©;
Simon Winchester ©; Image Source/Corbis ©

MIX
Paper from
responsible sources
FSC
www.fsc.org
FSC™ C021741

Paper in this book is certified
against the Forest Stewardship
Council™ standards. FSC™ promotes
environmentally responsible, socially
beneficial and economically viable
management of the world's forests.

AN INNOCENT ABROAD

Life-changing trips from 35 great writers

Edited by Don George

Lonely Planet Publications
Melbourne · Oakland · London

Contents

Introduction

Don George

Ilost my innocence in France. I went to live in Paris right after graduating from Princeton, following in the footsteps of F. Scott Fitzgerald, or so I fancied, and within two weeks I had fallen head over heels for a 22-year-old jeune fille from Grasse, who exuded a Provençal perfume of sunshine and *sexualité*.

A *jeune américain* unwise to the ways of the world, I spent two months panting like a puppy after this *fille fatale* before I realized that for her I was more bauble than boyfriend. But by then it didn't matter. I had found a new object for my passion – Paris itself – and this lover consummated my ardor with Monet and Molière, the Île Saint-Louis and Sacré-Cœur, and midnights wandering under the plane trees by the Seine, sometimes hand in hand with a *jeune américaine*, intoxicated by the moon and the swooning stars.

Then I lost my innocence in Greece. At the end of that Parisian summer, I rode the Orient Express through Switzerland, Italy, and Yugoslavia to Athens, where I would be teaching on a one-year fellowship at Athens College. Before classes started, I had a week free to sightsee, and on my second afternoon in the city, overheated and blinded by the stark sunlight, I took refuge in a shady bar just off Syntagma Square. No sooner had butt touched barstool than I was surrounded by three scantily clad sirens caressing my hair, arms, and thighs – and ordering and re-ordering Champagne from an attentive barkeep. I was besotted with the prospect of the night to come, until it came time to pay the tab – and the women disappeared, along with my entire reserve of emergency drachma.

But Greece repaid that lesson time and time again, with rosy-fingered dawns reading Plato on the Parthenon and bouzouki-brightened evenings sipping ouzo by the wine-dark sea, picnics with a mysterious muse named Gisela among the red poppies and white columns of Corinth, and soul-dancing connections and kindness on Crete.

Then I lost my innocence in Tanzania. It was the summer after my teaching year in Greece, and the parents of two of my students had invited me and a fellow teacher named John to visit them in Dar-es-Salaam. We were touring the Tanzanian bush when the clouds cleared and Mount Kilimanjaro suddenly gleamed on the horizon. The father impulsively asked if we wanted to climb it. John and I looked at each other. 'Of course we do! Why not?' We were 23 and invincible. What could possibly go wrong? Well, to start with, all I had for footwear were tennis shoes – we hadn't planned to climb the highest mountain on the continent – but we survived, and all these years later, I'd still climb it no other way.

That year changed my life. I learned the illusions and exhilarations of love, the enticements and terrors of adventure, and the importance of charting my own course. At the end of the year, I relinquished the student's hand-me-down desire to become a tweedy professor and chose instead the perilous path of becoming a writer. I had no idea where that path would lead; I just knew that I wanted to walk it wild and wide-eyed, daring to dream.

Looking back on all this now, I realize that something profound and utterly life-changing happened that year: I embraced my innocence.

Ever since then, through 40 years and 90 countries, innocence has been my steadfast soulmate, my platform and persona, skin and shield, the rose-tinted mind/heart-set with which I encounter the world. As it is still. Over the past few days, I have started to prepare for an upcoming journey to Sweden, Estonia, Finland, Denmark, and Russia, all countries I'll be visiting for the first time. As I read about these places and imagine being in each one, innocence pulses as powerfully through me as it did on that first foray to France in 1975.

Yesterday I wrote in my journal: What will Stockholm be like? What will I discover in Copenhagen? Who will I meet in St. Petersburg? What wonders await?

An innocent abroad.

Compiling this collection has also been an adventure in innocence. I started by reaching for the stars – the writers I most revere around the globe. To my astonishment, many of these award-winners and bestsellers, despite being deluged with their own deadlines and demands, responded to my invitation with grace and enthusiasm. I then sought out up-and-coming authors whose power and passion awe me – and whose stories enthralled me. The result is this beautiful, bountiful book you hold in your hands, 35 celebrations of innocence at large.

As I have assembled these tales, poring over each with ever-deepening gratitude and delight, I have been astonished to see a jigsaw-puzzle portrait compose itself, piece by interlocking piece, right before my eyes.

In one part of this puzzle, innocence abroad is the portal to a rite of passage. Dave Eggers discovers this in the backroom of a Bangkok brothel-cum-nightclub, and Sloane Crosley on a cliff overlooking a shark-infested Australian bay. Pico Iyer's passage unfolds as a succession of ill-fated initiations in South America, while Tim Cahill's coalesces over a series of rootless adventures in North America. And for Jan Morris, the portal is an unsolicited post-war assignment in Venice that unexpectedly transfigures her world.

In another part of the puzzle, innocence is a conduit to misadventure, as it is for Richard Ford in Morocco, when he and his wife embark on an ill-advised journey by car into the heart of hashish country, and for Simon Winchester when he and a team of fellow geologists are ice-bound by fjord-freezing storms in Greenland. Alexander McCall Smith's innocence guides him toward an unsuspecting brush with murder in Swaziland, and Fiona Kidman's to an almost deadly disaster in Vietnam. For Jane Smiley and her husband, unanticipated mishaps play a more benign role, eventually offering admission to off-the-tourist-path pleasures in France.

Sometimes innocence takes the form of a teacher, as it does for 19-year-old Ann Patchett on an eye-opening exploration of Europe, Mary Karr in the eco-wilds of Central America, Kerre

McIvor in the equally uncharted wilderness of Cuban conmen, Cheryl Strayed on an emotional odyssey in Andorra, and Stanley Stewart in the Italian capital, where he came of age on his first trip abroad, and where he has now returned for the birth of his first child. And for Torre DeRoche, coming home after a globe-girdling journey, innocence presents an old, familiar place in a new, unfamiliar light.

And finally, innocence can sometimes be a force for connection, as it is for David Baldacci on a visit to his ancestral homeland in Italy, for Suzanne Joinson when she's forced to spend an unscheduled weekend in Yemen, for Anthony Sattin as he searches for stories in Tunisia's Atlas Mountains on what he's determined will be his last writing assignment, for John Berendt when he befriends a widow with a determined dream in Venice, and for Marina Lewycka when circumstances force her to rely on the kindness of strangers in Yaroslavl.

These stories and all the other treasured tales in this collection, so vastly varied in setting, style, and subject, all ultimately illuminate one common truth: However it manifests itself when we travel, innocence can be a life-changing catalyst for discovery, connection, and transformation on the road.

Mark Twain discovered this truth in the course of writing The Innocents Abroad, that wise and witty account whose title our own humble collection echoes and honors. In describing the misadventures and marvels of his 1860s expedition by boat and train to Europe and the Holy Land, Twain penned one of my favorite quotes: 'Travel is fatal to prejudice, bigotry, and narrow-mindedness,' he wrote. 'Broad, wholesome, charitable views of men and things cannot be acquired by vegetating in one little corner of the earth all one's lifetime.'

That sentiment is one of the core messages of this collection as well: Innocence abroad expands our hearts and our minds, opens us to the splendors of serendipity, builds bridges between peoples and cultures, and lays paving stones on the path to global peace and understanding.

But now, as I contemplate the pieces in this book and in my own life's puzzle, I've realized another truth that I'd never completely understood before: Innocence and worldliness intertwine, in an intricate synthesis that enables each to thrive.

When I left Princeton for Paris, I believed that innocence was something you lost once, never to be regained. But then I lost it again, and again, and again, as I have continued to do, across six continents, over the ensuing decades. Now I understand that innocence is inexhaustible: The more we lose, the more we gain. Each loss, whether through ignorance or idealism, misassumption or misinformation, burnishes and broadens our understanding of how much more remains.

That's the truth these puzzles have finally pictured for me: As long as we continue to venture into unfamiliar situations, to open our hearts and minds to foreign ways, as long as we are able to keep losing our innocence abroad, that innocence will never end – and our appreciation of the world, our embrace of this unembraceable whole, will extend, and extend, and extend.

Caffe Strada, Berkeley
June 2014

Over the Edge

Sloane Crosley

This is the part where I jump off a cliff into choppy, shark-infested waters. It's the middle of the Australian winter and I am barefoot, wearing a wetsuit with neon stripes down the side. I have never been to Australia before and did not grow up in a surfing community. This is my first time in a wetsuit. As I crouch down against the evening wind, readying myself to spring off this pointy rock and into a part of the Sydney Harbor called 'Shark Bay,' I feel like a superhero, surveying her lands from atop a stone gargoyle. This is an unusual feeling. My traveling superpowers are generally limited to making trains arrive by losing my boarding pass and being impervious to caffeine before 7 a.m.

I'm not supposed to be here. I know this because about 40 feet inland from the cliff is a sign that reads 'Warning: Serious Injuries Have Occurred to Persons Jumping From Cliff Edge.'

But the sign has an inverse effect on me. Its very existence means that more than one person has done this and come out in one piece (more or less). Maybe, I think, this is what it feels like to be brave. As an adult, it's easy to get away with being so corporally unadventurous. Most careers do not require you to leap from tree houses or see who can hold their breath the longest. Therefore, to prove to myself that I'm as adventurous as a teenager, I'm going to fling myself off this cliff.

'We don't have to do this if you don't want to,' my new friend Jill shouts.

Jill is a classically fearless Australian blond who takes trips to New Zealand with the express purpose of jumping off that country's edges. She also has the dubious distinction of being my only friend in Australia. I came to her country on a book tour and almost immediately met Jill, who agreed to show me 'her Sydney' on my day off. But even she's having second thoughts about this particular activity.

'There could be sharks,' she adds. 'Honestly.'

'There's a Diamond Bay around here somewhere,' I try to be cool. 'I'm sure it's not covered in actual diamonds.'

'It's not like up north,' she concedes, referring to the Great Barrier Reef, 'but occasionally there are sharks.'

'Occasionally,' I mutter into the wind.

Below me, the water is opaque and violently stucco, concealing a more permanent terrain of rocks, tangled kelp and underfed sea monsters. In the distance, the Sydney Opera House looks like a folded linen napkin. The water knows I'm looking for a safe place to jump, that I'm trying to get through, but the darkness is like a busy signal. All of our representatives are currently busy assisting the sharks — please try back again later. I curl my toes around the cliff's edge as it releases the last of the day's warmth.

'This is Australia,' she clarifies. 'If there's a way to kill you, we've bred it.'

'Thank you,' I say. 'That's very comforting.'

'Oh God, I can just imagine the headline: Young American Writer Killed by Australian Girl.'

'We're not that nice,' I correct her. 'It would just read 'Idiot Bites It.''

The cliff itself is in Nielsen Park, near the eastern suburbs of Sydney. We took Jill's BMW to get here, zipping through a neighborhood of castle-like private schools with girls in knee socks and boys in ties meandering at the gates. They looked straight out of central casting for *Harry Potter: Rise of the Platypus*. I kept thinking: what could possibly happen to me in this neighborhood? But the terrain changes fast in Australia, even in Sydney. Jill and I parked, changed into our wetsuits, and quickly began hiking up into the woods. Soon the manmade stairs morphed into root-system stairs.

'Isn't it funny,' I panted, swatting away thorny branches, 'how long it takes to get places when you've never been there before?'

Jill stopped abruptly and put her nose in the air like a beagle.

'Follow me,' she said over her shoulder.

We broke off from the path. When there was no more shrubbery to dodge, I found myself looking at a stunning tree-framed view of Sydney...and a cliff that dropped off straight into the water.

That was about twenty minutes ago. Now cockatoos watch us from the trees above, dubious. I want to jump, I do. Badly. I keep blaming my hesitation on variables. Maybe if it was summer. Maybe if we had a better sense of the tides and the wind. Maybe if the sky was less ominous. Maybe if I had consulted my insurance plan first. I could break my neck if it's too shallow down there. I flip-flop between 'When am I ever going to be back here again?' and 'I'd like to keep enjoying my full mobility.' Jill and I are silent for a good minute, each waiting for the other to speak.

'Huh,' I say through blue lips, 'I wonder how we're going to get back up.'

The thing with nature is that it doesn't reward you with an escalator when you do something dangerous.

'That does it!' Jill throws her neoprene-covered arms into the air. 'I've never even done this in winter. It's crazy. I'm pulling the plug. I don't want to do it.'

'What?' My eyes bulge. 'You have to.'

'It's scary as hell,' she says, pointing at the water as if it knows what it did, 'and I know from scary.'

I think I have never been so grateful to hear a set of words. They have a magical, spell-lifting effect. This is what I've been subconsciously waiting for, to be released from my adventurous goals by a real, live Australian. I tell her that I understand, that I don't want to pressure her. She kindly lets me take on this role even though we both know I was the petrified one. We stop at a public restroom near the park's entrance to change out of our wetsuits, hopping up and down to get warm. When I get my suit stuck over my head, Jill and I laugh until there are tears rolling down our faces. It is perhaps the best time I've ever had not doing something. That said, I still wish the story ended differently. I wish I could say I jumped. Barring that, I could say I came to the realization on my own that it was okay not to jump.

Oh well. There's always Diamond Bay.

The Place I'll
Never Forget

Tim Cahill

The desert was located in, well, OK, I don't recall precisely where it was, but definitely somewhere in the United States. Certainly it was in a state west of Wisconsin, where I grew up and was, at the time, going to school, a junior in college and entirely innocent of America on the far side of the Mississippi. It was spring break and a couple of pals and I had decided, on the spur of the moment, that we should drive to California. It was going to be a long trip and we couldn't sleep a lot because we wanted to be back when classes started and, more to the point, we didn't have any money to waste on motels. Occasionally I caught an hour's worth of shut eye while someone else drove, but sleeping wasn't easy with three hulking jocks in a VW Beetle.

So I was, I suspect, deep into one of those sleep-deprived modes in which unexpected emotions assault the senses. What I recall most clearly on that drive was this, uh…place. Instead of the green rolling hills with grazing dairy cows that I had seen all my life, there was a lot of, ummm…sand. And rock. I think. And it must have been early in the morning because the sun was low in the sky (but it could have been sunset) and I looked out over these, well, I think they were mountains. And we were on a lonely road or maybe we'd pulled over on an Interstate. We could have been deep in a valley or high on a ridge top. And spread out before us – or perhaps rising above us – was all this…landscape…that I'd never seen before. I stood there, battered by the raw power and sheer magnificence of a land I'd never known. My friends gave me a minute. Or perhaps they told me to take a minute. In any case, my eyes stung, as if I was about to cry. I don't know why. I didn't think about it.

The mountain or the deep valley or whatever it was shimmered in my vision and it might even have been that I could feel tears, real tears, on my face. But maybe not. In any case, I stood stock still and looked at this strange earth – whatever it was, wherever it was – and I said to myself: I will never forget this place.

I could see it whole in my mind's eye for hours. Then I fell asleep and by the time we got to Los Angeles, it had vanished. I could not conjure it up again, not as I had seen it and felt it at the time. A place I'd never forget, gone in twenty-four hours.

A few years later, in 1967, I was living in San Francisco in what can only be described as a hippy crash pad. I was planning my first trip to Mexico and reading books on the culture and geography and food and music of that country. If you envision a mattress on the floor and a bunch of library books piled on all sides, you pretty much have the picture.

My crash-pad friends chided me in clouds of marijuana smoke. 'Man, you're doing it all wrong. Just go down there and let it happen, man.' But I'd learned the lesson of 'the place I'd never forget' and was determined to know as much as I could about Mexico before I left. And then, when things happened, I'd never forget.

That didn't work, either.

There are events I recall clearly but, unfortunately, they mostly involved problems with traveling companions and had little to do with Mexico itself. For instance, I know now that it is a bad idea to travel to Mexico with someone who is on probation for a dope bust in Texas. You may get to talk to local people a lot – but those people are police, and they are the ones asking the questions.

Some memorable events had to do with simple ignorance on my part. Back then, never having been a camper or backpacker, I had an inflated idea of the capabilities of an Army surplus sleeping bag. Sure, you can sleep outside in a pouring rain in such a bag, but soon enough you will be soaking wet and freezing, and in the morning the bag, drenched with water, will weigh 750 pounds and it will never dry out – but you might be able to give it to a local family who, in turn, will let you sleep in a shed with a couple of goats for a night or two.

These were tales my crash-pad friends found vaguely amusing, but I felt that my recollections were still misty and unsatisfying. At the time, I thought I wanted to be a writer. The Great American Novel would, presumably, spring into existence, whole and of a piece, directly from sights seen and emotions felt over the space of a lifetime, which at that time, was twenty-four years long. But here I was, trying to tell folks about a goat shed in Mexico, and I couldn't fully answer simple questions about the story.

'Oh, man, I bet that stunk in there.'

'It wasn't bad.'

'Cool. What did it smell like?'

'Well, you know, goats.'

'Goats? Goats? Do I look like I know what freakin' goats smell like?'

And it occurred to me that the stories I told would benefit from more detail. I couldn't just experience something and expect to have it etched indelibly into my memory. I had to give names to the colors and odors and feel of things. I had to assess my own feelings, which gave emotion to the landscape. And I needed to do it on the spot, because travel often doesn't allow you to backtrack. What color were the shadows on the cliff face? I felt confident with purple when it was right there in my notes. Nightfall, shadows purple down to absolute darkness. Ominous. Creeped out. Like that.

Northern California was all new to me and I spent what free time I had exploring. There were trips to Point Reyes or Mount Lassen or Big Sur. Every travel day, I'd make some time to sit quietly and take notes. And now, well over forty years later, I can open those old spiral notebooks, read through the notes, and feel the day come back to me with remarkable clarity.

Another benefit of note-taking is that even the things I didn't write about come vividly to mind. I can, for instance, recall the overlooked weather, feel the morning's damp chill and see a bruised sky finally break open into a downpour that sent me scurrying back to a tent that rattled in the rain and that flapped and quivered in the wind.

Some people are certain they can recall such physical and emotional experience through their photographs. I can't argue the point, though feeling through a lens is a rare talent and one that I don't possess. I need to put words to sensations and emotions in order to own them forever. Whenever I can't figure something out and take a photograph rather than a note, I know I'm losing the scene forever.

The lesson of the place I'll never forget went deep. Why had I cried at my first sight of desert? It would be interesting to know. I should have taken a moment at the time to assess what I now call the 'interior landscape.' Taking notes, I have discovered over time, is an art into and of itself. When I have both observation and emotion on the page, I am sometimes able to feel an inkling of 'what it all means'.

In time, I got a job writing about music for a little start-up magazine in San Francisco called *Rolling Stone*. Several years later, I was privileged to help conceive another new magazine called *Outside*. I did a lot of writing for *Outside* because I liked the work. A raft trip down the Owyhee River, a search for pre-Columbian ruins in Peru: I could scarcely believe people paid me to do this work.

And I was good at it. My obsession with notes served me well. Once home from a trip, all that scribbling turned itself into stories I could tell with a kind of sure-footed brio. Now, at seventy, I'm still writing about travel, still enjoying it immensely and still amazed that I earn a living doing it. Sometimes I think my working life is charmed and that it all has to do with a mystical desert valley. Or mountain. 'The place I'll never forget.' I'd like to say that it was a spiritual vortex of spectral beauty, but that's just a guess. In my mind, it is a combination of hard felt emotion and harsh desert land that exists solely in my flawed recollection.

Then again, maybe it was in Utah.

The First Time I Had So Many First Times

Pico Iyer

The beauty of any first time is that it leads to a thousand others: The first glance eases one towards the first meeting, and then, perhaps, the first kiss and the first love and so much else (the first divorce?). Every 'first time' opens a door upon a long corridor, down which you walk with the sensation, from experience now, that any other door might fly open at any moment, leading onto another corridor.

The first time I truly got to savor the world was when I was seventeen and, suddenly, almost free from high school, I began to put the different parts of my inheritance, as someone always a little bit abroad – a confirmed traveler for life – together. In the summer of 1974, my parents decided I should spend three months traveling around India, getting to know the cousins and uncles and grandparents, the ancestry, that I'd never had a chance to encounter before (except briefly, at the age of two).

I was as thrilled with the decision as any seventeen-year-old would be, and approached the trip with the sullen resignation of a prisoner dragged towards his last meal. But as the years went on, I began to realize how much that initial encounter with the world in all its chaos had formed me: The first time I'd tried to compose a love song on a guitar; the first time I'd ridden a train for two days and two nights; the first time I'd read the complete plays of Shakespeare – in a drafty library room in Elphinstone College in Bombay, birds flapping amidst the rafters; the first time I was lucky enough to visit the Dalai Lama in his home in Dharamsala. After that summer sojourn, suitcase heavy with barely readable books on Jung, hair falling down to my shoulders, worn cassette of Songs by Leonard Cohen clattering around in my guitar case, I returned to my school in rainy England for a final autumn to prepare for university examinations. That was the first time a teacher had us read Joni Mitchell next to 'The Eve of St. Agnes,' and the first time I was old enough to realize I was taking leave of a certain kind of innocence.

By the time winter came, I was back in my parents' home in Santa Barbara, California, eager to save money for a trip: Within weeks I was depositing plates of enchiladas in customers' laps and pouring hot sauce into their glasses of water at Pancho Villa Inn Mexican restaurant on State Street. I was spectacularly ill-equipped for my first job, as for every job that followed – my most constructive moments were spent, on slow afternoons, sitting in the sun outside the front door trudging through Adam Bede and Joseph Andrews from my university's reading list – but a kind friend of my parents was generous enough to offer me a position in his restaurant, and I was set loose in a world of bull-fighting posters and Herb Alpert and the Tijuana Brass (such was our image of Mexico in 1975).

In the mornings, I drove down to the restaurant, and entered into battle with tubs of lard larger than myself; the Mexican cooks in the kitchen cherished my appearances as the rare moments of comic relief in their hard lives (it might have been the arrival of a midget Falstaff). Then I staggered out from the back and started tending to the needs of our lard-filled guests. 'You can't make a silk purse out of a sow's ear' was the philosophical verdict of Joe, our senior waiter, as I tried – and failed – to juggle two plates and, dropping them both, began sliding and slithering on the newly slippery floor.

And then, at last, my year of spending every season in a different continent came towards its climax as I took the money I'd (technically) earned to the local Greyhound station and, joined by my friend Rob, an equally clueless classmate from my English high school, boarded the bus for the border. Very soon, we were bumping around the streets of Tijuana, brassy, and before long – free at last from all signs of adulthood, retired at eighteen and in the autumnal spring break known as the Gap Year – I found 'firsts' tumbling down on me at every turn.

The first time I fell into a ditch in the middle of a lightless Guatemalan jungle, as night was falling, never knowing if I'd make it out again. The first time I was more or less deported, as we stopped off in Panama, and my friend waltzed through Immigration, eager to savor the sights of the Canal Zone, while I was forcibly held back, and told that I had to remain in police custody for the duration of my stay, on suspicion of being an Indian.

The first time I'd stayed in a cheap hotel only to notice that all the other guests were friendly, pretty young ladies who somehow had new friends sharing their rooms every night; Rob and I sat in the breakfast room of the Hotel Picasso in Bogota, our first morning there, and wondered if we'd ended up in a nunnery, we were so surrounded by young women, and ones innocent enough (as we in our innocence surmised) to want to talk to us.

The first time I suffered altitude sickness, as our train jolted across a 15,689-foot pass on its way to Huancayo, in Peru, and the first time I'd seen Rob, who affected to be a gruff misanthrope out of Evelyn Waugh, hasten around a strange town, with his non-existent Spanish, gallantly seeking out medication for me. The first time I'd tasted a pisco sour – in a fancy hotel in Lima, where we deployed the 'emergency' American Express card my father had given me to potent effect – and the first time I'd ridden a horse through a jungle, when a chain-smoking ten-year-old persuaded us it was the only way to visit remote pre-Columbian statues near San Agustín.

The first time parts of me were sore for days on end, after our ride at the wily kid's hands, and the first time we'd seen women wearing bowler hats, and llamas among the snowcaps. The first time we resisted altitude sickness – veterans now, in La Paz – and the first time I'd gone shopping for jewels (in Rio, though only, alas, for my mother).

Finally, after ten weeks or so of traveling together, and at the culmination of my year of living a bit more adventurously, Rob and I separated, as he wanted to go to Sao Paulo and Iguazu before flying back to London, and I had to proceed up the eastern coast of the continent, towards Miami and a Greyhound home.

We shook hands manfully at the airport in Rio, and I flew up to Belém, at the mouth of the Amazon. When I arrived at the other end – it was just me, soft-featured, girlish, with hair down to my shoulders, in a cheap blue-and-yellow poncho I didn't have room to pack, hauling around a suitcase that was at least half my weight – I didn't know what cheap and unsavory hostelry from the *South American Handbook* to select, or how to get there. I'd already noticed how much Brazilians enjoyed being addressed in Spanish.

A man a few years older than I, in a business suit, trim, respectable – the very soul of responsibility – caught sight of me in my lostness.

'Where are you going?' he asked.

'Not a clue.'

'I'm here for work,' he went on, 'and I know a good hotel. Would you have any interest in sharing a room?'

Even a shared room in a good hotel was too expensive for me, my look must have said.

'My company is paying,' he explained. 'It's no problem.'

He spoke English, he knew the place, he'd taken pity on me: Some part of me was touched, my faith in human nature notched up a little.

That evening was the first time I'd eaten in a fisherman's hut along the Amazon, as my new friend took me to visit some retainer he'd known since he was a boy. It was my first time in a respectable hotel I could remember. It was the first time I'd entered a realm of tropical luxuriance that felt like a magical realist novel.

The firsts were crashing down on me as we completed our meal in the hut – I took pains not to find out what firsts I'd tasted there; there were some advantages to not speaking Portuguese – and went back to the room to get ready for bed. That was the first time a stranger ever loomed up beside me in the dark, on my side of the bed, and silently, with a hand on my knee, suggested that I really had been failing to understand a thing.

I came to believe, as the years went on, that in certain cases innocence is its own protection. That's the only way I can explain the miracle of somehow getting out of that locked room, my imprisonment within my foolishness, untouched. The man must have realized just how clueless I was – or how anaphrodisiacal is startled innocence. The next day, by the time I'd awoken – I had no trouble sleeping, though I would today – there was no trace of the man, and the hotel room had been paid for, as promised. That was the first time I sat by a hotel swimming pool as a guest.

I gathered my huge suitcase at checkout time and headed towards my next stop, Suriname, where – this was a first, too – I was pushed off my flight day after day, every time any 'VIP's' showed up, and was left to sleep in the airport hotel, which was the jungle floor across from the terminal, using my suitcase as a pillow. But the evening in Belém became the all-important first time in which I realized that taking in too many firsts, in a rush of ignorance, could have consequences, and that there was a virtue in second times, the moments when experience could temper the flush of discovery. So keen to look at the world around me, I'd never stopped to think about how the world around me looked back.

In the years that followed, I made variations of the same mistake again and again, somehow without tragic result. But the first time I completed a year of spending every season on a different continent was the first time I began to surmise – though my first time of acknowledging it would come many years later – that I didn't know a thing.

Innocence Abroad
Jan Morris

F or many people of my generation it was one army or
  another that first sent us more or less innocently abroad.
In my case it was the British Army which, at the end of the
Second World War, deposited me for a couple of months in
the very first city I had ever inhabited. I was twenty years
old, not all that innocent but decidedly provincial. The city
on the other hand was not only ultra-urban but also almost
inconceivably abroad.

I was 2nd Lieutenant Morris of the 9th Queen's Royal Lancers.
The city was Venice.

Can you imagine the culture shock when at our camp on
the River Po I was detached from our kindly old regiment,
a substitute home and family, and told to help organize the

requisitioned motor-boats of that legendary foreign city? It would not be for long, I was assured by my colonel, a gentle fighting Welshman from a home near my own home; actually, he said, he was not quite sure what I would be doing in the place, but you never knew, I might find it an enjoyable experience.

He was right. I am in a daze even now about the nature of my duties in Venice, which abruptly came to an end when we were all posted on to the Middle East, but it is a daze that has lingered deliciously to this day. Robert Benchley, when he first set foot in Venice, allegedly cabled home, 'Streets full of water. Please advise.' I myself felt I was entering some different dimension of life, in which I was an ignorant alien. Nowadays everyone knows all about Venice: In 1945, a twenty-year-old subaltern from the western islands, stepping onto the waterfront of La Serenissima for the very first time, felt a bit like Benchley.

It was a defeated city, of course, and I was part of an occupying army. This perhaps meant that Venice, 1945, lacked its habitual triumphal pride, but the misty melancholy that surrounded it seduced me almost at once. It was not the grandeur of the place that captured me, but the strange lapping of its waters, the secrecy of it all, the browns and ochres of it, the suggestiveness. Wandering the crooked maze of its streets in the misty evenings really was like exploring a city of another planet; a sudden burst of sunlight over the waterfront affected me like a melody direct from Mozart.

I was billeted in the requisitioned house of a French politician, full of exotic bric-a-brac, and I soon felt myself almost sentimentally at home in this gloriously foreign, unremittingly urban place. The foreign people, I discovered, were generally delightful, the foreign food was great, I enjoyed trying to talk Italian, I learnt for the first time seriously to look at buildings as works of art, and I still can't remember just what I did about those boats.

City life grew upon me. In the seventy years since then, I have never had a home in one, but I was to spend much of my life looking at cities, exploring the characters of cities, thinking about cities and making my living by writing about them – not least about Venice itself. In short, those couple of months as a semi-Innocent very much Abroad changed my life forever.

Oh, and here's an afterthought. The one military duty I do remember from that Venetian tour of duty is the task of conducting military bigwigs from their staff cars at the head of the causeway to their allotted billets in the requisitioned grand hotels. They were a hard-bitten lot of generals, hardened and perhaps embittered by their years of campaigning, and few of them had ever been to Venice before. They treated me as generals usually do treat second lieutenants, and their faces were generally unsmiling as we began our passage up the Grand Canal.

But lo! As the celestial waterway opened up before us, as one noble palace succeeded another, as we passed under the Rialto bridge and the generals found themselves disembarking beneath the campanile at the miraculous Piazza of San Marco – by then they were boyishly smiling at me, and their grizzled faces were aglow with delighted astonishment. They were like Innocents Abroad themselves!

In the Beginning There Was Paris

David Downie

It seemed sexy in a dangerous Day of the Jackal way: after an overnight ride on an unheated train I made my entry into Paris at dawn.

On that autumn dawn in 1976, Paris felt especially cold because the summer – which I'd caught the tail end of in Luxembourg and Switzerland – had been so hot. Somehow I'd never realized that the city was more than a movie backdrop – and that it lies north of Montreal, or so I'd been told on the train.

I was shivering. I'd already eaten two bars of milk chocolate for dinner and one for breakfast, but I was still starving. I was loaded with a duffle bag stuffed with enough stuff to last me a year, and I was also carrying another bag. It belonged to a friend on the move. He had lived in Paris, moved out for a time, and now was moving back. We'd traveled together from Switzerland. He and I trooped along, immigrants weaving down the platforms of Gare de Lyon. Mist rose from another film set. It showed glistening tracks, ice and overhead wires.

We followed rush-hour mobs down concrete stairs into a fluorescent-lit passageway. I looked up at the art nouveau cast iron and glass before being swallowed. The multicolored strands of the métro map appeared at the end of a corridor. Another movie started in my head.

Where had I seen the ticket-punchers of Paris? A trio stood by wide gates and snatched at our stubs and punched and muttered and yelled to keep the crowds moving. We were pressed bodily into a tin can of a train car. Wheels squealed. Compressed damp humanity filled the wooden seats and rocked like bowling pins as the car lurched out. The air reeked of burning brakes, dust, axle grease, nicotine, and pencil shavings. It was intoxicating.

Muffled in dark woolens and leather and topped by a rakish cap, my sophisticated friend had lived in Paris for nearly a year. He'd left for a stint in the Alps. Now he was retaking possession of the city. Paris was new to me. I knew it from words and screens and was largely satisfied with such expertise. I was three months into my first tour of Europe. I'd written my Parisian friend before leaving home.

He was different, changed. He seemed to move, walk and talk like a Parisian. What clashed was his Nordic-light hair and height. The peak of his cap rode a foot above the crowds. I was more Parisian in looks and size. But my short jacket, permanent-press bellbottoms, colorful polyester shirt and wavy-soled shoes looked funny. My expression felt funny. I couldn't help staring at everything and everyone and smiling stupidly.

Rows of beady eyes fixed me in mute amusement as the subway rocked. They could see I was freezing, dazed and had just arrived. It was the smell of pencil shavings that baffled

me most, like someone had emptied a big pencil sharpener
attached to the wall.

The ride to Odéon involved a transfer through tiled tunnels
swelling with overcoats, folded umbrellas and bent heads. Above
them floated my friend's cap. I raced to keep up, chasing The Red
Balloon. The funfair ride continued on another roller coaster.
The design and color were different, older. The car dipped under
the Seine, the overhead lights flickering, the scent of sizzling
electricity and grease taking me back to Playland at the Beach in
San Francisco. I struggled not to compare.

Disgorged, we flowed to the surface at Carrefour de l'Odéon.
The name sounded like something to sing over café au lait. It
sounded like olé and I imagined the bullfights in Hemingway's
The Sun Also Rises. We'd read it in high school. I hadn't really
liked it but had pretended to like it like everyone else. Now I
needed it. It spoke to me. My pasty mouth struggled to tease
out wispy grade-school French, separating it from the meaty
Italian and Spanish defaults from home and high school. Forget
phonetics, I told myself: olé, olé, olé and café. And warm clothes.

It was still dark. I could feel the sleety rain coming down
through the leafless sycamores. We had those back home too.
Umbrellas came open. With our luggage on our shoulders we
lumbered among them. Passing a café, I shouted. My friend
didn't stop. Around us wild subcompacts with slanting yellow
headlights swirled, engines whining. Trucks with corrugated
sides blasted horns and belched black fumes. Buses swung wide.
One had an open-air passenger deck out back. At the upper end
of the sloping street a ghostly white colonnade appeared. Was it a
monument or a theater?

The wide, straight street was Rue de l'Odéon. I wanted it
to sound familiar. The facades of the buildings had once been

white but were stained now by soot and damp under the eaves. They rose with dilapidated majesty into foggy rain. Each had a boutique or bookstore on the ground floor. Pushing through a weighty green door, my friend led us into the entranceway. Steam billowed from our mouths. I unslung myself. A concierge popped from a nook. She stood about four feet tall. Was she from Hôtel du Nord? An old black-and-white French movie, that was sure.

French literature I did not know, unless you counted the Existentialists or murder mysteries. But my movie repertoire was respectable for someone not yet nineteen. A rag wagging in one hand, the other on her hip, the concierge began interrogating felons. Who were we and what did we want, where were we going, what was this wet luggage and how dare we put it on the floor she had just cleaned? I understood but could not answer.

My friend's French was angular. He sliced a few words, dropping the name of the owner of the apartment we were to occupy. He glared down. The woman's wrath blunted, she egged us up a carpeted spiral staircase ten steps to the mezzanine.

Somehow I had imagined a top-floor garret from La Bohème or the crime novels of Georges Simenon. I had read them in translation. Inspector Maigret would have felt good. The door swung open on a grayish quadrangle. The ceiling was low. My friend had to stoop. In my stocking feet my hair brushed the plaster. It occurred to me I might fit in. I decided I liked the mildew scent. Voices rose up from the boutique underneath.

Grayness seeped through a low window on the street. An even lower window in back gave on the courtyard. I wrestled it open. The view was of garbage cans, rags and mops and brooms, a cold-water tap. Paris.

My friend seemed enviably blasé. He unpacked stacking sweaters and French books. There wasn't much furniture. I couldn't see a bed or sink or bathroom. The apartment was the size of my father's potting shed. How about showering and heading back out for coffee and croissants, I said? My friend shrugged. He made a face I'd never seen before. It wasn't his face. He said I could use talcum powder instead of washing. That's what Parisians did. There was no hot water probably, and he wasn't sure there was a shower or toilet either. They might be in the hall or the courtyard. We'd have to figure that out. Did it matter?

The rain wasn't so much rain as curtains of water in fog. I had not seen rain of this kind except on screen. It seemed wonderful, like the smells and the noises and the language and the looks on people's faces. My friend had acquired those looks – startled, amused, skeptical, blasé.

On Boulevard Saint-Germain we pushed into a corner café. People smoked back home but this was different. I couldn't at first see how to reach a table or the bar. The air was thick with blue plumes from yellow cigarettes. The same damp overcoats from the subway formed a beehive around the cash desk where a bony man with something hanging from his lower lip tore off tickets and swapped packs of Gauloises or Gitanes for large franc bills. They bore the face of a bearded man. Even I recognized him. Victor Hugo. Hadn't I seen *The Hunchback of Notre Dame*? One day I might read the book.

My friend had studied French for years. He fancied himself European. Technically he was, if you considered Great Britain part of Europe. He'd been born in England while his parents were traveling. With practiced insouciance he ploughed through the overcoats and I followed in his wake. With the same insouciance he tipped his cap back and ordered us cafés au lait and *sandwichs mixtes*. These were boiled-ham-and-Swiss on a crispy baguette more than a foot long. There was no lettuce, no ketchup. He spread his open and with a wooden paddle daubed it with moutard. Then he asked for cornichons and when the dinky pickles arrived we paid extra and were scolded for not having ordered them first so the cook could put them inside the sandwiches.

I was pleased. Even he could make mistakes.

My eyes and nostrils burned from the mustard. The cornichons were tart, vinegary. The cigarette smoke mixed with the strange scent of pencil shavings. What was it?

With practiced indifference my friend leaned down and spoke into my ear over the raucous voices. When you've been here a while and you use the talcum powder, he said, you will understand.

This was something I hadn't seen in the movies, beyond the mustard and pickles, I meant. And another thing: since when did French women have red hair?

My friend chortled. Can't you see it's dyed, he asked. They use henna. That way they only have to wash it once a month. He said this as if it was the most reasonable thing in the world. I wasn't sure what henna was and I wasn't sure I wanted to find out. He tapped me on the shoulder and shoved me close to a pair of twenty-something girls fighting past us to the bar. Pencil shavings, he asked. I sniffed and nodded.

The feline girls had hennaed hair. It stood up stiffly. I thought it was the rain. No, not the rain, he said. Washing isn't something people do here daily. We are obsessed. Here they are earthy, natural, sensuous, life-loving and less put off by strong flavors and smells. When you make love with a Parisian, he assured me, she doesn't rush to shower.

That explained the scent. No wonder everyone smoked. Even the dogs smoked. I saw a sign for one. It said 'Le Chien Qui Fume'.

I bought a pack of Gitanes like the ones the men in the cafe were buying. The logo showed a dancing gypsy girl. The packaging was beautiful. It was perfect, Parisian.

We strolled in the rain through the back streets of the Latin Quarter and Saint-Germain, then down narrow streets with art galleries and under an archway and across a wobbly half-rotten wooden bridge on the Seine, along the riverbanks lined by green boxes, past gurgling pissoirs also painted dark green, an expressway below full of cars. I said I'd go to museums later.

On the Right Bank near a place called Les Halles was a gaping hole and worksite bigger than any I'd seen. We feigned indifference inspecting the rows of prostitutes on Rue Saint Denis. It looked like the backdrop to Irma la Douce. But these women weren't pretty like Shirley MacLaine. Some looked like men. Pencil shavings and damp filled my head.

My friend became expansive telling me about his plans to stay in Paris or maybe return to Switzerland. He was reading philosophy and French literature, studying music, enjoying the richness of culture. Home seemed so bland, so banal, so uncouth in comparison. How could he possibly live there again?

I wasn't sure what syntax was but he no longer sounded American. It made my brain ache.

Over lunch in a bistro with a ceiling as low as the mezzanine, he told me something about his mysterious friend, the rich kid who had insouciantly given him the keys to his parents' Parisian pied-à-terre. Did the parents know we were here? Maybe. Actually he had no idea. He smiled wickedly. His teeth were stained by the red wine we were drinking. It came in small carafes. We had two, then a third. What did it matter if they knew or didn't know? If they threw us out, we could go to a hotel. Toss a franc and it'd land on one. Paris was cheap. It wasn't like home. Nothing was like home. We clinked together. The wine glasses were thick. Their bowls were round and they fit in the palm when your fingers were splayed around the stem.

Enjoy the mezzanine, my friend said, tucking into his gizzards, his livers, his kidneys in creamy mustard sauce. If you only knew how many places he'd seen in the last year. Rue de l'Odéon was a great address, it was a wonderful building, a fabulous theater.

I listened trying not to show my bafflement at the ordering of his words, or at what I'd seen so far in Paris. It was like the movies, sort of. The soundtrack came with unexpected smells and the lighting was gray and had a special flavor and gritty feel.

There were no newspaper vending machines or parking meters anywhere. There were no fire hydrants. Everyone had a dog. Everyone was in a hurry. No one said 'Sorry' when they ran into you. Smiling seemed to hurt people's faces. They squinted and spat. No berets. But everyone carried baguettes. I kept notes. This was important.

While walking down unknown streets full of unusual objects and signage and people heading to the Left Bank, I began striking strange waxy matches and finally got a cigarette to light. I took a drag. Coughing, I leaned on a wall. A pair of streetwalkers laughed. My friend laughed too. He took the pack as I was throwing it away.

There were no books I could read in the mezzanine. Even in English, *Madame Bovary* had not spoken to me in California. Here it was in French.

One day when my friend was out, I rode the métro a single stop to Place Saint-Michel. I wandered slowly up the coiling steel staircase in a deep iron drum, a *caisson* riveted like the Eiffel Tower. I knew. I had climbed the tower and stood in the numbing wind and wondered whether the city below could be mine. The city underground, too.

In the alleys near Saint Michel, I ate sticky fried doughnuts dripping with honey, or so I understood. The pastry shop was Moroccan or Algerian or Tunisian. The sweets I'd never seen. On a road paralleling the Seine was a bookstore everyone said I must visit. It was Hemingway's bookstore, they said. Had I read *A Moveable Feast*? I lied.

I found a paperback by Fitzgerald – the 'Ritz' caught my eye. Someone had once said, 'Oh, *Colette*, read *Colette* to understand Paris.' I bent to retrieve *Colette* and a flea bit my ankle. I hiked my pants to catch it. A tall, grizzled man watched me. This might have been City Lights Bookstore in San Francisco. I could not help comparing. The man asked was this it. I said what did he mean, this was just the beginning. I had another nine months to go. I had not meant to quip. He eyed me. People can stay upstairs and do volunteer work in the bookstore, he said. But I didn't need a flop.

Before paying warily, I added *A Moveable Feast* to the pile. I smuggled it into the mezzanine. My friend might ask why read Hemingway in English in Paris? *Ulysses* was the exception and Joyce had been Irish and so that was okay.

My favorite possession was a book-map of Paris streets and métro lines. I bought it at a newsstand. L'Indispensable it was called. Then I walked the streets between stations. I found the places in the books I'd bought. My friend was busy. I had days to myself. There was too much to see, too much to read. Fall was almost over. Winter would be colder. I returned to the bookstore and from outside watched the grizzled man. Young travelers moved stacks of books or swept. Was this really the place Hemingway had known? The name was right. A line from the book came back to me: 'You expected to be sad in the fall.'

But I wasn't sad. Paris was an amusement park in low season. I wasn't sure I wanted to come back in the spring. I wasn't sure I wanted to know French like my friend. But the sun of California had always blinded me.

In a cafe I reached the part in *A Moveable Feast* where Hemingway is always hungry. I was hungry too but didn't see why he enjoyed it. I read the address again, the address where Sylvia and Adrienne ran their bookstore. The name was the same. But it wasn't on the quay. It was on Rue de l'Odéon. The number was 12.

I walked fast, eager to get back before my friend. The concierge said yes, there had been a bookstore here. It was so long ago she never saw it. Yes, she said, or I thought she said, the mezzanine had been used by the bookstore. Here? I asked. This, I said, tapping the book and showing her the page with the address. 'Oui, oui, oui,' she said, 'c'est ici'.

Smiling I settled down in the mezzanine. *Ulysses* was published where I'm sitting. Hemingway was here. I dog-eared the page with the address and waited feeling warm. Should I tell him? Did he know? No. One day he'd find out. One day they'd put up a plaque. Until then, the secret would be mine.

The Paris Tattoo

Ann Patchett

A room with two beds usually meant a room with a bed and a cot. Marti Kavaler and I were very diplomatic about trading off – if I had the bed in Copenhagen, she got the bed in Strasbourg. I remember that she had the bed in Paris, but that was a small victory. It was a terrible bed, a terrible cot, a terrible fourth floor walk-up in the only pension we could afford. The bathroom was not just down the hall, but down the hall and down a flight of stairs. On the bright side, the location was good (the location was Paris), and we were nineteen, so our standards were still breathtakingly low. Marti and I scarcely had known one another before we embarked on our three-month summer adventure in 1983, but by the end of the first week we had become a single unit. We shared our toothpaste, our guidebooks, our croissants. We had one mass-market copy of *One Hundred Years of Solitude*, and when I finished a chapter I ripped it out and handed it to Marti, unless she was a chapter ahead and so ripped it out for me.

By the time we got to Paris, we had been traveling for more than six weeks. We were tired and in need of a laundromat. Even though the city was beyond our modest budget, we wanted to stay in Paris. We could pretend our nasty pension wasn't too far from an artist's garret. *Mi chiamano Mimi!* We walked along the soft, straight paths of the Tuileries, we stood in line for half the day to join the masses in the Centre Pompidou, we wandered from one arrondissement to the next, blissfully lost, until we saw the head of a giraffe poking up over the horizon. Then, because we weren't much older than children, we went to the Paris Zoo.

Where to eat, what to eat and how much we could afford to spend on a single meal were our favorite topics of conversation that summer. Given the size and the culinary importance of the city, it had been our plan to never step into the same cafe or boulangerie twice. So much for plans. Wandering through the Latin Quarter on our first night, we found a crêpe restaurant whose interior was constructed entirely from bright chunky pieces of broken tile. The walls, the floor, and the booths that pushed up from that floor like cement eruptions were all covered in a haphazard mosaic. Bulky strips of neon tubing pulsed light around the room.

Enough of looking at art! We were inside the art now. A waitress, who was tall enough and bony enough to call to mind the giraffe we had seen earlier in the day, led us to our booth, handed us our menus, and loped away without a word. She wore a black tank top and extra-long toothpick jeans, a starched white dishtowel tied around her narrow hips. It was impossible to comprehend that she was a human in the same way that we were human, two American girls grown chubby on a summer of pastry. Over by the bar, we watched her talking to her friend, another waitress every bit as tall and pale and angular as she.

'They must be artists,' Marti said.

'Or philosophers,' I said, because the second one was wearing glasses with thick black frames propped atop her delicate ears. The glasses made her look serious. We knew without speaking that we both wanted to lose weight, grow tall, move to Paris, and become waitresses. In an instant we saw the beauty of this life stretching out before us.

The second waitress, the intellectual, came to our table and held up her pad and pen, her arms so long and thin and white there should have been a museum built to honor them. In broken high-school French, we ordered crêpes. She turned away from us without a word of acknowledgment, and that was when we saw the delicate clutch of flowers inked into the sharp wing of her shoulder blade.

The year was 1983. Two nineteen-year-old American girls had gone to Europe for the entire summer with their saved-up babysitting money and whatever was left from birthdays and high-school graduation. They had no idea where they were going and so no one in their families knew where they were. They had train passes, and sometimes boarded a train without checking to see where the train was going. They occasionally sent postcards but did not receive any mail. Once, in the middle of July, they called home from a phone center and talked for exactly five minutes because it was so expensive. There were no cell phones, no Internet cafes, and no women with tattoos. Or there were women with tattoos, but until this night in Paris they had never been sighted by Ann Patchett or Marti Kavaler. The other waitress, the one in the tank top who walked us to our table, had one too.

Back in our lumpy bed and cot, we didn't even try to read García Márquez. The drunken French shouted from the street was easily heard four flights up, but we didn't notice it. In the dark, I asked Marti if she would ever get a tattoo.

'I don't know,' she said, but because we were one person, I knew she was thinking about it.

We are not the girls you knew before, is what our tattoos would indicate to the world.

The next day we went to the Musée de l'Orangerie to see the water lilies, and then for lunch we ate couscous near the Gare du Nord. At Notre Dame I spent two francs to light a votive candle. We worked out our day from the guidebook, but there was no question where we were going at night.

We never considered the waitresses might not be working. We expected them to be there the way a tourist expects to see the Mona Lisa. We were not disappointed. The philosopher led us to a different table without a flicker of recognition, her tank top purple.

'I think a fish,' Marti said after the waitress had given us our menus and turned away. 'A little fish on my shoulder blade.'

'I want a black and white cow, maybe the size of a quarter, right here –' I touched my biceps. A cow? Why a cow? Why not the Arc de Triomphe? There is no answer.

The next day we hiked up to Montmartre to find Degas' grave and see the Basilique, but they made no impression. Our heads were full of nothing but tattoos. I didn't have my ears pierced and was worried about how much the tattoo would hurt, but it wouldn't matter. The tattoos would establish us as free thinkers, sufferers for art, or at least sufferers for a fish and a tiny cow. With our French/English dictionary we hammered out the phrase, 'Where did you get your tattoo?' We practiced saying it to one another.

That night in the crêpe restaurant, the neon tubing blinking around us, a cheap bottle of wine consumed, we summoned our courage. It was really Marti's courage, since her French was better than mine. 'Qui vous a donné cet tatouage?' she asked.

The waitress – it was the first one, the artist – had never actually looked at us before. She was probably only two or three years older than we were, but her excruciatingly angular beauty, her fundamental Frenchness, made her in every sense our senior. She looked at us uncomprehendingly at first, and I was sure that Marti had botched the pronunciation. Then she touched the edge of her tattoo. It was a decorative scroll of flowers and curled lines that ran in a half-circle around the side of her arm. She made a little back and forth movement with the pad of her finger. 'Rub-on?' she said, with a heavy, questioning accent, as though those were the only two words in English that she knew and we shouldn't try to ask her anything else.

And so it came to pass that Marti Kavaler did not wind up with a small fish on her shoulder, and I, at fifty, do not have a cow carved into my arm.

But that is not exactly where the story ends. In the early part of August, our Eurail passes expired, our language skills exhausted, and our funds badly depleted, we decided to spend the weeks we had left hitch-hiking through the UK. One day in Donegal, we got a ride with a vacationing family who were on their way home to Londonderry. Would we like to go to Londonderry?

That was how we ended our summer vacation in a war zone.

We rode to Northern Ireland in the back of the family station wagon. It was raining the first time we were pulled out of the car at a checkpoint by boys who looked younger than we were, boys with automatic weapons slung across their backs and pistols shoved into their belts, boys with tattoos that cut from wrist to shoulder, tattoos inching up their necks and spreading out across the tops of their fingers. I had seen boys with tattoos before, but none as wrathful as these. I had seen boys with guns before, but had never thought it possible that one of them might shoot me. We were told to get out of many cars in Northern Ireland, our passports checked, our backpacks poked through with rifle-tips. I can hardly remember seeing a boy without a tattoo in Northern Ireland that summer, or, for that matter, a boy without a gun. When I didn't see the tattoos and the guns it was easy to imagine they were there, waiting. They were there in Coleraine and in Bangor. In Belfast we had lunch at the White Horse Tavern. The next day it was bombed.

Marti and I flew home two weeks before school started. We tended to study together, either in her room or in mine. We had gotten used to the sound of the other one breathing. We were never able to keep each other from making bad decisions, but at least when we made them we were together.

Lies of Passage, Zurich 1973

Lloyd Jones

At the age of eighteen, fresh off the beach from the other side of the world, I arrived at the railway station in Zurich as green as can be, but with all the self-assurance of the seasoned traveller who has been there and seen it all.

I had an overnight bag and a few Swiss francs stuffed in my corduroy jeans pockets, exchanged at a breathtaking rate from British sterling at Gatwick Airport.

I was very excited – although not about Switzerland. I would have been just as happy shoved into a wardrobe, so long as it was with my girlfriend, Susie, whom I hadn't seen in six months. She and her older sister were staying with their aunt in Bern. They were expecting me later that afternoon. I had a telephone number to call when I got there. I was in no doubt that everything would fall into place, that somehow I would get there and through the usual means of telepathy, Susie would be at the station to meet me off the train.

We'd made these arrangements by letter written in longhand. There was no mobile or email, no up-to-the-second contact. Our separation was more or less as it had been for couples in the nineteenth century. However, there had been one phone call where her voice sounded tiny and husky at the end of a very long line.

She must have been baffled by my own brisk tone. I was terrified of any emotion leaking out, since the phone call was taken in the Surfers Paradise office of a business acquaintance of my older brother. Paddy sat behind his desk grinning through his glasses. I hadn't said anything about this gorgeous girl my own age, with dark hair and dark eyes, and for whom I would have swum to Europe that afternoon if it meant seeing her.

All that summer I had worked on a building site, digging out sand from the flooded car park of an apartment building, to save for my airfare. Paddy assumed I was saving up to do something really useful with my earnings, like make more money. Whenever he found his useless son lying all over the couch, he would kick him in the butt and wonder why the hell he (a year my junior) couldn't be more like me, and show an appetite for hard work, and be conscientious, and thrifty. He never realised I was saving for another reason. I had no interest in making money or turning myself into something, as he put it, as much as an overwhelming desire to deliver myself back to the bed of the girl with whom, as people used to say back then, I'd lost my virginity.

I was living in a hostel crammed with middle-aged failures, and shared a room with a forty-year-old bankrupt. I can't remember his name but all these years on, I can still see him, with a fine gold chain around his neck, lying on his bed, propped up on an elbow smoking a cigarette. His girlfriend worked in real estate and whenever she visited, I had to take a hike.

In the main hall of the Zurich station I looked around, surprised to find men in suits drinking beer and eating frankfurters at a kiosk, amazed to find that no one was drunk or behaving badly, and no fights had broken out.

I went and stood outside the station for a while and stopped to watch city workmen in distinctive orange overalls. I was outraged by the bright colours. It was as though workingmen carried the stigma of being workingmen.

Back inside the main hall I didn't quite know what to do with myself. I felt awkward and conspicuous, and every time a Swiss person glanced my way, I was quite sure of the thought that crossed their face. It was 'You dirty little bastard, I know why you are here'. Desperate for a cover diversion, I came up with an excellent idea. I would buy a frankfurter.

I started towards the kiosk, but stopped as more customers bunched up to the counter. I anticipated an embarrassing moment when the man behind the counter would not understand what I wanted and like a moron I would have to point. I waited by a florist until the customers moved away; with the counter clear, I shot across the station to the kiosk, held up my forefinger and said, 'One frankfurter'. The man behind the counter said something in reply, which of course I didn't understand, but nonetheless I nodded back with supreme confidence. A moment later, he demanded an astounding amount of money. I discovered I had ordered a very tall glass of beer with my frankfurter.

Three or four other customers stood silently eating and drinking. I found a table. Within a few minutes they had peeled away to leave just myself and a man in a suit. He was also eating a frankfurter, but his was chopped up and he ate with a toothpick. His beer was in a moderate-sized glass. Everything about my frankfurter and the outlandish glass must have singled me out as someone ludicrous, a foreigner with a surfer's tan and beach clothes. The man in the suit smiled a few times at me, nodded at my beer, grinned, and prodded another piece of frankfurter on to a toothpick. Then, in excellent English, he asked me where I was from.

The answer was New Zealand. But all of a sudden, and quite unexpectedly, such a reply seemed insufficient, as though it didn't quite represent me in the way I saw fit. It hadn't ever presented as a problem before – although the word 'problem' doesn't quite get to the nub of what was at stake. 'Opportunity' is perhaps more accurate. I'd been asked where I was from, and here, in Switzerland, where no one knew me – apart from my girlfriend and her sister, and they were hours away – there was no one to contradict me. I could say I was from anywhere, and for the time being it would be as though I really was; I would have all the benefits of migration without the tedium of the journey and arrival.

I possibly sound more reflective now than I really was at the time. But I'm still grappling, all these years later, with why I said 'Hawaii' rather than the truth.

I can only guess that I seized on an opportunity to present myself differently to the world, and although I'd never visited Hawaii or anywhere in America, I felt I knew it, and that here in Zurich of all places the man in the suit would surely be impressed, or at least surprised in the right way of being surprised, by this blind landing of mine.

But then the man in the suit, very confidently and equally disconcertingly – while still smiling directly at me – asked, 'Where in Hawaii?'

His expression had changed. He looked interested. It occurred that, unlike me, he might actually know Hawaii. Perhaps he had visited. It was too late of course. I was stuck with my bullshit.

From reading surf magazines I was familiar with all the famous surf breaks on the North Shore, but no actual places, so I said 'Waikiki', which of course was like saying I lived in a shopping mall.

He didn't quite laugh aloud, but his response was just as deflating. He stabbed another piece of frankfurter, grinned down at his beer, and fell silent.

I was very aware that I had failed myself, and that a stranger with whom I had barely exchanged five minutes of conversation had seen right through me.

The man finished his beer and departed without a word, and I was left with a gigantic glass of beer, my frankfurter, and the paltry remains of the first character I had tried to create independently of myself.

Song

Dave Eggers

The man is in a hotel just outside Nairobi. A local friend of his has set him up here, saying the hotel was clean and cheap.

It is indeed cheap, $45 a night, but it does not seem safe. The locks on the doors do not work, and the clerk sits behind bulletproof glass. The man's room is small and smells of paint, and the outlets don't work, so he goes down to the hotel bar, which is unadorned and empty.

He orders a gin and tonic from the Kenyan bartender, who is wearing a red vest and white shirt and black bowtie. The visitor drinks his first drink down, feeling sad about so many things, wanting to be home, wanting to be doing something else, and then orders another. He takes this second drink and, not wanting the bartender to feel compelled to talk to him, he walks to the other side of the bar and sits in front of a large flat-screen television. There is a music video on, in which eight African women in traditional clothing are singing and playing instruments. The song is jangly, buoyant, joyous.

The man goes back to the bartender to ask who the band is, this all-women band in the music video. The bartender says he has no idea, so the visitor goes back to his seat and finishes watching the music video. When it's done, he sees the name of the band in the bottom right corner, writes it down, and finishes his drink. He looks up to find the bartender at his side.

'You need company?' the bartender asks. His smile is genial, his tone expecting the answer to be yes.

'Excuse me?' the man says.

'You want a woman to keep you company?' he asks.

And because the man is naive and often slow to grasp obvious things, it takes him another few seconds to realize that the bartender is offering him a prostitute.

Everywhere in the world, men who are alone or who seem alone get off airplanes or leave their hotels, and they get in taxis, and they ask the drivers of these taxis to take them to bars, or nightclubs, or to hear live music. And these taxi drivers, without heed and almost without exception, take these men to brothels.

Once, in Bangkok, accompanying a few friends, one much older and Russian and one younger and American, both of whom thought the whole enterprise — the brothels, Thailand, life altogether — absurd, the visitor found himself in a nightclub where young Thai women danced on steel stages; their attentions could be rented by the hour. A slightly older Thai woman, holding a clipboard, urged the visitor to spend some time with a young woman in the back room, and the Russian said, Do it, do it, and laughed maniacally.

Because he was a young man seeking any new experience, the visitor took his notebook and he went with the young Thai woman, feeling wretched as he followed her away from the lights of the club and through a back passageway. The young woman was tiny, shy of a hundred pounds, and led him through a series of narrow hallways, everything lit indigo, and into a white room. She closed the door. In one half of the room there was a shower, white-tiled and so big a dozen people could wash themselves at once. In the other half there was a kind of bed, high like one found in a medical examination room, with a plastic white mattress.

The young woman motioned him to sit, and he did. She quickly disrobed, revealing a body that looked much like the man's own, at age twelve. With a stern downward motion, she suggested the man take his clothes off, too, but he disabused her of any obligations to work his flesh. He told her he would still pay her for her time, but he wanted only to sit and rest and talk. She understood immediately; it was not an unusual turn of events, it seemed, for a visitor to want no part of the whole thing, to instead want to buy an hour of respite for them both. She scooted back and rested her back against the wall.

He asked her name, and she said it was Song.

'Song?' he asked.

She nodded, then took his pen and wrote the word in his notebook, in careful, impeccable English letters: 'SONE.'

Oh, Sone. The visitor assumed some clever English-speaking madam, maybe the woman with the clipboard, had devised this name, knowing it would be intriguing, sounding like something between a song and a moan, something between music and despair.

The visitor nodded, smiled, told her she wrote very well in English, and found there was nothing more to say. He drew her a few pictures in his notebook, and then, the two of them frustrated by their inability to say anything to each other, they lay side by side for the remainder of their time, the music thumping through the walls, the room otherwise as still as a grave. He briefly fell asleep.

In the bar of the Kenyan hotel, the man smiles and tells the bartender no, he needs no company tonight. He goes up to his room and tries to get online, where he looks up the all-women band he saw on the television, hoping to buy the music they made.

Extract from Song © Dave Eggers. Used by permission of Dave Eggers.

In Swaziland
Alexander McCall Smith

A lot of people are not at all sure where Swaziland is. There is no shame in that: there will always be places that any of us might find hard to locate on the map. I am less sure of where all the various '-stans' are, even if I can put my finger unerringly on Afghanistan and Pakistan. Of course even the most tolerant of us will feel vaguely hurt when we encounter people who have no idea of the location of our own countries. I have met people on my travels with no idea where Scotland, my homeland, is. I have been complimented on my ability to speak English. I have been asked whether we ever have elections, and so on: geographical uncertainty appears to have survived the proliferation of information that marks the wired age.

Of course there is a good excuse for some forms of this unawareness. In the case of at least some countries, there have been changes of name that cannot have helped. This was a major issue in Africa, where colonial names were shrugged off – understandably – on the attainment of independence. So those who knew where Basutoland was might be forgiven for not realising that present-day Lesotho is in exactly the same place. Similarly, you will search the modern map in vain for Bechuanaland, Northern Rhodesia or Nyasaland (respectively modern Botswana, Zambia and Malawi). There is a book on the subject, in fact, Whatever Happened to Tanganyika, in which Harry Campbell explains the fate of many of the country names with which those of us with stamp albums used to be so familiar.

Swaziland, if you are amongst those who are unsure of its whereabouts, is in southern Africa, sandwiched between Gauteng in South Africa (formerly the Transvaal Province) and Mozambique (still Mozambique). It used to be one of the so-called High Commission Territories administered by a British commissioner based in Mafeking in the Cape Province of South Africa. Mafeking for a spell became Mmabatho when it was part of the generally unrecognised state of Bophuthatswana, and then became Mafekeng (changing one i to an e) when Bophuthatswana disappeared off the map altogether. Simple.

Swaziland did not feel the need to change its name on independence, as the name Swaziland accurately described it as the land of the Swazis. It had always been a rather peaceful country in a sea of trouble. Both South Africa and Mozambique had tragic histories – Mozambique was a colony that experienced a bitter war of liberation from Portugal; South Africa narrowly averted what would perhaps have been a bloodier war, but had a well-known sad history behind it. Swaziland, for the most part, managed to avoid being sucked into both of these conflicts.

Swaziland is not a democracy in the Western sense. For much of the twentieth century it was governed by a king, King

Sobhuza II, who reigned for the longest period of any recorded
monarch. Although no democrat, King Sobhuza ruled wisely –
in a paternalistic way – and there was little of the civil conflict
that beset many newly independent African states. To his great
credit, the King was reluctant to allow capital punishment – in a
region where enthusiastic use was made of the death penalty. He
was also a great friend of old traditions, particularly polygamy.
The King had a very large number of wives, requiring a bus
to transport them to the more important events. His clan, the
Dlamini family, occupied most important positions, and there
was a presumption that a government minister's name would be
Dlamini – unless otherwise advised. Dlamini was, in fact, the
most common name in the country, there being royal Dlaminis
and then lesser grades of Dlamini.

That is the country where I went to work in 1980, sent by
my then employer, the University of Edinburgh, as part of its
programme of partnership in legal education with Swaziland,
Botswana and Lesotho. Our small plane dropped down over
a landscape of modest green hills and meandering dirt roads,
landing on an airstrip that saw a couple of planes a day from
Johannesburg over the border and nothing much else. This was
Manzini, a sprawling and uncluttered town, on the edge of which
was the neat cluster of low white-washed buildings that made up
the university campus.

There were two hotels in town at that time: the George on
one of the three or four streets that made up the centre, and the
splendidly named Uncle Charlie Hotel on the outskirts. I stayed
at the George for the couple of nights before my house on the
campus became available. I was young, and a bachelor at that
stage, and could have done with a small apartment, but a few
days later I was given a three-bedroom bungalow with a veranda

and a couple of acres of garden. This was to be my home for the next six months, and all I needed was a car to get around in and I would be well set-up.

A car was proposed by a colleague. He knew of an orange VW Beetle that had a good history, having been owned by a mechanic at the local garage. This vehicle was for sale and Swaziland's hyper-efficient bush telegraph had notified the mechanic that I was in the market for a car. Every African country has an unrivalled system of ensuring that news gets to where it needs to reach. There is no such thing as anonymity in these small African countries: everyone who needs to know who you are and what you want will be told – and usually very quickly.

The orange VW started first time and continued to do so for the full six months I was in the country. It made strange sounds, but so did many cars in Swaziland: indeed I should have been suspicious had it not made any odd noises. It had seen better days, of course, but I was not really going anywhere important.

So now I was in the house, with a car, and a job to do. I sat on the veranda that first evening in my new accommodation and looked out over my garden to the fence at its end. Beyond the fence was uncultivated bush of the sort that is so common in Africa – scrub with tall grass and narrow paths that wind off in directions known only to themselves. In the distance, beyond gradually sloping ground, rose a small range of mountains. One of these mountains was forbidden territory, as in one of its caves the kings of Swaziland are buried in their leopard-skin robes. It was a romantic setting by any standard.

I had a kitchen and kitchen equipment, of course, but there are ways of doing things in Africa and one of them is that a single man is discouraged from cooking for himself. Things have changed by now – to some extent – but in those days there was a very strong expectation that if you were in a position such as mine – a householder, and particularly a foreign one – you would make your contribution to the local economy by employing a maid or cook to look after the house and somebody as well to look after the garden.

So it was that the day after I moved in I was visited by people wanting domestic work. I had no means of distinguishing between applicants and so I employed the first two who presented themselves and seemed keen. The maid was a young woman in her early twenties. She had the friendly smile and good manners that are so typical of southern African countries. She was delighted to be offered the job, although there was one major drawback: the house had almost no furniture. All that I had was a bed, a couple of chairs and a table. There were not even any curtains – a lack that became significant later on.

The maid rose to the challenge. She seemed to spend a lot of time polishing the floors, with the result that they soon resembled an ice-rink. I slipped several times before I worked out that the best way of ensuring safe passage was to walk around the edge of the rooms and never in the centre. She was keen to cook, although I did not really want her to do that. However, the pressure was intense and I agreed that she could cook me one meal a day and leave it in the fridge for me to eat in the evening after she had returned home. Unfortunately the food that she cooked for me was largely inedible, being composed, for the most part, of grease and unidentifiable lumps of meat. It remained in the fridge and seemed to be eaten during the day – presumably by the maid or her friends. It was, I think, a satisfactory arrangement all around. I paid for the food, of course, but I understood that this was just another form of local taxation.

The garden was looked after by Simon, a young man who was very keen on the job but not a natural gardener. He had, however, a few strawberry plants that had been planted by a former tenant, and he guarded these diligently. When the strawberries ripened, he ate them. Again I did not mind as this was, I imagined, an old tradition.

I took to having my meals in a curious, rather run-down restaurant about a mile away down a side road. This place had a Portuguese name and was owned by a charming and agreeable woman who was highly regarded in the area. She employed a competent chef who excelled in the making of peri-peri chicken. That was what most people ate when they dined there; in fact, I do not think the other options on the menu were ever ordered.

The same people were there every day. One of these was a professor from the university, a man who came from a nearby African country and who had little time for any students who dared to enter. 'This place is not for students,' he said. 'It is for us. It is our place.' He also made a peculiar remark that I have remembered very clearly over all these years. 'Here I sit,' he proclaimed one evening, 'exuding knowledge.' Modesty was not his most obvious quality.

Another regular was the sister of the local Roman Catholic priest who played cards every evening with the owner of the café, slapping the cards down on the table top under the creaking ceiling fan. There was little else to do. The only other option was to go to the George Hotel or to the Uncle Charlie. That was it. But everybody was happy enough in these Graham Greene-like surroundings, and I was too, being a devotee of the seedy settings of Greene's novels. I had no idea that I was about to meet a murderer.

This is how it happened. I had driven the orange VW into Manzini one day to have lunch in the George Hotel – the week's big treat. Getting into my car in the car park after lunch, I was greeted by a local man somewhere in his late fifties, wearing a battered wide-brimmed hat. He came up to me as I was about to close the car door. 'There you are!' he said. 'It's very good to see you.'

Like most of us, I like to make an effort to be polite when accosted by strangers who appear to recognise me. After all, you can hardly remember everyone you come across. This, I thought, was such a case.

I returned his greeting. 'Of course!' I said. 'How are you?'

'Oh, I am well, thank you. And you?'

'I am well too. Very well.'

There then followed a silence that was eventually ended by him. 'You remember me, don't you? I'm Albert Dlamini.'

I should have said that I did not. I should have said that he was making a mistake and that I was busy and had to go. Instead I said, 'Yes, of course, Mr. Dlamini.'

This pleased him. 'Would you mind taking me out to Kwaluseni?'

Kwaluseni was the village near the university campus. The fact that he knew I would be going in that direction made me think that he must have met me before – otherwise, how would he have known my destination. The answer to that, of course, is that there are always eyes watching in Africa. They see more than we imagine.

I could not refuse to take him as my car was manifestly empty apart from me. So he got in and we set off up the hill and along the winding road that led to the campus. Our conversation in the car was general – and not every extensive. His English was good enough, even if not all that fluent. It demonstrated, though, that he was a man who had benefited from a certain level of education.

He said that I could drop him near my house, and I agreed to do that. That, I think, was a mistake. If you drop somebody near your house, then he knows where you live. I was naïve. But I dropped him off and I thought that was that. I was to be proved wrong.

Behind my house was a small flat-roofed building that was intended for the occupation of domestic staff employed in the main house. The maid lived with her family, as did Simon, the gardener; neither needed the one-room accommodation that these staff quarters offered. Word had got out, though, that I had an empty staff room, and I had been approached by a female clerk in the university who asked whether she could possibly rent the room. I agreed, but said that I did not need to be paid rent. That was well-received and she moved in, her accommodation problem neatly and very satisfactorily solved.

I noticed, though, that she had a lot of male visitors. It was not for me to take an interest in what my tenant did, and so I paid no attention to any of that. When you are a guest in other people's country, you should, in general, mind your own business.

Now, a day or so after my encounter with Mr. Albert Dlamini, I was sitting one evening in the small study that I had at the back of the house. Because there were no curtains I could have been seen by anybody standing outside in the African night. The only protection given from watchers would be the riot of bougainvillea that grew outside the window, but that was hardly enough to afford privacy.

It was about eight at night, and pitch black outside. I was working at my desk, which was so positioned that I was facing away from the window. Suddenly I had the feeling that eyes were

upon me. It is a curious feeling, inexplicable and quite chilling.
I froze.

When I turned around I saw a face at the window staring in
at me. It was Mr. Albert Dlamini in his broad-brimmed hat. My
heart seemed to stop for a moment.

I stood up and went to the front door.

'Yes, Mr. Dlamini,' I said. 'What do you want?'

He took off his hat and held it as a supplicant might, fingering
the brim. 'I need money to go to the funeral of my brother. I have
no money.'

It was a common hard-luck story – utterly unexceptional in
that part of Africa. I realised that the only way of getting rid of
him would be to give him something, and so I did just that. He
thanked me and disappeared into the night.

The next day I happened to see my tenant in the university
offices. 'Somebody came to my window last night,' I said. 'He
gave me quite a fright.'

She frowned. 'Who was it?' she asked.

'He's a man called Albert Dlamini.'

She said nothing for a moment, and then, 'Describe him.'

I embarked upon a description, but she soon stopped
me. 'That is Albert Dlamini, the well-known murderer,' she
announced. 'If he comes back, you call me – understand? Just
call me in my house and I will deal with him.'

Two days later, a Sunday, I saw Mr. Albert Dlamini walking
towards the house. Without letting him spot me, I went out a
side door and knocked on my tenant's door. She was entertaining
at the time, I think, but came out wrapped in a large white towel.
I told her that Albert Dlamini was on his way. Her brow set, she

wrapped her towel around her more securely and made her way down the front path to intercept the unwelcome visitor.

I heard a terrible shouting. Looking out of a window, I saw my tenant shaking her fist at Mr. Albert Dlamini while screaming at the top of her voice. He cowered before the verbal onslaught. He took one step backwards and she advanced. She was a very substantial lady – traditionally built, in fact. He retreated, all the while under a barrage of what I imagined was choice and unambiguous Siswati language. Then he turned tail and fled.

My tenant came in and smiled. 'We will have no more trouble from him,' she said.

And she was right. I often think back on those six months in Swaziland and reflect on my good fortune in being able to spend some time in that lovely country and amongst those kind people, where even the murderers, if spoken to sharply enough, will leave one in peace to look out over the mountains.

Innocents Abroad
Richard Ford

I can't remember why we had to go to Morocco. We'd never been abroad. My wife, Kristina, had lived in Japan and Hawaii with her Air Force family, but she had been a child then. And that was not true travel anyway; just a version of removal. I'd been to Mexico, but only to play basketball for my church team. Once I'd crossed a bridge to Canada just to drink a beer at the age of eighteen. But I came right back. Europe, however – never; never England; never to Asia. Double-never to Africa.

We were in our middle thirties. Suburban Jersey-ites, transplanted from the South. I'd written a novel and had a romantic idea that I wouldn't 'go abroad' until my books paved the way. They hadn't yet.

Morocco was, however, vividly on my screen – along with Timbuktu, Trieste, Annapurna, Bali; exotic names which, if you went to the places they represented, would signify something interesting about you, even if they were hell-holes. 'We were in Annapurna – you remember, sweetheart…' 'We took that long, dusty drive down to Timbuktu. It was that long year it didn't rain.' I thought like that. Travel was good because you could tell about it – sort of the way many boys think about sex.

But I'd read Gavin Maxwell's book, *Lords of the Atlas*, about Thami El Glaoui, the ruthless Pasha of Marrakech, who well into the twentieth century savagely guarded the mountain passes into Morocco from the Maghreb and knew no mercy. I'd also read Paul Bowles, who lived in Tangier and was American and mysterious and brilliant. Like everybody else, I'd seen *Casablanca*. It was all enough to make me want to go there.

The reasons you decide to go someplace are rarely logical. Ideally, I suppose, one's first foreign travel would move you outward from home in widening, concentric circles. From America to Canada and Mexico. Then to… well, Greenland and maybe the Caribbean? That isn't how it happens. Something draws you – a name, a book you read, a friend's tale of adventure, a movie, something you fantasize. An impatience with your own ignorance.

So, in 1980, we went.

First, it must be admitted, we went to Tunis. I had to find Tunis on the map. A friend from New Jersey had been posted in the US embassy there, and he invited us. Parties on the parterre. Handsome, lacquered people. A trip into an actual desert. Tunisians idling in cafes, drinking coffee, sniffing fragrant flowers. The ruins of Carthage were nearby. Everyone was nice. I'd never been in an embassy. But my eyes were tending west.

What we thought we were going to do in Morocco, I don't know. Be there. Soak Morocco up like a sponge. Don native garb, figure out what and where the Kasbah was (or a Kasbah, if there were more than one), lurk around the steps at Paul Bowles' house. We didn't know how to travel. We could've got guidebooks, like Brits. Read some history. But I didn't like the too-planned feel of that. Tourists read guidebooks, but only got to see the usual stuff. We weren't tourists. We were Americans abroad. We'd find and see things others wouldn't.

Our flight from Tunis to Tangier – on Royal Air Maroc – was not to be without incident. In subsequent years – due to seeing too many movies – I've always found crossing international borders to be fraught, disagreeable ordeals. Even in Europe today, when to go by train from France to Germany is barely noticeable, it still feels risky. As if stiff-necked, crisply-uniformed border police were about to enter one's compartment, barking orders, requiring documents.

As soon, however, as we were inside the wobbly old DC-7 and buckled into our Royal Air Maroc seats, someone began shouting in French from the back of the plane, insisting a certain Arabic-named passenger was on board but unaccounted for. A very uncomfortable silence lingered inside the cabin. We were all looking around to see who was who. What was this all about? Then all at once we were noisily told – all of us – to depart the plane immediately. Something was highly irregular. With us out on the blistering asphalt in the whistling desert wind and the beating sun, our luggage was piece by piece tossed from the plane's cargo hold down onto the tarmac. We were rather rudely told to go stand by our bags until all pieces were matched to passengers. Which proved not to be possible. Mr. Ali or Mrs. Ali wasn't actually on our plane, though his or her luggage was. This fact was presently certified, and the Ali luggage trucked away. We were all told to climb back on, which we did.

Why, though, I asked Kristina once were re-belted in, why would it make so much difference if a simple piece of luggage without its owner went on our flight? A short flight over to Tangier. What was the problem? Whoever owned it would catch up sooner or later. That's how people thought then.

In Tangier all was extremely agreeable. A bit of Arabia, a bit of Africa, a bit of Europe – everything nicely sized down. Two distinct and beautiful oceans. Not too much of anything, only quite hot. Our hotel – I want to call it the Mediteraneé – was greenly bowered and stuccoed above the city, though not all that high. There were ceiling fans and a greenish tint to the air, tiny red birds in the eucalyptus, non-poisonous lizards on the viney walls. We enjoyed a spacious balcony over tree tops and roofs, and far in the distance the silent, green Mediterranean. There was no atmospheric mosquito netting on the bed and no one wore a turban or a white suit, but there was gin in the patio bar and the other guests – whom we didn't talk to – seemed interestingly preoccupied and to have all been there before and know the staff. To me, it was perfect. We imagined Paul Bowles probably came there on weekends, although we didn't know what he looked like.

In the many hours of the day and night, the muezzin recited the Adhan from a mosque, the starkly tall tower of which we looked straight toward down the hill. Its presence and willowy call were comforting and reliable and good. I knew nothing about Islam, but felt sure it was unfairly thought about where I was from. I could easily live in Tangier.

Something about the presence of the Rif – the northern-most lowering spine of the Atlas Mountains – made us feel, after a day or two, in need of adventure beyond what we'd so far experienced. We needed to go there. The word alone – Rif (say 'Reef') – bespoke ancient, isolated, craggy places and the blue-eyed Berber ancestors of the terrifying Glaoui. We were told at the hotel that if we went by the easterly route, we could reach Fez more quickly and pass along the Rif. In Fez, I'd been told, you could enter the medina and never be heard from again and not really care if you were never heard from again. It was like in a Bowles story.

A car was required. Euro-car at the airport had these, though not any good ones – no Renaults or big, powerful, deep-throated Citroens to mow down the mountains. An ancient gray, snail-ish Deux Chevaux was the best we saw in the dusty lot. It would hold what we brought and would be economical, if pokey. It was cute, in a way – foreign. In the 60's, we'd once driven an ancient Beetle with slick, rubber-band tires from Texas to Montana, right up through the Rockies. All had gone well, then. This would be like that.

Someone must've told us about the kief merchants. Morocco was all about drugs – we knew that. Weren't those men in djellabas, sitting around hookahs in the Kasbah, smoking hashish? Back in the States, the strongest, most bliss-inducing, brain-crunching black-tar rock was said to be 'Moroccan'. We understood you could have it shipped right from here to your house in Princeton, where we lived (assuming the Postal Service wasn't wise to you). Of course you didn't want to get caught with drugs in Morocco, and definitely didn't want to buy anything here. The police were ghoulish and violent (distant relatives of the Glaoui). And Moroccan jails – full of luckless American youth, wasting away forever – made Mexican jails look like Holiday Inns. We were on our guard. We weren't druggies anyway. Kristina was a professor at NYU.

Today, the thought of driving an old rickety, underpowered French rent-a-car through treacherous, mysterious Moroccan mountains seems poorly-advised on the face of it. Much has happened in between then and now, of course. Back in 1980, though, I didn't give it much thought. Moroccans drove on the right. There was good hardtop. The stop signs all said STOP. Traffic lights were the trusted red-yellow-green. The rest you'd just deal with. I'd driven a station wagon through Mexico to play basketball, and we'd done okay there– at worst, a few laughable miscues with the natives. But if you had a flat someone would always help you for a little dough. There was a universal language of amity. People were more or less the same wherever. They were good.

What we'd heard, somewhat darkly, however, was that if you drove the highway (it would be the N2, today), you very well might see citizens standing on the side of the road, holding big chunks of hashish up in the air, wanting you to stop and buy it. This was very different from the rustic, rural farm stands we had in New Jersey, where every fall we bought red tomatoes, eggplants and mums, plus decorative ears of corn to hang on the front door. Selling hashish was known to be illegal – even in Morocco. These sellers were breaking the law. The fact that they did it anyway, that everyone knew they did it (including the police), that it was a local custom and vital spring for a trickling revenue flow – that didn't really change things fundamentally. Any attempt by us to participate in the colorful local micro-economy wouldn't be a good excuse if we got busted for buying drugs on the side of the road.

Don't Stop was thus the order of the day. Have no business with these people. Yes, the often disheveled, usually smiling, impoverished-appearing man (or woman) might be a local villager scraping along by selling the odd brick to passing Americans hoping to get innocently loaded at day's end. But that impoverished appearing man also might be someone else. A policeman. Or a policeman could be waiting in the weeds just behind him to arrest you. Or he might be a desperate character scheming to kill you, steal your money and leave you in the weeds. Many things could happen – almost all of them bad. It wasn't our country. It was theirs.

The road out of Tangier was clear and straight and everyone, indeed, drove on the right. There was modern traffic and the mountains rose out ahead of us. Along the way we passed hand-drawn carts and people carrying things on foot and on their heads, and many just standing on the dusty shoulder, watching us go by. It was the undifferentiated, third-world interface of urban, ex-urban and rural – pretty much the way I expected it. Mexico in Arabic.

After a while, the road turned south but still angled easterly toward the mountains. What had been the flat, oceanic plain of the Mediterranean began to be rising land, rocky and characterlessly delving – like the back-lot where American Westerns were shot. Big boulders on the roadside, low scrub trees, nothing growing, no one living anywhere in sight, no animals or buildings.

Which was where we saw the first human being selling hashish. He was standing atop one of the big sand-colored boulders, holding what must've been a brick of dark hashish in the air for us to see and immediately stop and buy. 'Jesus,' Kristina said, as I kept on driving, possibly a bit faster, 'it's just like they said in the hotel. It's amazing.' By then – by which I mean immediately – other men became visible atop other big boulderish rocks or else scuttling out from behind them, flagging at us and similarly holding up what we assumed to be entirely illegal chunks of hashish – which, were we to stop and make a purchase, would land us in jail or worse.

I wasn't stopping. Indeed, I pushed the little French sewing machine right up into its highest measurable speed – possibly 60. The roadside soon became quite cluttered with people – men and women, young and old – wanting to sell us contraband drugs. We didn't see anyone else stopping. Indeed, ours seemed to be the only car on the road. It didn't seem really feasible to turn around and drive back to Tangiers, since we'd have had to slow and stop to turn around. And that, we felt, would've given the kief sellers a chance to swarm us and block our way. And so as the road became narrower and devoid of traffic, and unhappily rising into the first elevations of the mountains, and as I persisted in my unwillingness to stop, the whole experience of 'being abroad' began to be decidedly and quickly creepy – and dangerous.

'I don't think this is such a good thing,' Kristina said.

'No,' I said, pushing my face nearer the narrow windshield like a fighter pilot, taking a better grip on the oversized steering wheel.

Some of the hash dealers by this point – we were far from any town or settlement – were darting brashly out into the roadway, shaking their chunks of hash at us, then dancing back onto the dusty shoulder as we hummed past. Rather like a matador brushing a passing bull. Only there were quite a few matadors. And I noticed that when we didn't stop, the smiles they were showing us when we faced them, were all changing to barking, scowling frowns of resentment as we disappeared on down the highway – headed where, we couldn't really have said.

It is not an exaggeration to depict this, almost thirty-five years later, as a very bad scene. I saw no police; though the appearance of police would've been as anxious-making as heart-calming. Why were we here, they'd have wanted to know. Did our car contain contraband? Was this chunk of high-quality kief in the boot not ours? Did we think it was all right to buy drugs here? Let's have a look at your documents? As panicked as I was beginning to feel, I actually didn't mind not seeing a police car.

Though I was suddenly fully alarmed to see in the rearview mirror a pint-sized white pick-up pull out from behind one of the big boulders and grow quickly in size as it sped up behind us. In pursuit. 'They're following us,' I said.

'What are you going to do?' Kristina said, craning her neck around to view the truck – a dilapidated Datsun of the sort I've since seen members of the Taliban use to transport prisoners to their execution sites. 'You assholes,' Kristina said back at the truck, which had a driver and also a rider who was leaning out the side window waving another big block of hashish and of course smiling. The driver began honking his horn, and I could see through the several panes of dusty glass between us, that he was also talking animatedly, possibly shouting, occasionally waving his arm out his own window and clearly wanting us to pull over.

Which I did not intend to do. By now the road had further narrowed and become windy up into a low revetment of mountains. Off to one side was now a steep fall-off. It would be easy, even without being chased and harassed, to drive right off and never been found again (a theme, here). I was now driving faster. The white Datsun had begun making radical automotive attempts to pull alongside of us, its tires scattering gravel and dirt and risking its purchase on the perilous road. The driver was going on shouting at us. The rider with the brick of hashish was all the way out the passenger window to his waist, waving and flourishing the brick in the hot mountain air. Our Deux Chevaux was maxed out in both speed and maneuverability – hitting the sudden curves precariously so that I had to drag on the steering wheel to keep the wheels nearer to the mountain-side shoulder than the cliff side, where the Datsun was doing its best to pull even with us.

I had never been terrified before. I realize that only now. I was thirty-six. Kristina was thirty-four. I hadn't gone to Vietnam – though I'd tried. I hadn't done especially perilous things in my life – dived deep into an ocean, raced motorcycles, sky-dived, committed crimes that got you killed, risked my life for either good or bad reasons. But up there on that mountain road in the Low Atlas – the Rif – with my wonderful young wife in my charge, and my own ignorance and imprudence on vivid display, I was extremely scared to be where I was and doing what I was doing, and hadn't the slightest idea what I should do to save us. Keep driving and faster? Don't stop? Hope something happens to make all this bad shit go away? Those seemed to be about my best choices.

At about which point, the Datsun with the two men inside went churning right past us on the left – dizzyingly tempting the abyss – and swerved hard to the right in front of us, so that to avoid a collision, I cut the Deux Chevaux wheels sharp to the right, slammed the brakes and came to a rattling stop half on the shoulder and half up the side of a rocky embankment that almost flipped us over but didn't.

The two men in the Datsun were already out and walking toward where we sat in our car, shaken up and badly discomposed. These men didn't look like anybody special. They were ordinarily dressed – soiled-looking trousers and t-shirts – not large, not menacing, not particularly intent. They were just walking toward our car. And they were murderers. These were what murderers looked like: guys who worked in your backyard at home.

'They're going to kill us now,' Kristina said, staring straight out at them.

'Yes,' I said, 'I think they are.' Or I said something like that – something movie-ish and grave sounding.

I didn't have any sort of weapon. We were Americans abroad. We weren't armed in any way except with poor judgment. The two men stopped twenty feet from the Deux Chevaux. They weren't apparently armed either, although I assumed they were armed. In the back seat of our car was a 64-ounce glass bottle of Coke – empty. This, I grasped, holding it like a cudgel, by its neck, and without more movie-ish words, barged out onto the roadside and into the heat and still-settling dust – bent on doing what, I'm not sure: die defending my wife and self with an empty pop bottle.

'What's wrong with you?' one of the two men shouted at me – in French. My French was somewhat better than infantile, but wasn't set up for this kind of impromptu give and take. And yet it sprang forth – to my rescue. 'You're scaring us to death,' I shouted at them – in French (I don't know where it came from). My big Coke bottle was gripped at my side.

Both men started laughing. 'What are you going to do with that bottle?' one of them said.

'I don't know,' I said. 'It's all I've got.' I wasn't laughing. I was angry. But I was more afraid than angry. Kristina said they were going to kill us, and I thought she was right and this was how getting killed probably always got underway. Nothing glamorous. They shot you while you were holding a big Coke bottle in your hand, then went and had a nice lunch.

'Why won't you let us sell you some kief?' the one man said. The driver. 'That's all we want to do. It's what we do for a living. You won't let us do what we do.' He'd begun speaking English now and seemed – they both did – extremely good-natured and agreeable.

'I don't want to buy any kief,' I said. 'Kief's illegal. It's crazy.'

'Well, all you had to do was say that,' the driver said. 'You were being extremely unpleasant and unfriendly.'

'I'm sorry,' I said. 'You scared the shit out of us.'

This man now advanced toward me, while the other with the ingot of black kief began walking back to the Datsun. Kristina hadn't left the car. It was very hot and the air was thin in the mountains, and we had no idea in the world where we were. Morocco.

'Look,' the man said. He wasn't tall, wore a faded, smiling-Mickey t-shirt and sockless dusty shoes – he was possibly thirty, near my age. 'Let me just give you my business card,' he said. 'When you get back to where you live – in America or Canada or England – if you write to me and order something, I'll send you some hashish. It isn't expensive. I'm Mike,' he said. The card, which was softened and had been in other hands before mine, said, Muhammed 'Mike.' Businessman.' An address was provided. I don't remember it now. I long ago lost it.

'Yes,' I said. 'That's probably what I'll do. I'll get home and write to you.'

'Then I can do my business properly,' he said. He still had his big beaming smile. He extended a small hand to me. We shook each other's warmly. Then he turned and walked back to his Datsun. He honked and waved as he and his friend drove away. I waved back. Kristina did not.

Some years ago I read that Emerson, the Ur-American genius of the here and now, wrote that 'travel is a fool's paradise.' I understand that. And although I've gone many places in these intervening years – not yet to Bali, it should be said, not

Timbuktu, not Annapurna or even Trieste – I've never 'traveled' again, never gone someplace I didn't have good business to be, where I couldn't have asked myself the question, 'Why in the world are you here?' without knowing the answer. It doesn't seem too much to ask.

Two Angels in Anatolia

Candace Rose Rardon

'For truly we are all angels temporarily hiding as humans.'
– Brian L. Weiss

When I decided to walk the Evliya Çelebi Way, a 220-mile trail across northwest Turkey, named after the 17th-century Ottoman traveler whose pilgrimage to Mecca it follows, I didn't exactly stop and consider whether doing so as a woman on my own would be safe.

I did question if my decision not to purchase a pricey GPS in Istanbul beforehand was foolhardy – the authors of the only guidebook to the route had deemed the item 'essential,' after all – but for the most part, there was little that gave me pause before embarking on the journey. Not the fact that my backpack tipped the scales at nearly half my own body weight; nor the fact that sleeping alone in a tent along a mountainous path might prove more frightening than fun; nor the fact that I spoke no Turkish and would be passing through remote villages where my chances of coming across anyone who spoke English were incredibly slim. In fact, my only real concern on the day I left Istanbul had been finding an appropriate pair of waterproof trousers to wear on the trail.

For the first three weeks, however, my time trekking through Anatolia was a brilliant success. I befriended farmers and shepherds, was invited to sleep in local families' homes, listened to the call to prayer ring out across the olive groves and tomato fields, reveled in ruins over 2000 years old, picked up dozens of new words in Turkish, and every day, grew a tiny bit closer to the route's final destination of Simav. And yes, the waterproof pants had held up remarkably well against all manner of rain, wind, mud, stream crossings, bushwhacking, forest navigating, and encounters with curious goats.

One Sunday morning, my twentieth day on the Evliya Çelebi Way and just two days from Simav, I arrived in the village of Gürlek. There wasn't much to distinguish it from the scores of villages I had already passed through. A small sign at the entrance to the town read Hoş Geldiniz – one of the first phrases I'd learned, Turkish for 'welcome'; all the narrow dusty streets led to a silver-domed mosque with two minarets, the sapphire tiles on their pinnacles gleaming in the bright sunlight; and when I came to the village *kahve*, or teahouse, I was quickly ushered inside by several gray-haired men for a steaming cup of *çay*.

Like the countless other villagers I'd met during the trek, they laughed away any attempt to leave a lira or two in the saucer of my tulip-shaped teacup.

By the time I left Gürlek, my belly was warm from tea and my heart from yet another gesture of kindness from strangers.

I had heard stories about Turkish hospitality before arriving
in the country, but it had been altogether different – and
profoundly humbling – to experience it for myself, time after
time. So caught up was I in my reverie, reflecting over the
generosity I had been shown on my journey thus far, that it
took me longer than it should have to notice two young men
following me out of the village.

They seemed to be in their early 20s, and I recognized one
of them from the *kahve*. He had offered to accompany me over
a mountain, claiming it was a shorter way than the stabilized
road I planned to take, but I'd declined. Apparently he hadn't
accepted my answer. No matter how fast I walked, they held my
pace. This went on for fifteen minutes, until I turned around and
thought I might as well confront them head-on. I planted both
feet in the ground, Superwoman-style, and held my walking stick
as though it were more than just a long branch I'd found on day
eight and carried with me ever since.

'What do you want?' I asked, hoping I looked far more
formidable than I felt. 'Why are you following me?'

Sly grins broke out across their faces. 'We go to our fields.'

I couldn't argue with this, but still I was shaken. I passed
a small farmhouse and saw an older couple sitting outside.
We waved hello to each other, and though I contemplated
stopping and waiting for the guys to pass, I kept going.
Minutes later, a car pulled up and lowered its window. It
was the same couple, offering me a ride to the next village
of Üçbaş, some two hours away on foot. This wasn't the first
time I had been taken as an unsuccessful hitchhiker. People
were constantly slowing down beside me, and I was forever
having to tell them that I was *gezmeye gitmek*, or taking a
walk. A very long walk, you might say.

I didn't know if this couple was merely being kind, or if they had seen the guys on my trail and taken it upon themselves to convey me safely to Üçbaş. As we talked, I watched the pair come into view and turn down a side road between fields. I watched them until they crouched to the ground and disappeared out of sight. I thanked the couple, explained that if at all possible, I wanted to walk every mile to Simav, and continued on the path. A little voice inside me asked if I was being stubborn or just stupid.

After a few minutes, I glanced behind me and saw the men cutting across the field, once again heading in my direction. That's when my annoyance turned to fear.

It isn't something I experience often in my day-to-day existence as a writer and artist, sitting at my desk or sketching on-location. But here there was no mistaking it – the pulse-quickening, blood-thickening instinctual feeling of fear, pumping a steady surge of adrenaline into every cell in my body. I could feel it at the tips of my fingers, coursing through my veins, making every hair stand on its unwashed end. The last time I'd felt fear so physically was at the edge of the Nevis Highware Platform in New Zealand, as I was about to throw myself off the country's highest bungy jump. But there had been a safety cord around my ankles then, and despite official warnings and waivers, I had every reason to believe I would be just fine.

There was no such assurance on the road out of Gürlek. Again I had thrown myself off the edge of a safe life into the unknown, and for three weeks, by the grace of God or chance or some uncanny combination of the two, I had stayed out of harm's way. The villagers I met never failed to warn me of the dangers I faced – of dogs and bears, wolves and wild pigs, and those they called 'bad people.' The first question they always asked was *korku*? Was I afraid? Every time, I blithely assured them I was not, that I had met nothing but good people, but deep inside me that same voice spoke – was I trusting or just naïve?

I couldn't help but think that maybe my luck had at last run out. Had the limits of my innocent faith in the world and its ability to take care of me been stretched too far? I was alone on a deserted road in rural Turkey, I hadn't checked in with my family for days, and I didn't even know if the road I'd taken was the one I needed to be on. Behind me were two guys whose intentions for following me were anything but clear. Did they have their eyes set on the expensive camera swinging from my neck? Perhaps the wallet one guy had seen me take out of my backpack in the *kahve*? Or was their objective much darker? As a woman who usually travels alone, I am all too used to conjuring up a hundred worst-case scenarios in my mind.

I didn't want to let the guys know I was worried, so I forced myself to keep my gaze fixed straight ahead. I walked as fast as I could until it would be considered running. I came to a stretch in the road where it partially bent back on itself, and when I crossed a short bridge that was sheltered by oak trees, I cast a quick glance behind me through the branches.

Not only were the guys still there, now they were the ones running.

And so I did what I'd done a few other times on the path when things were getting desperate. I stopped walking, looked up at the big blue dome of a sky stretching out above me, and said three words: 'Please help me.'

What I had hoped would materialize was another car – preferably one aiming for Üçbaş – but what I couldn't have known to pray for were two middle-aged men suddenly emerging from the forest, walking sticks clicking in time with their stride, ambling towards my path as though this were a perfectly normal place to be on a Sunday morning stroll.

'Merhaba!' I called out to them. Hello!

I waited for them to reach the road, and was relieved when they said I was heading in the right direction. We said goodbye and went our separate ways – me to Üçbaş, they to Gürlek. I felt some of the stress begin to fall away, knowing there was now a buffer between the two guys and me. I was even wondering what the guys might say if they encountered the men when I heard a loud voice booming from above.

I looked towards the top of the bluff and saw it was the same two men. I didn't understand what they were saying, but again, I stood there while they made their way down the road. And when they got to where I was, they carried on walking with me as though we hadn't just parted five minutes earlier. I didn't get it. Had they, like the couple from before, come across the guys and realized I might need help? Or had they simply discussed the situation between themselves – this blond-haired, fair-skinned female foreigner walking on her own – and decided she could use some company to the next town?

They walked with me for an hour, and as we walked, I got to know them. Their names were Ismail and Murat, and from what I could tell, they had been friends since they were kids. Ismail was 62, with salt-and-pepper hair and a matching mustache. Murat was five years younger and several inches shorter. They were each dressed in the standard male villager's outfit – button-down collared shirt, pressed pants (or jeans, in Ismail's case), and a blazer with patches on the elbows. Although they had both grown up in Gürlek, Ismail said he now lived in the seaside city of İzmir, and was back for two weeks seeing family and friends.

Walking with Ismail and Murat, I'd never felt safer on the trail. In an instant, the pendulum of my fear had swung to the other side. I could relax and finally notice how beautiful the countryside around us was. The open rolling hills, which before had seemed almost too open, too quiet, were once again inspiring, their slopes a pastoral patchwork of autumn's glory. The two men laughed a lot, and I imagined it to be the laugh of old friends ribbing each other. They introduced me to a few shepherds we passed, and every so often, Murat would stop and dig around in the soil along the road with his walking stick. I didn't know what he was looking for until, at one point, he kicked away dirt from what appeared to be a round white stone, reached down, and wrenched from the ground the largest mushroom I had ever seen. He carried it with him proudly, his walking stick in one hand and the mushroom held high in the other. It took Ismail 45 minutes to remember he had a plastic grocery bag in the front pocket of his blazer, which he then ceremoniously fluffed open and gave to Murat to transport his prize in.

Soon after Üçbaş came into sight on the horizon, we arrived at a junction. I would go right, the men would go left and return to Gürlek. I wanted to hug them, but settled for modest handshakes. With each man, I placed both my hands on his and tried to communicate – through osmosis if not by words – just how much I appreciated their company, just how much of a gift and a godsend it had been. I'm not sure they understood, for when they walked away, I only saw them shake their heads and mutter, 'Maşallah, maşallah.'

God has willed it. God has willed it.

I will always wonder why Ismail and Murat turned around that morning, why they decided to go two hours out of their way to walk with me. I will always wonder what would have happened if they hadn't.

One of the things I've learned in my wanderings is that travel demands a certain amount of trust from us. This trust may sometimes seem naïve, but if we were to let our fear of fear have its way, we would never set off on a trip – indeed, we might never leave our homes. For as soon as we step out the door, off the edge, and open ourselves to the world, we also open ourselves to the possibility that things may not always be safe.

But I have found the rewards the world offers us are almost always worth the risk. As they were on that Sunday morning in Anatolia, when two angels walked with me on the Evliya Çelebi Way.

A Walk with a Cave Man
Jenna Scatena

The sun lowers over the mountain ridge ahead, the highest in Thailand, leaving a sudden chill in its wake. As the ember-red bus slowly climbs toward the darkening sky, I review the few things I know about John Spies: He's earned the nickname 'Cave Master of Thailand' for mapping more than two hundred caverns, some of the deepest in the world, in the northwest corner of the country. He built his guesthouse, The Cave Lodge, in 1984 mostly with his own two hands, and by paying local villagers with beer. He's Australian and married to a Thai trekking guide whom he met when he was 22. He's now 58. He's discovered ancient tribal coffins in the area and is still on the hunt for a rumored stash of World War II treasure.

Traverse the backpacker circuit in Thailand long enough and you'll hear his name. Some say he's crazy, even dangerous, and tell tales of guests at his lodge who have vanished in the nearby jungle or narrowly escaped with their lives. Others hail him as one of the very few authentic explorers left in Southeast Asia – no maps, no sponsorships, no bullshit. Just boots and a feeling he follows. But all the tales are hard to trace to their origin, leaving the man himself an alluring mystery. Which is why, on this chilly December evening, I have impetuously decided to take a five-hour bus ride from Chiang Mai to John's lodge in the jungle on the Burmese border.

The bus drops me at a dusty bench on the side of the road, where a group of women in tribal garb are dismantling their food stalls for the day. There are no tuk-tuks or taxis here; I must rely on strangers and my gut to tell me who I can or can't trust. I hitch a ride with a gentle-eyed villager in a rusty pickup. We bump along a narrow winding dirt road for miles, the sky darkening until the only lights are from the pickup's one functioning headlight and the occasional fires warming families on the side of the road. We drive so far that after thirty minutes I begin to question the driver's intention. Then we come to a halt at a weathered log cabin.

A figure opens the porch door. Scrawny shoulders slouch in a canvas German army jacket and clumps of peppered chest hair struggle out of a low, white V-neck. The first thing that comes to mind is delusions of grandeur. But there's no turning back; the truck has already disappeared into the jungle.

I evaluate the mad-scientist hair, the face that possesses a shark's sharpness. 1980's rock blares from inside.

'Well, eh, hurry up. Dinner's almost over,' he says.

This is the man I've come to meet. I hand him the equivalent of nine US dollars in jade-colored Thai baht for three nights in the main dorm.

Inside, the bamboo walls are covered with photos of local hill tribes and scrolls of butcher paper listing tours written in colorful ink. There's kayaking, caving, hill tribe treks. John's wife, Diew, scoops chicken curry from a giant wok into small bowls and hands them to the five other lone travelers and me. I eat in silence, leafing through a copy of John's self-published memoir, *Wild Times: 30 Years on the Thai Border*. It begins with a chapter about a young Australian woman who was murdered while staying at the Cave Lodge in 1988. The case was never solved. The rest of the book is riddled with titles that tease at the dark tensions of his reputation: 'Blind Drunk', 'Head for the Hills', 'Paralysis', and 'Cold Blood'. I think maybe I don't need to go on a trek with John to find the answer I am looking for. But before I can confirm this decision, John hands me a tin cup of whiskey, inviting us to a bonfire on the other side of the lodge.

'Tomorrow,' he says, prodding the flaming logs with a stick, 'I'm heading just over a ridge, above the nearby village. A friend there said he saw a new opening in the mountains. Should be back by early afternoon. Any takers?' The five other guests, all men, ignore him.

'I'll come,' I say, tossing back another swig of whiskey.

'You, eh?' he says, surprise in his gaze. I see his point: Between four burly Dutch men, one German, and me, an American woman in yoga pants, I seem the least likely choice to respond emphatically. He looks me up and down, then heads off to bed without another word.

The next morning I'm in the back of John's old pickup truck, sliding around like a load of loose cargo. We whiz past villagers boiling water over fires, turning up debris in the brisk morning breeze. Dust-cloaked children wave their hands wildly, and barefoot elderly women in black and neon garb smile at us.

The crowns of the mountains we're heading for, foothills of the Himalayas, bob on the horizon. This is the outskirts of the Golden Triangle – a remote region where the terrain is as tumultuous as the history.

The forbidding topography is riddled with gaping caves and rogue 2000-foot cliffs. Water combines with decayed plants to form a carbonic acid that leeches into tight limestone crevasses, slowly eating away at them and eventually carving out hollow valleys and some of the deepest known caves in the world. Above ground, black scorpions, tarantulas, and centipedes scuttle about, but John tells me they aren't poisonous to the point of death, unlike the snakes, such as the ill-tempered Malayan Pit Viper or the king cobras.

Inside the caves is a world even more mysterious, unpredictable, and baneful. I recall the ominous way John explained the caves by the fire the night before: Tunnels twist through the earth like an intestinal system, leading to vertical drops that plummet 1000 feet. Carbon dioxide festers and is even exhaled from some of the caves, a fact that inspired John to sarcastically recount a near-death incident in one: 'Slow death by suffocation – bloody hilarious!' And this world exists in a darkness blacker than outer space, a shade found only in the bowels of a planet.

Ten minutes into our trek, I'm barely keeping up with John as we hoof it up a barren, craggy formation toward the lush jungle and the deep blue sky. I glance below us, at the small hill tribe village where he parked the truck. John's pace is one stride per second – swift and not breaking a beat, even when a renegade rock or branch crosses his path. He reminds me of an old but sturdy train chugging up a hill, his breath deep, short, in steady bursts like a locomotive.

Given John's haggard physique and affection for whiskey and cigarettes, I'd concluded I must be in twice as good shape as him. But not even a single mile in, my chest is already tightening and my calves are cramping, while John ascends into the elements without hesitation.

'What I like about Thailand,' he says, not breaking stride, 'is that there's no permits to go into the backcountry. You can just do whatever you want and no one will stop you.'

As if on cue, a gunshot blasts in the bushes next to us. A villager emerges with a rifle slung over his shoulder and passes us, shining a smile. John grumbles the only thing that scares him are guns, the long-muzzled automatic ones, which the hill tribes surrounding the Cave Lodge carry in abundance. Luckily, John says, he's on their good side. He befriended most of the local tribes, and even lived with a Black Lahu tribe in the late 1970s, when opium addiction was rampant and kids as young as five smoked rolls of rough homegrown tobacco.

John rolls a spliff between his fingers, sucks in a steady drag and says, 'Onward, mate.' I take one last look at the thatch-roofed village below, a sight I never thought would indicate such civilization compared to what's ahead.

Three hours later we are trampling leaves the size of elephant ears as branches with the girth of a python reach toward us from every direction. My forearms sting. I look down to see hair-thin trails of blood lashed across my arms. Lime green vines twist and tighten around my ankles, as if pleading me not to go deeper, but I pull my way in. With no focal point to rest my eyes on, the jungle feels unreadable – just a shapeless nightmare of green.

I ask John if he has a knife, but really I'm hoping for a machete. 'Knife? Eh, why in bloody hell would I have a knife?'

John replies, furiously battling his way through the brush. 'That's what you got hands for.'

Then I ask if he has a compass and his response is asking if I have the time. When I realize he doesn't have a knife, a compass, or a watch, I conclude that I've just found the unfortunate answer I came here seeking: I've followed a crazy man into the wilderness. And I'm getting the feeling he has no plans to return in the early afternoon, as he'd promised. So I begin to weigh my chances of turning back on my own.

'The only thing more dangerous than going forward is turning back,' he says with the conviction of a preacher. 'But you can go whenever you like. Luck to ya.'

I survey the terrain we've covered and consider the possibility. But we've wound around too many cliffs, scaled too many peaks, and crossed too many valleys for me to be able to find my way back through this limestone labyrinth. And in the chaos of the jungle, a city girl like me wouldn't last long. I look at my water bottle. There's three ounces left. The gravity of the situation starts to set in. Every few steps I stop to gauge my chances of making it back on my own, and each time I do, a tar-like dread bubbles in my gut, telling me this time I've followed my curiosity too far.

I look behind me one last time, and confirm that I have no chance of getting out of the wilderness on my own. I must commit one hundred percent to wherever the whims of John's internal compass take me.

By 4pm we're in a poppy field, crouched below the fading sky on a corroded bamboo platform John says hasn't been used since the area was farmed for opium in World War II. For the first time I take a moment to appreciate the beauty surrounding us.

Grass almost as tall as me sways in the wind. Jagged slate grey cliffs jut out of the blond and violet brush. The sun hangs low and a streak of navy blue is widening on the eastern horizon. My last ounce of water slides too easily down my throat, a cold reminder that we're running out of time.

This must be the turnaround point, I think. But no. I should know better. Soon we are at the edge of a steep slope. John takes a step forward and his foot sinks ankle-deep into loose dirt the color and consistency of espresso grounds. He grabs a flimsy bamboo stalk for support. 'We have to move fast down this, no stopping,' he says, then charges down the cliff like a warrior sprinting into battle.

I stop at the bottom of one of the ravines; the climb up the next pass looks sketchy, with loose boulders and rocks unavoidable on the ascent. My mouth is dry and my knees are weak, from both exhaustion and fear. John sees me hesitate and pulls a small bottle of water from his pack. He's been holding out on me. 'You can have this,' he says, placing it on a rock, 'but you have to come get it.' Then he disappears over the ridge.

Dangling with one arm twisted in vines, I stretch for a distant root sprouting from the side of the cliff. But when I grab a hold, it loosens, releasing a plume of spiders with plump marble-sized bodies and toothpick legs. Dozens pour out, scurrying up my arm and scattering across my body. I feel their feathery feet tickling me as they scamper.

I look at the void below that I will fall into if I let go of the root, and I cling tighter. The water bottle is glistening in the orange sunlight, just a few feet above. I must reach it. I don't even care that hundreds of spiders are crawling on me when my other option is plummeting to a rocky death. I suddenly realize that this is all it took to overcome my lifelong fear of spiders, and start laughing. They are the least of my worries.

As we begin our descent down the next pass, John tells me he wasn't this intrepid when he first came to Thailand. He was a young backpacker, the same age as me, drifting through Southeast Asia on a shoestring when he met Diew, a beautiful Thai woman, in Chiang Mai. Diew was the first female trekking guide in the region, and the deeper she lured him into the mountains, the more he fell for her. Soon they were exploring every nook of northwest Thailand, despite the turbulent nature of it, both topographically and politically. Then the allure of undiscovered caves and rumored treasure drew them 120 miles down a dirt road, originally made as a World War II Burma invasion route, to the spot where the Cave Lodge sits today.

Now, he admits, 'It's hard to stop. The deeper I go, the greater the temptation to continue.' For John, hunting for a new cave is not unlike a junkie seeking his next fix. Realizing this, as the darkness descends around us, makes me question if he has an exit strategy, or if he will blindly follow this impulse until he finds his next cave – even if that means we're trekking for days.

We finally reach the bottom of the cliff, and discover, a few yards to our right, the dark gaping mouth of a cave the size of a grand ballroom. A foul smell wafts around us, like a monster exhaling the stench of rotting prey. I press my hands against a boulder with the texture of petrified lace and pull my way up. I cobble over a pile of four other boulders with that same ancient feel, then stop where the ground levels out inside the cave. I feel like I'm in the jowls of a sleeping beast.

The 'plunk… plunk… plunk' of condensation falling from fang-shaped stalagmites echoes around us. One, as tall as a three-story house, drips onto a patch of perfect emerald ferns and ivy. The unlikeliness of this little Eden, in this dark and foul cave, surges hope and joy through my chest so quickly it catches me off guard, and I start to choke. 'It's the only place the sun touches,' John says.

I ponder the time it took for this to form. A time incomprehensibly beyond my experience. I think of the few things in this world that are untouched. I feel a sense of the scale of the universe and for the first time in my life, I kneel down on the earth and worship something.

But my state of euphoria is short-lived. Just as the bruise-colored sky turns to black, the animals of the jungle come alive in a clamor of hoots and hollers.

'Where's your headlamp?' John asks, as he cinches his around his head.

'I don't have one. I thought you were bringing me one.'

'Eh, why would you think that?'

He turns around before I can answer, his light revealing a thick, tangled wall of thorn bushes, with no way around. John desperately beats them down, but they're resilient and slowly close up behind us, encasing us in a daggery tomb. 'Bloody fantastic,' John says, looking defeated. 'It's too thick and could go on like this for miles. Turn around.' I realize we are lost.

When we emerge from the brush, I'm pulling thorns from my sleeves while John hinges over a river as black as the moonless sky, a look of intense contemplation on his face. 'Oh, hell no,' I think. The dark watery highway rushing by four feet below feels like the edge of the universe. John hesitates, leaning forward, then back, then forward again. Tufts of whitewater scatter across the river, like puffy clouds on a black oil canvas, signs of rocks and logs beneath the surface.

John jumps and sinks chest deep, grabs a protruding branch to keep from being swept away, and begins a slow and unsteady journey across the river. When he reaches the other side, the light from his headlamp rotates around like a lighthouse and pauses on me, shining in shattered brightness through the trees. But it quickly turns back around and continues on.

I'm left with no time to weigh options, and dip myself into the rushing water. My feet slip and slide on the slick rocks beneath my sneakers. I gain my balance and slowly, inch by inch, without lifting my feet from the rocks, begin to shuffle my way across when I feel something slick coil around my ankle. I want to scream and writhe and flail like an infant, but a calm voice within tells me that will result in me being pulled down the quick-moving river, so I keep going, one inch at a time, the opposite bank looking like the farthest finish line I've ever seen. Steady, steady, I repeat to myself, while the slick wiggling body around my ankle tightens and tugs.

When I reach the other side, there's a cliff one foot higher than my upstretched hands. With no hope of pulling myself onto it, I plunge my fingernails into the dirt and begin clawing away at the cold moist earth until I reach the icy corpse of a root and curl my fingers around it. I pull myself up, prepared to rip a water snake from my ankle. But it's only a vine.

I look at my watch. Midnight. We've been in the jungle for fifteen hours, and out of water and food for seven. And now John is beginning to move on without me. My mind starts to slide into primitive desires – fire; water; a road; a path. I think of my backpack, sitting on my bed in the lodge, with my flashlight uselessly inside it, my toothbrush still moist on the bathroom sink.

Will we be the final chapter in the lore of the Cave Lodge? Or will we make it back, escaping with another story that a few will believe and spread on the backpacker trail, strengthening John's reputation and luring more naive backpackers hungry for real adventure, not heeding the warnings of those who've lived to tell the tale – don't go, he's crazy – and instead hearing adventure – wilderness – become a real man.

Just as I'm plummeting into the darkness within me, just like the cave – dark and foul beyond belief, housing a trove of beauty – a light emerges. John sees it too and starts running. I follow. My dragging feet feel light again, and soon we're both running, stumbling, savagely tearing through the jungle like the beasts it's made us.

As we approach the light, I see it's coming from a lone corroded wooden shack on a narrow dirt path. John gets to the door first and furiously knocks on it. An old man with labyrinths on his face that seem as deep and brown as the canyons we just trekked through answers it. He squints his eyes at us then chuckles, revealing only a few yellow teeth, and motions us inside.

He seats us at a table fashioned from an old splintered door, piling tepid Chang beers in front of us. We clamor for them like starved animals and guzzle, foam streaming down the sides of our mouths. The floor is dirt, iron pots are piled on white ashes in one corner, a cot with an old woven rug in the other. A single lantern rocks in the midnight draft. He's a Karen refugee from Burma, who moved here to escape the violent military junta,

John says, translating. His smile is radiant, contagious. 'He says he has a truck and can drive us back to mine.'

John climbs into the bed of the rusted Ford truck and for the first time, extends his hands to me. They feel big, weathered, and sturdy as he pulls me in. The old man offers us a few warm beers for the road.

The truck grinds up steep grades and curves around the mountains whose other side we've just braved. Stars dazzle in the sky like distant diamonds. I'll think about this experience the next time I encounter something difficult in my life: that even when we feel like our legs are giving out beneath us and there's no way we'll be able to carry on – not only can we keep going through the darkness with barely a flicker of light, but we can climb mountains and cross rivers. And still keep going. That in the world's darkest caves, there are verdant untouched gardens. And in the most remote decrepit shack, there is a jovial refugee who helped a couple of crazy strangers in the night.

I look at John, who's sitting next to me, clutching his straw hat to his chest.

A smile spreads across his face and I suddenly wonder: Was this his plan all along? I study his face hard, trying to determine the answer, but the darkness is obscuring, and I can't tell if it's a smile to be out of the jungle alive or the smug satisfaction that he's pulled off another successful stunt.

El Clavo

Amy Gigi Alexander

Glistening like gems, blue frogs hop on my path as I make my way up the mountain. I'm living in the Comarca Ngäbe-Buglé, a reservation belonging to the indigenous Ngäbe people of Panama. As resident English teacher, latrine builder, and runaway pig catcher, I walk nine miles each way every few days to visit schools below my base village at the top of the mountain. Tonight I am returning with important supplies: medicines, canned fish, coffee and books, as well as news from the rest of the world – we are too remote to have radio or phone reception.

The path before me stretches almost vertically, and my companions, a young girl who serves as my trail guide and a malnourished packhorse carrying our supplies, look as though they cannot possibly complete the journey. Yet the three of us – the most unlikely of companions – seem to have found an alliance in one another as we walk quietly without stopping through a night filled with stars and stories. Each tree we pass, each star, each twist in the road, has a story to tell for the Ngäbe. The hungry snake. The angry wife. The woman who looked at the moon. Each tale wraps itself around me like a blanket, making me feel safe and content, despite the gnawing hunger in my stomach. We haven't eaten for hours and I'm out of water, but these things seem normal now, unimportant.

I see a shape moving on the side of our path. It's so quiet that it seems like a ghost. The ghost runs alongside us, turning into a frightened and painfully thin dog. I can see the dog's pockmarked body, jutting ribcage, and fearful eyes. Suddenly, it bites the back of my leg, and we whirl about frantically as I try desperately to shake it off. As the dog lets go and disappears into the jungle, I find myself on the ground, afraid. The wound seems shallow, but I'm bleeding and there's no clinic within twenty miles. The child is more capable than I am in this moment: her face shines with intensity as she carefully wraps my leg with my extra t-shirt. I stand up to walk and see that my ankle is twisted and swelling like a Ngäbe child's pig bladder balloon toy.

Gingerly we continue to the village, walking up the steep dirt path, trying to avoid holes and ruts left by the rains and other travelers. I should feel worried about my throbbing and swelling leg, but somehow I don't; instead, I feel calm and methodical. The night sky calms me with its bright stars, so close I feel I could reach up and touch them. The usual cacophony of animal and bird sounds floats over us and leads us home.

When we finally arrive, I make my way immediately to my hut. There's no door, only tree branches holding up a bit of battered metal roofing. A few boards nailed hastily together make two walls, and my bed is a narrow sagging plank board held up by a few rickety stumps. I gratefully sit down and examine the wound. It looks as though it will need a few stitches.

When I decided to live in this remote place several months ago, I knew I would be taking risks. I wanted to be in a place with no soy lattes, no hotels, no guidebooks, no tourists, and most likely, no hospitals. I've learned that I can handle almost anything – but now I begin to feel overwhelmed. Where is that bottle of whisky that I've been lugging about? It's been tremendously handy for bribing border officials – perhaps it will prove its usefulness tonight as an impromptu painkiller! I open my pack and fish around for the bottle, and happily discover it is almost half full. Taking a noxious swig, I search for the medical kit I'd bought a few months earlier off an irritable Peace Corps worker who had told me he was fed up with the Ngäbe and was going home. I'd actually never looked inside the medical kit and am relieved to discover a tiny surgical set.

I've never sewn up a wound before, and the mere sight of blood on the average crime television show used to make me ill. But I tell myself that this will be similar to darning a sock as I thread the needle, douse the wound with some horrid brownish disinfectant, and shoo some curious chickens out of my hut. I take a big breath, take an even bigger swig of the whiskey, set the flashlight beam so that it's shining towards my leg, and get to work. Nine stiches later, I'm done – as well as a little drunk and dazed.

I change into a *nagua* – a typical muu-muu-style dress worn by the Ngäbe women – and stumble out into the village's main compound. The trees overhead and the tall sugar cane growing around us make the compound feel like an enclosed outdoor room, brightened by scattered cooking fires. I make my way over to the closest one and am invited to sit down. A tiny child hands me a gourd bowl filled with scalding hot coffee mixed with cane juice. My injured leg is well covered by the nagua, but my swollen ankle is immediately noticed by the family sitting around the fire.

A crowd gathers, poking my ankle, as the village elders decide my fate. Everyone watches as an elder takes a piece of thin metal wire and casts it into the hot fire until it turns a deep red. He then sticks one end of it firmly into a dried corncob, which will serve as the handle. He explains that this treatment is called *el clavo*, and that the Ngäbe use this hot metal rod on the skin as a curative for parasites, pain, and fatigue. As I watch the *clavo* heat up, I realize that this is a defining moment for all of us: no longer an outsider, I am becoming part of this community. I want to be brave, but part of me wishes I was back at home in a comfortable bed with no *clavo* in sight. I feel as though I'm on the outside of myself, looking in. Then I have an epiphany: I realize that the way I see the *clavo* might be very similar to how the Ngäbe see the Western medicines I've brought back with me tonight.

I'm told that the *clavo* procedure must be done by either a man who has been bitten by a snake and survived, or a pregnant woman. A pregnant woman volunteers for the task, and holding the *clavo* in one hand, she grabs my head with the other, holding me firmly in place. I immediately wonder if she's going to burn my face, for I have seen many Ngäbe with scars on their faces from burns. Am I ready to question my Western idea of beauty? I am relieved to discover she's not going to burn my face; instead, she tells me to remain very still and not show any sign of pain. This would be easier if I had drunk more whiskey, but I gather my remaining wits together and attempt to look stoic. First she burns my ankle eight times, followed by the small of my back, my stomach, and my arms. I feel dizzy as the pain sears across my skin, now an angry reddish color, sprinkled with blistering welts. As I am led back to my hut, I feel blank and empty, as if I am falling down and cannot stop. The world goes black and silent.

I awake early in the morning to the sound of the neighbor's daily evangelical sermon. Every morning I have awoken frustrated and sleep deprived by the piercing sound of his preaching. This morning I limp out of my hut and see his family listening in rapt attention, his children stroking pet doves on their laps. His wife is at the kitchen fire, and silently hands me a gourd of steaming coffee. The evangelist sounds different to me today, and I realize he's a lyrical poet, a rock star, an everyday saint. For the first time in my life, I understand that I understand nothing. For the first time in my life, I realize that everything I thought was right is most likely not right. For the first time in my life, I don't know.

I sit on my bench by the fire and drink from my gourd, listening to the morning.

Into the Puna

Virginia Abbott

We drove for hours through a vast frigid desert littered with silver rubble and scraps of ancient lava. A solitary dirt path stretched before us endlessly. It snaked past incinerated volcanoes cloaked in black ash and mountains of red earth before dissolving into a tidal wave of purple peaks bobbing in a metallic sea. A fierce sun clung to every rock, mountain and grain of sand, causing my vision to blur and my temples to pulsate. There was a sinister quality to this place that permeated my body to its core.

We were in the Puna, a high-altitude desert in the extreme northwest of Argentina near the border with Chile and Bolivia. Along with the Atacama Desert to the west and the Bolivian Altiplano to the north, the Puna comprises one of the driest regions on earth, a place so hostile to life that it is frequently compared to Mars. I had come to this region drawn by the

visual spectacle of otherworldly landscapes and had chosen the
Puna, in particular, because it is by far the most remote and
least visited of the three border regions. Now that I was here, I
felt deeply unsettled. I cringed at the glaring monotony of the
surroundings.

And yet, the Puna beckoned to me. At every turn, I would
spot a dozen stupefying images that I wanted desperately to
capture on my camera or describe in my journal. This bleak land
was stranger than I could have ever imagined and every scene
that horrified me fascinated me in equal measure. My curiosity
propelled me forward.

My journey to the Puna began a world away in Salta, a bright
and vibrant city with pleasant palm tree-filled plazas and lively
cafes. There, as I lounged with my husband, Jorge, on the terrace
of the elegant finca where we were staying, I fantasized about
our journey to the Puna. The Puna had become the focal point
of our two-week vacation to northwest Argentina after I had
chanced upon a photograph of its hypnotic clay-colored dunes
a few months earlier on the Internet. I had been immediately
captivated. I imagined myself with Jorge, driving through the
windswept dunes in a jeep, exhilarated by the magical solitude of
the desert, exploring a place that few had ever seen.

Once in Salta, I immersed myself in a book about the history
of the Puna. An ancient plateau of hard crystalline rock, it
had originated at sea level. During the Tertiary Age, with the
formation of the Andes, the Puna erupted to its present height of
13,000 feet. Long before Spanish colonists arrived, the Puna was
settled by indigenous peoples, including the Incas, who asserted
their control over northwest Argentina for roughly sixty years.

The book interspersed this historical account with spectacular photographs of dazzling salt flats and pink flamingos, both legacies of the Puna's maritime origins, as well as volcanoes, lava fields, and undulating expanses of sand. I marveled at the exotic beauty of it all.

The day of our departure for the Puna, we awoke early to meet our guide, Pompon, a jovial, middle-aged Argentine with rumpled hair, dark shining eyes and a manic energy he derived from consuming large amounts of *yerba maté* and coca leaves. Pompon possessed the wildness of a man addicted to extremes. He thrived in the harsh conditions of the Puna. He had been there hundreds of times and his skin bore the scars of life at high altitude, creased and leathery, with red cheeks permanently scorched by the sun.

As we drove south, to the province of Catamarca, the landscape emptied. Salta's verdant tobacco fields and posh vineyards gradually disappeared, replaced by barren stretches of concrete and dust. At midday, we stopped for lunch in Hualfín, a desolate village with a fate intricately tied to the rise and fall of a nearby goldmine. Not a single restaurant was open. The truckload of groceries that arrived on a weekly basis from Salta had not come that week. Exasperated, Pompon knocked on every door until a woman at a corner store with a sign advertising empanadas agreed to scrounge through her kitchen for leftovers. She reappeared with fried eggs, mayonnaise and cold slices of breaded veal cutlet, peasant food in a land where beef is plentiful.

Leaving Hualfín, Pompon announced we were beginning our ascent into the Puna. Giddy with anticipation, I watched happily as the sad concrete houses and passing trucks slowly vanished until no signs of human presence remained. Pink mountains coated with silky white patches of sand swirled before us and unfurled into plush plains carpeted with lime green and mustard-colored grasses. Herds of vicuñas, graceful mammals of the alpaca and llama family highly desired for their soft wool, galloped in the distance, camouflaged by the muted earth tones of the plains. Eventually, the grasses cleared and only sand remained. Here, the Puna unveiled milky ponds with yellow currents flashing like electricity.

At the summit, we caught our first glimpse of our destination for the night, a tiny patch of wispy trees amidst a turbulent sea of gray rubble and scattered boulders. This oasis, Pompon told us, contained a village of shepherds called El Peñón and a spartan inn where we would be the only guests during our two-night stay. I stepped out of the jeep with my camera and struggled against a ferocious wind to photograph the village and desert sprawled beneath us. Face to face with the Puna, I suddenly felt anxious. This was not the dreamy desert of my imagination. It was a dark, foreboding place in which small pockets of life were overshadowed by monstrous emptiness. I shuddered.

On our second day in the Puna, we awoke early to drive to a large lagoon with snow-white shores, known as Laguna Grande. Our journey was bumpy and long and with each passing sand dune and field of blazing yellow grass we dove deeper into the Puna's hollow netherworld. A glaring sun cast an eerie haze on our surroundings. I recoiled at the accelerating immensity and monotony of this strange world, feeling as if I were plunging into a black hole from which I would not be able to return.

From the barren stillness, a colony of flamingos emerged suddenly, pastel pink with a flare of yellow on their beaks and black ruffles on their wings. They waded calmly in a lagoon of cobalt-blue water and coarse white salt. Pompon told us the lagoon contained high doses of saltpeter, a toxic chemical used to make gunpowder. Intrigued, I crept softly from the car to photograph the flamingos. Startled by my presence, they squawked and flew from me like nervous children. They knew only the pond in which they lived, and were not accustomed to interaction with any other species. I commiserated with their isolation, feeling light years from the safe contours of the world I knew.

My discomfort intensified that afternoon when we drove through another interminable desert to a wasteland of dormant volcanoes and strewn chunks of lava, a cemetery of ancient volcanic eruptions. Here, the air choked with death and disaster. The yellow grasses of the morning, the lagoons, the vicuñas and flamingos had all disappeared. All that remained were shades of gray: dull gray mountains, silver rubble, pearl-colored boulders and charred volcanoes so black they appeared to be permanently obscured by passing clouds.

From among the shades of gray, our destination materialized: a sprawling city of jagged pumice stone nearly two stories high known as Campo de Piedra Pómez. I entered the city cautiously, as if surveying the aftermath of a terrible tragedy. A roaring wind thrashed against the boulders and sprayed them with faint red sand. Before me, a maze of pathways unfurled. I chose one and trod heavily through its fine gray gravel, my shadow consumed by the boulders towering overhead. In the distance, the foreboding Carachipampa Volcano stared at us vacantly. Terrified, yet mesmerized, I pressed ahead.

On our third day in the Puna, we awoke for another long drive, this time to Tolar Grande, a village about ten hours from El Peñón. There, we would behold the clay-colored dunes that had inspired our trip to the Puna. Yet I did not look forward to this journey. Anticipating the long hours trapped in a car in a blistering desert, I felt only dread.

Even in the early morning hours, the sun beat down on us with ferocious intensity, scorching the passing hills and empty plains. The landscapes followed the same familiar pattern from the previous days: flat expanses of seared lava and freakishly black volcanoes displaced by mountains of green and yellow grasses, rising like stairs, and then uncoiling into rolling plains of pinks and browns.

This time, however, the pink plains shattered and reassembled into a long swath of luminous white salt, the first of the Puna's giant salt flats. Two lumpy islands floated in the middle, one long and narrow, the other only a small stub, like the body and head of a giant alligator. Half buried in the salt, the alligator appeared to furtively plot his attack as we made our way across the salt flat.

Occasionally, we would pass a flowering of vegetation in the midst of a stark desert. Wherever there was green, there were people, either a hamlet or a single shepherd herding llamas. In one such oasis, amidst a sea of metallic mountains accented by purple peaks, there lived only two people – brothers – who, according to Pompon, refused to speak to each other. In another oasis, home to the village of Antofalla, we stopped for lunch. Less than fifty people lived here in wall-to-wall stone houses with miniature windows overlooking the dusty main street.

One lone tree loomed over the main street of Antofalla. Pompon had planned to spread our picnic lunch in its shadow, the only available escape from the suffocating sun. However, when we arrived, we discovered another car parked beneath the tree. Desperate to avoid the sun, we lay our picnic behind this car and teetered with our sandwiches along the tightrope of shade that remained. The sun assaulted me all the same. Overcome by a wave of nausea and fatigue, I sank woozily onto a nearby cooler.

The rest of the journey was excruciating. A powerful migraine had seized control of my head, causing my temples to throb and tears to stream from my eyes. Nausea and dehydration gripped at my throat. Pompon and Jorge repeatedly insisted I stuff my cheeks with coca leaves, the panacea for all forms of illness in the Puna. I refused. Early in the trip, Pompon had told us coca leaves produce a sensation of dryness in the mouth. I worried the coca would exacerbate the dehydration debilitating me.

Miserably slumped across the back seat of the jeep, I felt my hysteria rising. Yet I still felt compelled to document this place. One moment, tall heaps of blackened rubble rushed past us, and the next, the largest salt flat yet materialized, the Salar de Arizaro. In the opposite corner of the salt flat, a perfectly shaped pyramid soared like a cathedral 800 feet into the air. This, Pompon told us, was the Cono Arita. Though no one knew its origin, Pompon explained that many believed it to be a sacred ceremonial site built by the Inca.

I pleaded that we stop. My head pounding and my stomach on the verge of explosion, I stumbled towards the pyramid with my camera. Astonished by the presence of such a precisely shaped structure in the midst of this forbidding desert, I wondered if it was really manmade. What humans in their right minds would have chosen to construct a massive ceremonial site in this desiccated land?

By the time we reached Tolar Grande, a village of terracotta knolls and matching adobe houses, my agony had escalated to the point of crisis. I rushed past Jorge and Pompon and locked myself in the bathroom of our hotel. The rest of the night passed in a blur of vomiting, crying and collapsing into brief spells of fitful sleep. Everything I tried to consume, even water, I would immediately expel violently.

Soon, word had spread across the village that I was *mal de la puna*, the term for those who fall ill there, especially from altitude sickness. I awoke to Jorge insisting that I drink a steaming cup of coca tea. Several villagers had urged him to give me coca. This time I obeyed. I lifted the cup to my face and let its vapor cloud over me. The coca smelled pure, like earth, but in my nauseous state, it repulsed me. I drank it quickly and then bolted for the bathroom. There, I exploded in a final horrific convulsion. Minutes passed. Then, at long last, I sensed relief. I drifted into a deep, peaceful sleep.

The coca calmed me, but the following day I was still too weak and nervous to venture beyond the oasis. I remained in my hotel room with the shades drawn, ecstatic to lie swathed in darkness while the hot sun harassed the world beyond my windows. At the end of the afternoon, I agreed to join Jorge and Pompon for a drive to the nearby Desierto del Diablo, home of the glowing dunes that had appeared so magical to me from the screen of my computer. This would be our final excursion; the next day we would leave the Puna.

As we drove to the dunes, past mounds of clay and the tracks of a deserted railroad, I reflected on the barbarity of this place. For the past three days, the Puna had slowly devoured me, rattling my nerves and ultimately ravaging my body. Yet in doing so, it had aroused me intensely, heightening my awareness of the passing world in a way that rarely occurred when I was in my comfort zone. Was this, in fact, what I had craved?

Eventually we reached our destination, a crumpled sea of wind-shaped ridges spread as far as the eye could see. Dark storm clouds reeled through the sky, casting a damp chill in the air. I separated from my companions and climbed a small hill with my camera. From this vantage point, a harsh, angling light pierced my skin and a flurry of sand whipped at my hair and settled on my face. A vast emptiness enveloped me. This time, I did not resist. The following day, I would once again be in a world of gentler elements. But for now, I was alone with the Puna. I closed my eyes and surrendered to the wind.

A Walk
on Thin Ice

Simon Winchester

It was in the summer of 1965 when I saw my first ice floe. When our ship scraped past my first iceberg, when I glimpsed my first Arctic hare, met my first Eskimo, ate my first seal. It was the summer of '65 when I snacked on my first little auk, roasted my first musk ox and – I promise an explanation is to follow for this – when I shot my first polar bear.

And when matters got so dangerously out of hand, it was also the year when I underwent the first major crisis of my life, and had my first brush with the possibility of an extremely chilly death.

Yes, indeed, my twenty-first year – for I was born in September, 1944 – was the time of the loss of all kinds of personal innocence. Not a loss in terms of sex, nor of the consumption of drink or drugs or the understanding of the baser arts of card playing – all of these had already diminished me when I was nineteen, and had lived briefly in Oklahoma, where all manner of amusing and innocence-robbing wickedness befell me.

No, it was in 1965, when things went so badly and dramatically wrong, that I was made fully aware of something of which I had been quite innocent all of the two decades prior: I came suddenly to know the awe-inspiring power of Nature, and most especially, the power of bitter, bitter cold. This is what happened, to the best of my recollection, fifty years ago.

We were in Greenland, six of us, all in our twenties, all students on our summer vacation from Oxford. Back in those more muscular days, British universities liked to toughen up their youngsters by sending them on expeditions to remote corners of the world. I remember in my year a group of anthropology students took off for Borneo, some Biblical historians climbed Mount Ararat and a party of strapping Oxford medical girls went off to collect blood samples from the still-lightly cannibalistic jungle country of West Papua.

But we were geologists, all young men, and we went off to the Arctic. Specifically to East Greenland, where there is a great abundance of interesting geology, most of it back then still waiting to be discovered.

Young and damp-eared though we may have been, there was a real scientific purpose to our trip. It was seriously planned, and, until the Incident, impeccably executed. Moreover, it yielded results – scientific results, the listing of which does not really belong here, though I happily repeat what has been so often and so proudly said of us, that close study of the rock samples brought back by The Oxford University Expedition to East Greenland, 1965, helped prove the theory of continental drift and confirm the existence of the world's tectonic plates.

The rock samples. These were the key to our purpose. Once we had performed, high on the Greenland ice cap, the tasks for which we had come – the details of which do not belong here either – we found we had in our possession six heavy boxes filled with carefully drilled cylinders of dark-grey basalt, each cylinder an inch in diameter and six inches long. For us these boxes of rocks were precious beyond words. They were our raison d'etre. They simply had to be brought back to Oxford.

And it was that compulsion, to bring a quarter of a ton of dark-grey rock back home, that very nearly led to our undoing.

We had been performing our fieldwork along what was then an almost wholly unknown tract of the East Greenland coast, a section of the ice cap crouching behind a high wall of mountains situated to the south of the great embayment known as Scoresby Sound. This system of fjords, named for the English whaler William Scoresby, and visible on all maps, is world-class massive – it reaches eighty miles into the heart of Greenland and is fifteen miles across at its mouth, widening to twenty miles in places.

The only nearby settlement, a modest clutch of shacks housing a hundred or so hunters and fishermen, stands on the northern side of the sound. This settlement – back then called Scoresbysund – is where the icebreaker hauling supplies and colonial personnel from Denmark arrived a couple of times a year. It also brought our party up to Greenland in late June. It would take us back to Europe when we were done. The last sailing of the year would be in mid-September. After that the pack ice and the Arctic night would close in, and the region would become quite cut off from the outside world.

All this we knew. There was one small complication stemming from a simple fact of geography: that while the icebreaker docked at the northern side of the fjord, our fieldwork was to take place in the mountains on the southern side.

There was a simple solution at hand. In June we had hired a local boat, a fishing smack called the Entalik, and for a small sum in dollars she, with her Lister diesel chugging merrily, carried us southward across the mirror-smooth waters between the two coasts. The journey took just four hours. We spent our time trying to learn Greenlandic from the crew, or watching seals cavorting in the sea, or marveling at the fantastic shapes of the icebergs that had drifted down from the inland glaciers.

The crew put us ashore beside a weather-beaten shack, a former hunters' refuge, that stood drunkenly at the base of the mountain wall. We left word with Entalik's skipper to meet us back at this same place in ten weeks' time, in September. He agreed to come on a date exactly one week before the icebreaker's scheduled departure. That, we supposed, would be time enough.

And in ordinary circumstances, seven days would have been ample.

But the summer of 1965 in East Greenland was by no means an ordinary summer. For one thing, down in the coast, at sea level – and completely unknown to us, working as we were scores of miles away, and high up on the ice cap – there had been a succession of formidable storms. Storms that had the effect of moving millions of tons of pack ice out from the open sea and thrusting them into the mouth of the sound, clogging it solid.

We came to apprehend this fact only on the very September morning that we had marked for our rendezvous with our boat.

We had had a long and trying final week of trekking, trying to make it quickly across an immense coastal glacier. We had been racing to make our appointed date, and were quite tired – our sleds groaned under the weight of our rock samples, and pulling them across the ice-ridges proved almost impossibly arduous. But finally we came to the top of the line of cliffs that marked the southern margin of the sound. Down below them was the hunters' hut and the prospect, at last, of a four-hour voyage across the fjord, the first stage of our long journey home.

At first, as we approached the ridge looking northward, we could see clear across to the far side of the fjord. We could easily spot the settlement, twenty miles away, glittering in the clear blue air. With my binoculars I could even make out the bright orange hull of the waiting icebreaker, the ship that would carry us back to Copenhagen.

And then we reached the very crest of the ridge, where we could look down into the sound itself – and saw in a moment what we had never imagined. That the stretch of water was no longer blue and mirror-smooth. The little scarlet-hulled fishing smack was not, as we had supposed, bobbing happily a few yards off the beach. Instead the waters were crammed with the wreckage of an endless vision of cracked and heaped-up ice sheets, stretching across to the horizon. And the little boat was nowhere to be seen.

I was the expedition radio operator. I hurriedly assembled the set and strung an aerial between two pinnacles of basalt. I called the Danish coastal radio station at Cape Tobin. A voice answered immediately. It was not good news. 'Ice conditions in Scoresbysund bad and forecast to become worse,' the operator said, dispassionately. 'MV Entalik unable to reach your position. Call him in two days' time.' He gave me the little boat's own radio frequency, and told me the captain, named Daniel Pike, was Inuit, but spoke good English. He would tell us more of the situation.

It was dark by the time we reached the hut – the gloom making the last few hundred feet challenging, especially since we had to bring down the cliff-face our two Nansen sleds, laden now with all the rock samples. It was also becoming very, very cold.

These last few days we had noticed the deteriorating weather, only to be expected as we headed toward the autumn equinox. Until recently we had been bathed in perpetual Arctic summer daylight ¬– we had almost forgotten what night was all about. But now the sun was dipping below the horizon for longer and longer periods, and the concepts of night-time and darkness came flooding back, and with them a shivering memory of the consequent chill. Once the drawing-down of the shades had begun, those of us who shaved each morning had liked to play games with their shaving-water, tossing it into the now-freezing air of dawn, and watching it fall slowly back as ice-crystals, pale clouds of new-made snow.

The old hut, its boards creaking in the gathering wind, offered us shelter. But this was scant comfort, for the main problem was that we had almost no food. Our provisions, carefully selected for weight, had been rationed with the assumption that we would be met on this September day. All that now remained, aside from coffee and sugar, was one large box of Weetabix, a dozen tin drums of Van den Bergh's specially-formulated low-temperature-spreadable margarine, and a cardboard box of bay leaves. We had to find food locally, and since I had control of the expedition rifle, as well as the radio, it was left to me to go hunting.

Luck brought us a goose the very next day, shot incredibly while it was in mid-flight. But one goose among six does not a long way go, and we had to hope for more. Which is where the polar bear came in.

It was an elderly male, half-deaf, with bad teeth and yellow fur, and it had the ill-fortune to come sniffing around our campsite the day after the goose had been reduced to bones simmering in the soup pot. I stalked him as he limped among the fallen boulders, then shot him, so far as I can recall, at close range. He went down with a sigh of relieved exhaustion. We skinned his half-starved carcass and cut him up for boiling. His thighs, the meatiest part of him, should have been ideal (we knew well enough never to eat polar bear liver, lethally rich in Vitamin A); but as it happened this beast was so antique and so unwell that his leg muscles were infested with planarian flatworms. We had no choice but to extract them with tweezers, and so long as the worms remained alive, we staged macabre races with them along the floor of the hut. I can't remember who won, but it passed the time.

Time that was most decidedly running out. Six days passed like this – we were bored, getting ever more hungry, irritated. We kept trying to reach the Entalik, but our radio was a weakling, and it seemed to me the crew weren't listening out for us as keenly as they might.

We heard Cape Tobin radio, though, and we heard chatter between the station and the waiting icebreaker indicating that they might delay their departure and wait for us. But hours later we heard what we most feared. As best we could understand with our poor command of Danish, the icebreaker's captain decided he had to leave after all. With the temperature now dropping fast, new sea-ice was forming out in the Denmark Strait, and the weather was worsening, and even he, with his powerful ship, might well be stuck for the winter. He offered his regrets; it would be up to the Air Force to drop supplies to us, he thought.

Next morning, though, our radio crackled into life. It was Entalik at last, and she had news. Skipper Pike had managed to find a pathway through the ice and was now in sight of our position. He could see our hut. His little boat was four miles away from us, lashed up against an ice floe, and as close to us as was possible.

The ice conditions were getting thicker, he said; the night-time cold was gluing the floes together. He dared not stay much longer for fear of being crushed. This was our last chance. If he turned back now we would be quite on our own for the remaining six months. If we wanted to get back to the settlement, we had only one choice: we would have to take our chances on the ice floes, and get to his boat by walking out.

There was no option, no time for debate. Besides, the Weetabix, margarine and rancid polar bear meat diet would last for only a day or so more, and then it would be bay leaves alone. And soon thereafter, nothing. So I radioed back to the boat, asked them to wait, promised we would do our best. We couldn't yet see them through the crush of ice, but knew roughly where they were from the direction of their radio signal, and would try to get to them by nightfall. The skipper wished me the best, though I sensed a sardonic note to his voice.

We put on our foul-weather gear, strapped crampons to our boots, hoisted the iron-heavy rock-boxes onto our backs, roped ourselves together, grabbed our ice-axes. We left most of our personal gear in the hut, imagining that some future expedition, years hence, might make use of it. We left a note, outlining our plans and giving the date and time. Just in case.

Shuffling clumsily in line ahead, we then walked down the beach to the separation point where the land and sea met. Here we paused briefly at the first of the ice floes. It was a monster, gleaming white in the low sun, but corroded and cracked, and it was tipped up at a steep angle against the beach shingle. It also seemed to be half-alive, moving, twisting back and forth under the influence of the currents beneath it.

The floe was perhaps fifty feet across. It was immediately clear to all six of us that once we stepped out onto its surface, and once we had walked down its slope and out to its distant edge, we would be fifty feet out over the water – water so cold it would be lethal in seconds to any luckless one of us who might fall in. We glanced at each other, gave thumbs-up for mutual encouragement, stepped one after the other up and over the rough edge and, very gingerly, moved out onto the raft and then down the abraded surface of its sloping ice.

We knew a little about the shape and nature of late-season ice floes, not least because we had seen so many of them piled up on shorelines. In the center they can be very thick – six feet, maybe, solid enough to support a bus, difficult for even the heaviest icebreaker bow to smash through. But that was at the center. In profile, and as a result of weeks of summertime melting and smashing against other floes, many of them were now mushroom-shaped, thick in the center, then thinning out at the edges.

Walking on top of a floe thus had its perils. In the center all felt stable, secure. Towards the edge, though, the ice became spongy and flexible. You stepped onto it and it bowed under your weight, seawater flooding over it. Or you might break through, your foot suddenly dangling uselessly, trapped over the deep, ink-black waters. The whole floe might tip up and lurch alarmingly, sending you skittering to one side and threatening to turn turtle completely. And then again, the floes were shaped irregularly, and though they might be locked against one another, or grinding past each other in the tides and currents, seldom did one floe merge seamlessly with another. There was often a few inches or feet of open water between each one – and so, mindful that the edges of each raft of ice were weak and unstable, we had to run and jump across the water from one chunk of ice to the next, hoping to land securely and not to go through the ice, either on take-off or landing.

And each of us was carrying sixty pounds of rock, strapped on our backs.

Yet we did make progress, slowly but surely. One by one we leapt from floe to floe, the last man belaying the others, the first man to land doing the same for those to come. You belayed by sticking your ice axe into the center of the floe and looping a bight of rope around it. Providing the axe was secure and the rope was sound, it should hold, we thought. But the ice was old and rotten and soft, and an axe was only thirty inches long or so. It was as good as we could make it.

And it was tested just once.

We took six hours to cross. It was late afternoon, the shadows were lengthening fast once again, and the wind was starting to rise. But there, at last, was the little boat – hidden behind a spur of ice, her red hull appearing dramatically out of nowhere. Daniel saw us, and his crew waved frantically for us, and yelled with delight.

His motor was running, but for a moment it stopped and the sea was filled with silence. A deliberate quiet, it turned out, for the skipper wanted to shout a message to us.

There was one problem, he yelled, and pointed ahead of him. Entalik was standing bows-on to an enormous floe – but a floe that was separated from its neighbor, to which we were heading, by a lead of water that was a good eight feet across, maybe ten. It was the best he could do, he said. He had been pushing with his bow for the last few hours, when the lead had been twenty feet across, impossible for us to jump. His hours of pushing against the thousands of tons of frozen water had reduced it to this eight-foot gap. But now the floes were locked solid against one another, and the evening freeze would lock them together even more securely. There was nothing for it, he said, as we reached the last-but-one floe. You'll just have to jump.

They were now so near. No need to shout anymore – they were close enough to speak in normal tones, and we could smell the comforting mix of diesel smoke and the cookhouse. The six of us assembled on our floe, in its very middle. Our expedition leader thrust his axe deep into the ice, until just the steel headpiece was visible. He looped our rope around it, and the four strongest of the group gathered around, holding loops of the rope in their mittened hands. I was to be the first to attempt the crossing.

I made sure I had a good length of free rope, then walked to the distant edge of the floe, closest to the land behind. I turned, started my run toward the little boat. I could see the crewmen were reaching out for me from the bow, hands extended. I was running now, as fast as I could.

I reached the soft edge of the ice, felt it give beneath my weight, saw the black gurgling waters in front of me and, with as much might as I could, launched myself and the huge box of rocks behind me high into the air, soared across the open water and crashed onto the ice beyond. A score of hands grasped my parka, my hair, my pack, and within seconds I was hauled roughly across the boat's prow and into the foredeck. I was safe. The crew looped my rope-end around a stanchion, double-tied it off. This was the new belay.

And one by one the others followed. One by one they ran, they jumped, they crash-landed without dignity or care, and were hauled roughly aboard. Five of us were now aboard, or standing on the ice beside the boat. Only our leader remained, now all alone on the ice.

He made sure he untied the rope from his own belay, and freed the axe from the ice. He walked steadily back to the starting-point, turned to us, began his loping run, passed the center point, started down towards the edge. And then suddenly, with a soggy cracking sound, the ice gave way beneath him – and he vanished, plunged deep into the waters.

For a second we stood transfixed, horrified. After all we have been through, this surely couldn't happen now. But then the sound jerked us back to reality – the whirring, buzzing sound of the belay rope, as it unspooled over the bow of the boat, down into the water. As one, we jumped onto it, slowing it with burning hands and then stopping it abruptly – and hand over hand, all working as one, we hauled it back upwards, as fishermen hauling in a net. After no more than ten seconds, he broke surface.

We hauled him out of the water. He was conscious enough to splutter – a good sign. We threw him down onto the deck like a mackerel, and three of the Inuit boatmen promptly jumped atop him. To keep him warm, they said. The only way he'll survive, they added. They knew.

As many of us could do so then joined in, arms around arms around freezing arms, while he choked and coughed and his color changed from blue to purple to dark red – and finally to pink. Parts of his beard had begun to freeze as the cold bit in; but as he warmed so did his beard, and after half an hour of a kind of demonstrative camaraderie seldom experienced in Britain, he opened his eyes, started to cough, to complain, to curse, to return to life. In an hour he was normal in all respects.

Daniel Pike went to the wheelhouse. The Lister engine started to throb, Entalik eased ourselves away from the ice pack and turned about, out into clear water, and we headed cautiously through the night for the lights of the settlement.

It was not until dawn that we found the quayside; and yes, the icebreaker was long gone from it. We still had to wait for a few more days. But then, by dint of a combination of sorcery and charm, good luck and a small sum in ready money, we managed to escape from Greenland by quite another route – the basis of a further part of this story, but one to be told on a later occasion.

For that is a story not quite relevant here. In undertaking that later journey home we were no longer quite the same innocents abroad that we had been, at the moment when we had stepped from the beach out onto that sloping raft of sea-ice, and had placed our lives into the hands of Nature. We had known all too little about Nature then – and yet now we did, we had enjoyed or suffered our brush with her caprices, and as one, we now tendered her the most profound respect.

We had placed into Nature's hand our lives – and the fate of those precious brown boxes of rocks. The six of us lived, shaken but safe. And a quarter of a ton of our hand-drilled basalt samples duly arrived back in Oxford also, safe and sound, just as promised. Once the technicians performed their magic on them, so their sober conclusion was drawn, one that is worth repeating after all this while: that close study of the rock samples brought back by The Oxford University Expedition to East Greenland, 1965, helped prove the theory of continental drift and confirm the existence of the world's tectonic plates.

We had made, in other words, a contribution. We had advanced, if ever so slightly, the sum of human knowledge. And if our innocence was the price we paid, then consider, as most of us have thought down the long years since, consider not its price, but its value and its worth. Far greater, surely. By far.

Lights Out
in Hanoi
Fiona Kidman

For almost a lifetime, I have been fascinated by the work of the French writer Marguerite Duras, born in Saigon in 1914. Duras has taken me to strange places. I have followed in her footsteps around Southeast Asia, and in France, as if nearness to where she lived would somehow infuse my own writing with the strangeness and difference, the passion, that characterize her work. In the early 1990s, along with my husband Ian, I braved South Vietnam when there was still a wild untamed atmosphere following the war, journeying along the Mekong in an open flat-bottomed boat in search of her family plantation. The better part of twenty years had passed when we set out for Hanoi, the last destination in my Duras quest.

Ian and I met up in Bangkok Airport. He had flown in from Cambodia, where he did aid work, and I from New Zealand. Ian is normally a cheerful traveler, but that day he looked tired and was unusually irritable. By the time we had checked through for our flight to Hanoi, I had begun to worry that dashing from one place to another was an ill-conceived plan. But we seemed past the point of no return and so we boarded.

The age of our innocence was long past, or so we thought. Neither of us was young. We had been to Southeast Asia a score of times, sometimes together on holiday, often alone on business, or in my case, for research. We were vaccinated, insured, and equipped with medical supplies, all the usual stuff, and on this trip we were booked into a comfortable hotel in the heart of the city.

The chaos on arrival was greater than I expected, and it took a long while to locate our driver. The night was thick around us when we began the ride from the airport into the city. The driver spoke no English, and the dark seemed overwhelming and endless. Every now and then a light flickered in a field. I had no idea whether we were headed in the right direction or not. I was aware of a bridge, water beneath us. I figured it was the Red River. Ian slid sideways, his head resting on my lap, his eyes closed. At the hotel he handed over his passport and told me to do the business.

I slept a little between the cool cotton sheets in our wood-paneled room; they were very fine, embroidered with drawn threadwork as if plucked from an old French linen cupboard. Yet though it had been some thirty hours since I left home, Ian was restless and distressed, and sleep was difficult for both of us. In the morning I could see that he was feverish, and he said he felt sick. He had, he told me, eaten with friends at a dirty noodle shop in Phnom Penh, a meal he hadn't been able to refuse. I went through the first aid kit and found Lomotil and Panadol and administered a mix of them. To my later shame, I felt impatient that he was not up to exploring. I found my way to the charming dining room and ate a good breakfast. If Ian was left to rest, I decided, he would soon be well enough to venture forth.

Out in the street I stepped around the little pavement cooking fires, the small children, the piled dragon fruit, the rambutans and longans, accustoming myself anew to the heavy odour of durian. I breathed deeply, inhaling that scent of Asia that has always excited me. I came to the elegant old Opera House, otherwise known as Nhá Hát Lón, that I had been planning to explore. And then, some inner sense told me that I should go back, that I was in the wrong place. I turned, and all of a sudden I was running.

Back in the room I could see that Ian needed a doctor. At the desk the receptionist said she would call a taxi, but I said that it was not possible for my husband to go to a doctor. A doctor must come to him.

A strange nightmare began unfolding around me. Two young women doctors arrived. Their faces were grim. They put on masks and gloves and called an ambulance, and within minutes my husband was being carried on a stretcher through the lobby of the Sunway Hotel with an oxygen mask over his face. The ambulance drove at furious speed, honking its horn at swarms of oncoming motorcyclists, bearing us to a clinic. At the clinic we were rushed into a side room. Ian was violently ill.

A young French doctor appeared. 'What has your husband been eating?' he asked. I didn't know. He looked at me as if I was simple. Had we not eaten together? I explained, as best I could, that we had met in Bangkok after some weeks in different countries, and that I hadn't seen what my husband had eaten in previous days in Cambodia, although what he had described didn't sound good.

The afternoon passed and night fell. I tried to stay cheerful, to tell Ian jokes, but he has always said, 'Leave the jokes to me.' I could see that he was right; nothing I said sounded funny at all. The young doctor said, 'We think your husband has cholera.' I began to cry then, in a stupid, futile way. We have been married, my husband and I, for a very long time. Over half a century. My plans seemed pointless and capricious. Did it matter that Duras had lived beside a lake in Hanoi when she was four years old? This obsession of mine had brought us to this. The Frenchman observed me with tired, hooded, very intense eyes. The plan was to transfer Ian to a hospital some distance away where he would be made more comfortable.

Before that happened, there was the small matter of the bill. As we left the hotel, I had flung some things in the safe and grabbed my shoulder bag. At the clinic desk, I showed the woman on the till my insurance details. She read them and phoned the company, back in New Zealand. But it was still night-time there too and nobody was answering the phone. She was sorry, she said, her voice cool, but I would simply have to pay. The amount required was five thousand American dollars. Unless I could pay it, my husband would not be transferred.

I opened my purse containing a few hundred dollars and one of our two credit cards; the other was back in the safe. The one in the safe was loaded for five thousand dollars; this one was not. A series of complicated calls with our bank's twenty-four-hour help line in New Zealand ensued before we were able to leave.

We drove again through the night, this time in an ambulance. I saw that the citizens of Hanoi used very little electricity. The heavy drooping power lines were relics of the war. The streets were dim and, like the lights in the shops, the street cooking fires were being extinguished one by one. This time I really didn't know where we were or might be going.

Eventually we arrived at the French Hanoi Hospital. This is a place I remember now with affection. I would come to think of it as one of the best hospitals in the world. But what can I say of the building that night when I first encountered it? Just that it appeared barren, bleak, concrete-walled and without any comfort in sight. A young man stood alone behind a vast desk in an empty room. I was required to do paperwork here, to present my own and my husband's passports, to answer questions.

'I hear your insurance is not good?' he said.

'My insurance is good,' I said. 'But it is night-time in New Zealand.'

'It is night-time here,' he said by way of reply. 'You come from this place New Zealand without any insurance?'

'Yes, please listen, it will be all right when it is daytime, you'll see. Ask the clinic, I paid them their money. I can pay any money. I can give you my credit card.'

'Credit card is not good. You will give me five hundred dollars.'

'Cash?'

'Yes, dollars.' He made a folding motion with his hands.

I opened my purse again, counting out the notes. Three hundred and fifty, that was it. 'This is all I have.'

He eyed it, and me. 'Give me that money then.'

'May I keep fifty, perhaps? I don't know where I am. I have to get back to the hotel.' I was aware that my voice was cracked and high.

He sighed and relented. And while all of this was taking place, Ian had disappeared. The ambulance had gone; the reception area was deserted.

'Where is he?' I shouted. 'What have you done with my husband?'

'The doctor will come. You wait for the doctor.'

An hour passed. A Vietnamese doctor appeared. 'You will now see your husband,' he said.

'Is he going to be all right?'

He shrugged, his expression impassive. 'Perhaps not.'

'He has cholera?'

'Not cholera. Rotavirus. It is very bad.'

I was led up some stairs and then I was given a mask and a door was unlocked. On the other side of the door was a room where nurses sat at a table. Beyond that was a glass cell. The naked body of my husband lay on a plastic mat on a high bed. Tubes were inserted into his nose, and drips were feeding into his arm. I moved as if to enter this chamber. Someone grabbed my arm. This room was locked too. My husband was in isolation, and only authorized people could enter. I saw through the glass wall that he was barely conscious. It would be nearly two weeks before I was allowed to touch him again.

Back in the reception area, I said to the doctor, 'Will he die?'

'Perhaps.'

'Not tonight, he won't die tonight,' I heard myself say, as if from a distance.

'Prob'bly.'

'He will probably die tonight, is this what you're saying?'

'You go home now,' he said, the interview over.

I was overtaken by a sudden wild fierceness. 'I'm staying here,' I shouted. 'You can't send me away. I won't go without my husband.' I lay down on the concrete floor, sobbing in a mad, disconnected way.

The man at the desk came over. 'You can lie on the bed, here in the emergency room,' he said. 'If there is an emergency, you must leave the bed.' And it was this unexpected kindness that jolted me into some semblance of reason. I rang our children and told them where we were. Not long after, the man at the desk came over to tell me that someone from my embassy was on their way to help me. Our daughter had rung the help desk at Foreign Affairs and the operator had rung our ambassador in Hanoi.

While I waited for them to come, an American woman came in with her husband who had had a heart attack, only she didn't believe it and got angry with the man on the desk. 'They don't know anything here,' she said. 'He'll be out of here in the morning. Say, you don't look too hot.' After we had had a brief conversation, she volunteered to meet me the next day. 'We could play a little,' she said, giving me her card. Her name was Nancy. I have the card still.

A four-wheel-drive arrived, carrying three people from the embassy. I have never been so happy to see my countrymen in my life. They had brought emergency food, a translator and assurances that they would handle everything from there on. After they had talked to the staff, they insisted on taking me back to the hotel for proper food, a shower and some sleep. When I had rested, they would bring me back to the hospital.

I did all that they asked, except that I didn't sleep. I sat down and wrote a letter for the nurses to give my husband to tell him what had happened and where he was and that I loved him and would for all time. I hoped he might be able to read it, though that was madness too – I had his spectacles in my shoulder bag.

Over the next weeks I would ride in a taxi from the Sunway Hotel to the hospital forty-one times. Nancy's husband didn't leave, even though she raged and fumed that she was going to have him airlifted to Bangkok. The husbands of two more foreign women were brought to intensive care. We became a kind of club, the women who sat in the corridors, helpless as our men lay in the locked rooms.

But Ian was getting better, and during the day, between my twice-daily visits to view him, I walked by the lakes, and burned incense for my husband, who is a Buddhist, at the tiny temples beside the water. I learned to say 'hullo' and 'thank you' in Vietnamese: *xin chào* and *cảm ơn*. They were useful words, and I used them often. The people at the embassy helped me recover my five thousand dollars in cash. I slipped my hand in and out of the hotel safe, helping myself and ordering silk jackets. In the evenings I ate fusion cuisine in the dining room and drank the house wine, Luis Buñel rosé, while I listened to the resident jazz band in the bar. A space in my head was letting go of an obsession. Farewell, Marguerite.

Some weeks passed. One of the husbands died; Nancy's husband stayed where he was. Finally the day arrived when Ian and I could take a plane to New Zealand, accompanied by a French nurse and an oxygen tank. The insurance company paid for Ian, the nurse, and the oxygen tank to have three business class seats, and one for me at the back of the plane. As we were being transported by ambulance to the airport, I pointed out of the window. 'Look,' I said to my husband, 'there's the Red River.'

Friends We've
Not Yet Met

Kerre McIvor

The first night I met the man who would be my husband, we
talked for hours. We met in a bar – of course. Where else
would an Irish man and a Kiwi girl meet but a bar?

We were the last ones left and the bartender was slumped
in a corner waiting for us to finish our bottle of wine and our
conversation. The wine came to an end but not before we had
decided – within hours of meeting one another – that one day
we would travel to Cuba together. We'd both seen Ry Cooder's
film *Buena Vista Social Club* and the soundtrack to the film
was ubiquitous that summer. I had read and adored *The Mambo
Kings Play Songs of Love*. Both Tom and I were champagne
socialists and we loved the idea of Fidel Castro sticking two
fingers to the United States administration in the face of the
Americans' trade embargos and tourist restrictions. Cuba was a
country that valued the important things – freedom, education,

equality – we affirmed to one another (while topping up our glasses), and while the people may have been poor, they were immeasurably rich in all that mattered, we insisted (as we had another drink).

Within days of that first meeting, we were a couple – a relationship that has endured for more than seventeen years – and just a few years later, we fulfilled the promise we had made that night and travelled to Cuba.

Living in New Zealand, it's an epic journey to almost anywhere in the world bar the Pacific, and the United States government's restrictions on travelling to Cuba made it even longer. From Auckland, we flew to Chile and spent a night there before the ten-hour flight to Havana. The woman at Immigration in Havana glanced at my passport and then up at me.

'You look very happy', she said. We were travelling in the utopian pre-9/11 days, when people were allowed to smile for their passport photos.

'I am!' I beamed. 'I'm so happy to finally be in your country'.

She stamped my passport and waved me through. 'Enjoy,' she said, and if she sounded doubtful, I put it down to my jet lag.

We had booked ourselves into the Nacional, the iconic hotel on the hill, for our time in Havana, and I was awestruck as we walked through the lobby in the footsteps of Winston Churchill and Josephine Baker and other historical luminaries. We had been given the Ava Gardner room – Ava had honeymooned in Havana with Frank Sinatra and there were portraits of Ava on her own and of Ava with Frank on each wall of the room.

I could barely contain myself with excitement. We were in Cuba! In Havana! It also happened to be my birthday, December 27, and I couldn't believe I was with the man I loved in a city I'd always dreamed of visiting. We went for a walk, hand in hand, along the Malecón, the sea wall that winds its way along the coastline from Vedado to Centro Habana. The late afternoon light suffused the old buildings opposite the sea with a golden glow, glossing over the cracks in the facades and gilding them in a way that made their peeling paintwork and crumbling masonry heroic and timeless. We turned and made our way back to the hotel, as most of the restaurants were still closed for the Christmas holiday. Near the hotel, we found a bare concrete square with tables and chairs set up and a little stall offering burgers, toasted sandwiches and soft drinks. My birthday dinner comprised a cheese toasty and a bottle of lemonade. My husband bought me a glass rose from an opportunistic peddler, who was winding his way through the tables. Within the rose was a pair of dusty off-white nylon knickers that looked like they'd been made when Che Guevara was a boy in shorts. It was the best birthday present I'd ever had.

By the morning of the 29th, Havana had roused itself from its post-Christmas celebration siesta and had started to come alive. The husband and I set off early from the hotel, wanting to soak up everything the city had to offer. The vibrantly coloured buildings were spectacular, the people were beautiful and music was everywhere. It was just like the movie. We stopped; we stared; we took photos; we consulted our Lonely Planet guide. Had we had 'Tourist' tattooed across our foreheads, I doubt we could have been more obvious. As we were having a discussion on a streetcorner about the direction we should take, we heard a voice behind us.

'Aussies?'

We turned, and there was a well-dressed man, newspaper tucked under his arm, smiling at us. 'No, no, we're New Zealanders,' I replied. 'But well spotted.'

Beside me, I heard my husband give a low growl. He grew up in Northern Ireland, during the Troubles, and is much less enthusiastic about mankind than I am. He is innately suspicious and distrustful. I, on the other hand, grew up in a bucolic paradise and believe utterly in the maxim printed on the poster of my religious studies classroom: 'Strangers are merely friends you have not yet met.' They do say opposites attract.

The nice young man turned his attention to me and we started chatting. He asked us how long it had taken to get to Cuba from New Zealand. He asked us how long we'd be staying in Havana. His name was Gerado, he was a teacher of English and he was married with two girls and a son. And then he asked us if we'd like him to be our personal guide for the next few days. Anticipating (correctly) that Tom would be sceptical of his motives, he cut him off at the pass. He didn't want money – how could we think such a thing! He was no *jinetero*, out hustling for every dollar. No, it was the school holidays, he had plenty of time to spare and he would love to practise his English.

I was delighted. We'd been in Cuba less than two days – and already we'd made a friend. And a friend with whom we had much in common. Tom too was a teacher of English. Both he and Gerado loved soccer. One of his girls and my daughter were the same age. It was a genuine connection. We were not just tourists. We had become travellers.

Gerado was true to his word. He was a knowledgeable and witty guide and we enjoyed his company. He took us to a friend's paladar – an informal restaurant in the front room of the friend's house – and over a delicious lunch of authentically home-cooked rice, beans and pork, he told us more about his family. They lived in a tiny apartment, he said. His wife's family had been on the wrong side of the revolution and accordingly, the accommodation they'd been allocated was basic at best. It was a shame, he sighed. His wife had to carry buckets of water up three flights of stairs and it made life very difficult for her. Cuba was an extremely low wage economy and there was no way he would ever be able to afford to pay to have water piped directly to the apartment on his teacher's wage. Still, he smiled bravely, he was lucky to have such a beautiful wife, healthy kids and to have made two such wonderful friends.

I heard Tom give a low growl again and I glared at him. Gerado reached for his wallet when the bill for lunch arrived and I stopped him. 'Please!' I said. 'No. Allow us to pay for lunch. It's the very least we can do given how generous you've been with your time and your knowledge.' Gerado protested but then gave in gracefully. Yes, we could pay for lunch but tomorrow, before we set off for another day's sightseeing, we must come and have morning tea at his home and meet his family.

The next day, we arrived at the address Gerado had given us and made our way up the flights of stairs. The building looked as though it should have been condemned a decade ago. I couldn't possibly imagine carrying buckets of water up the uneven slippery concrete stairs to the three-room apartment. Gerado's wife, Arecelys, was indeed beautiful and the children were gorgeous. They were polite and courteous and immaculately dressed. As the adults talked over coffee, the little girls played with the stickers and the sparkly hair ties I'd given them, their feet constantly moving in salsa steps to the music on the radio. After half an hour of coffee, cake and conversation, Arecelys and Gerado insisted that we join their family for New Year's Eve celebrations the next night. It would be a very simple celebration, Gerado said, and here he flung an arm about the tiny apartment with a deprecating smile, but it would be their great pleasure to host their two new friends.

After a busy day racing around Havana in Gerado's wake, we arrived back at our room at the Nacional. It had been beautifully made up and two fluffy white bath towels had been twisted and folded to represent swans and had been placed at the foot of the bed. However, I couldn't appreciate the charm of the room.

'It's a disgrace!' I expostulated. 'Look at us, in this beautiful room, and Gerado has never ever been able to afford to visit the hotel, far less stay here. We have water flowing from every tap and his family must resort to carrying water in buckets. This is wrong. We should pay to have his water put on! It's only right!'

My husband's face turned to granite and he did his best Easter Island statue impersonation. He proceeded to tick off the reasons why we would not be paying for Gerado's water. Firstly, we were on a budget. Yes, we were staying for five nights at the Nacional but the next ten days would be in private homes, casas particulares. We had allowed a certain amount of money for each day and that did not include paying for a local family's plumbing. He was deeply suspicious of Gerado's motives – he might be a very nice guy, but most conmen were.

'How could you be so cruel?' I wailed. 'We'll be leaving here in a fortnight and going home where we live in luxury by comparison.

We could increase the limit on our credit card. We could extend our overdraft. We simply have to help Gerado and his family!'

But the Easter Island Statue would have none of it. 'I think you're a bit jet-lagged', he said calmly. 'I'm going for a swim in the hotel pool. I'll be back soon.'

And out he went, closing the door to the room somewhat more firmly than was necessary.

'Oh, go and swim, you insensitive bastard!' I bellowed, throwing myself onto the bed and crushing the swan out of shape. 'Swim in all that water while Gerado's wife is struggling up the stairs with the water she needs to cook for her family.'

I burst into tears. Ava Gardner looked on implacably in the photo above me. She'd probably cried a few tears in her time over Frank. She understood.

Tom returned and I dried my face and we made up sufficiently to have a civilised dinner in the hotel restaurant. We agreed that we could afford to pay Gerado two hundred American dollars for his time as our personal guide but Tom insisted that was it. We would go to Gerado's home, we would celebrate New Year's Eve with his family and we would enjoy ourselves. We would not be paying him a cent more than the two hundred dollars and I was not to promise to send more when we returned to New Zealand. As marriages are all about compromise, I agreed – but as I lay in bed that night I did wonder how on earth I'd ended up with such a hard-hearted husband.

The next morning we spent with Gerado visiting museums and monuments, and then we left him so he could help his wife prepare for the party. Havana is a city that knows how to have a good time and it was clear as we were driven through the streets back to our hotel in a 1950s convertible Cadillac that people were looking forward to a big night. Women and men were dancing in the streets and spirits, fuelled along by spirits of the liquid kind, were high. As the day melted into night, Tom and I changed into party clothes, bought a couple of bottles of rum to contribute to the good times and headed back to Gerado's.

We knocked on the door. Music was coming from every apartment of the building – except, we realised, from the apartment of Gerado and Arecelys. The door was opened by one of the wee girls and we could see Gerado through the skimpy curtain that shielded the main bedroom from the lounge. He was lying on the bed, his hand covering his eyes. Arecelys and a couple of other people were sitting, chatting quietly, sipping from glasses.

'What's wrong?' I asked and Gerado called us through to where he was lying. It was a complicated story but in a nutshell, Arecelys had got into a terrible fight with one of the neighbours over the water. This neighbour had hit Arecelys and now he, Gerado, had to find a way to get the money to pipe water directly into the apartment or else he and the family would have to leave. Where they would go, he had no idea. There wasn't actually anywhere for them to go. The situation was untenable. He was sorry he wasn't in a party mood, on this of all nights, but he was sure we would understand.

Tom handed over the envelope with the cash and a thank you card. 'Well,' he said, gruffly, 'this might go some way towards paying for the plumbing. Thank you for looking after us the last two days.'

Gerado opened the envelope and rifled through the notes, ignoring the card. 'But my friends,' he said, looking up at us desperately, 'the plumbing will cost at least one thousand dollars. This' – he waved the money at us –'is of no use to me.'

'Well, that's all we've got for you,' Tom said implacably, while I stood silently, mute with embarrassment – for both Gerado and ourselves.

'Could you perhaps – is there any way', Gerado said haltingly, looking from me to Tom and back again, 'that I could borrow the money from you? I would pay it back.'

Tom turned into the Easter Island statue again. 'I'm sorry but one thousand American dollars is a lot for us too. Now if you don't want the money, we'll take it back and forget about the party.'

Gerado leapt to his feet, transformed. 'No, no, my friends,' he said. 'Where are my manners? Let me find my shoes… Arecelys, put on some music. It's New Year's Eve – come and meet my brother and my friends.'

We handed over the rum and Arecelys began mixing a concoction into a bowl with other liquids on the small table. The music started and Gerado's brother gestured to me and said to Tom, 'Permisso?' Permission granted, Gerado's brother proceeded to teach me how to salsa, good humour was restored and we had a splendid New Year's Eve in the company of Gerado and his family. When we left after the stroke of midnight, when kisses had been exchanged and promises of goodwill declaimed, we made our way down the stairs to walk back to our hotel along the Malecón.

'Be careful!' cried Gerado. 'It's customary to throw water out the windows at New Year's Eve – there will be water coming from all the apartments!'

We walked back slowly. I glanced up at my husband and by the set of Tom's jaw and the turn of his mouth, I knew he was dying to say, 'I told you so.' For my part, I was trying just as hard not to suggest sending Gerado and his family money from New Zealand on a regular basis until the plumbing had been paid for. So neither of us said anything. And the sound of the waves crashing against the sea wall and the faint strains of music coming from the apartments beyond us accompanied us back to the Nacional.

Fiora's Niche
John Berendt

It was fifteen years ago, while I was working on a book set in Venice, that I encountered the remarkable Fiora Gandolfi.

Fiora was, and still is, a journalist, an artist, a fashion designer, and a warm-hearted eccentric. When she discovered that we were both making inquiries into the same local news stories – including the murky suicide of a Venetian poet – she invited me to come to tea.

I already knew a little about Fiora, having seen magazine photo features that showed her in dramatic poses in her enchantingly cluttered palazzo. She was elegantly exotic, with high cheekbones, large inquisitive eyes, and mocha-colored hair that was pulled back in a bun. She designed art that could be worn – clothes that one could bunch up and stuff into carry-alls, adaptable items of apparel that had multiple uses such as a shoulder wrap that could sprout a hood or be turned around and worn as a skirt. She was adventurous in her choice of materials as well – a molded plastic packaging insert, for example, that she pounded, twisted, ironed, and extruded into a crinkly, eye-catching shawl.

By chance, I had witnessed a piece of performance art that she had staged as a tribute to Giacomo Casanova. Spectators had gathered in the street, and were looking up expectantly at an open window twenty-five feet above them.

The performance began as a man in a nightshirt appeared in the window and tossed out a rope made of knotted bed sheets. He lowered it until it touched the ground, then exited the window backside-first, descending hand-over-hand in great haste, to laughter and applause from the audience below. That, in its succinct entirety, was Fiora Gandolfi's homage to Casanova.

Fiora was best known as the widow of the famous soccer coach Helenio Herrera, who had died in 1997 at the age of 87. Herrera was widely acknowledged to have been the greatest coach in the history of the game. Journalists dubbed him 'the wizard' and 'the father of modern football.' His teams won three European championships and two back-to-back World Cups. His defensive strategies fundamentally changed the way the game is played.

Fiora lived in a Gothic palazzo on a quiet canal near the Rialto bridge. Its large central salon basked in the sunlight that poured in through tall windows, illuminating an array of brightly colored chiffon banners and swags that hung from the walls and ceiling, draped over chairs, pooled on the floor, and wound loosely around the neck and shoulders of Fiora Gandolfi herself.

She was wearing a jacket of wheat-colored canvas when she came to the door. It had brush strokes of red and orange paint on it. She noticed my eye traveling to the paint. 'They're the colors of war,' she said with a smile. 'In life you have to insist if you want results.'

I followed as she led the way into the kitchen where we were to have tea. The kitchen had been a chapel in the fourteenth century, and it still had a cloistered feeling. Pots and pans hung from the ceiling, and a lamp over the kitchen table was festooned with what seemed to be years' worth of notes, letters, photographs, fabric swatches, and postcards. Fiora poured two cups of a fragrant kiwi-juice tea.

'I enjoyed your "Casanova" very much,' I said.

'Thank you! I did it because Venice has neglected him! Casanova was born in Venice, you know, and his memory should be celebrated. Yet there is no monument to him.'

Fiora's concern over postmortem tributes was a deeply felt passion, and I soon realized her passion was deepest when it came to the disposition of her husband's ashes, which were currently in limbo.

Herrera had wanted his ashes to be buried in a tranquil, sunlit place within the sight and sound of water. He and Fiora searched for a spot on the cemetery island of San Michele and found what they were looking for in the Anglican section: a niche in the wall, with the waters of the lagoon lapping on the other side. The tombs of Ezra Pound and the Russian poet Joseph Brodsky were a few feet away. Igor Stravinsky and Serge Diaghilev lay nearby in the Orthodox section.

When Herrera died, Fiora wrote to the Anglican officials in Venice, asking for permission to place an urn with his ashes in a niche in the cemetery wall. The church gave its consent. Fiora put Helenio's ashes in an urn shaped like a football cup and made a frame for the niche from slabs of antique Istrian marble. Then she waited for the permits to be issued.

'I went to see them every day for two months,' she said, 'and every day they told me the permits were not ready. I wore a different brightly colored scarf each day, so they wouldn't forget me.'

'Then finally they sent me another letter. They had changed their minds! Now they refused Helenio's ashes! They said that anyone admitted to the Anglican section had to be a member of the Lutheran, Methodist, or Valdese church, and that an ordained minister must have officiated at his funeral.'

'Ecco! Helenio was born a Catholic, and he became an atheist. A thousand people came to his funeral, but it was not a religious service.'

Securing Helenio's niche had become Fiora's sacred mission. She would not consider looking for another site.

Their son, Helios, went to see a member of the committee who told him flatly that she objected to a soccer coach being buried in the Anglican section.

Fiora was enraged. 'The British are classists!' she said. 'Soccer is a sport for very poor people, and the high-class Anglicans do not want such types mingled with their precious dead. I was angry. I told them, "But you have Nazis, pederasts and atheists in your cemetery!"'

In the meantime, the authorities moved Herrera's ashes to a drawer in another part of the cemetery, high up in what appeared to be a marble filing cabinet, too high for Fiora, standing on a cemetery ladder, to reach the drawer or put flowers on it.

Over the next three years, Fiora and her friends tried a number of approaches without success. Hoping that I might be able to help, I called on the widow of Sir Ashley Clarke, the former British Ambassador to Italy, who was himself buried in the Anglican section. Lady Clarke was the most respected member of the British community in Venice, and she was also on the Anglican committee of San Michele. I did not tell her the purpose of my visit until ten minutes into our conversation. Then I asked if she was aware of Fiora Gandolfi and her predicament.

'Yes, I certainly am,' she said. She then picked up a letter that was lying on top of a pile of papers on her desk. She glanced down at the letter, then with an almost imperceptible sigh she looked back up at me. 'I'm afraid it's hopeless.'

I told Fiora what Lady Frances had said when I joined her for dinner the next night. She fell silent for a full minute before she spoke.

'Would you write a letter to Queen Elizabeth for me?'

'Fiora!'

'She's the Supreme Governor of the Church of England. That's like being the Pope, isn't it?'

'Yes, but…'

'She doesn't have to follow any rules made by stupid classist bigots. She doesn't have to answer to anybody. And she's a woman!'

'True.'

'Allora! Will you write to her for me?'

'Of course,' I said, 'but you must promise me you won't pin all your hopes on it. That you won't wait month after month for an answer. And that after a reasonable period of time, you will let me help you find an even better niche for Helenio.'

'Queen Elizabeth will read the letter, and she will give her consent!' Fiora was adamant.

I went to Fiora's desk and slipped a piece of paper into the typewriter.

'Madam,' I began. In two short paragraphs I told Queen Elizabeth who Helenio Herrera was, described his importance

146

to the world of sport and to Italy in particular, and explained that the Anglicans in Venice had given their permission for his burial in San Michele and then abruptly rescinded it. I handed Fiora the letter.

As she read it, she smiled. Her shoulders relaxed as if a great weight had been lifted. I worried that she was setting herself up for another disappointment.

'Don't forget your promise, Fiora.'

Three weeks went by without a sign. Then, one afternoon, as I was walking past the newsstand in Campo San Stefano, I caught sight of a poster displaying the day's headline in La Nuova: 'QUEEN ELIZABETH FINDS A TOMB FOR HERRERA.' I blinked to make sure I'd read it correctly. Then I called Fiora.

She was triumphant and went to work at once arranging for the installation of Helenio's niche. The day it was completed, Fiora, her daughter, several of her friends, and I all took the five-minute vaporetto ride to San Michele to celebrate. Fiora brought a basket of flowers. She put several in Helenio's niche, then placed one each on the tombs of Ambassador Clarke, Ezra Pound, Joseph Brodsky, Serge Diaghilev, and Igor Stravinsky.

We stood for a while admiring the urn and the niche.

'Fiora, I have to hand it to you,' I said. 'I don't think I know another person who would have written to Queen Elizabeth.'

'I know millions,' Fiora replied.

'Really? Who?'

'Children,' she said. 'And every one of them would have been as certain as I was that Queen Elizabeth would give her consent. Does that tell you something about yourself?'

'I'm not sure what, exactly.'

'That you are a worldly adult,' she said. 'You have spent your whole life letting go of the innocent dreams that made your childhood so warm and hopeful and full of certainty. Dream by dream you let them go. We all do it, to shield ourselves from disappointment. It's easy to shed them. Not so easy to get them back.'

Mauve
Marina Lewycka

Two hundred miles northeast of Moscow, at the first stop on the Trans-Siberian Railway or the final stopping-point along the perilous trade route from seventeenth-century China into Europe, on the confluence of the Kotorosl and Volga rivers, sits the remote fairytale city of Yaroslavl. You can imagine the ancient travellers' wonder, after months at sea, or descending from the frozen wastes of the Siberian Urals, on catching their first glimpse of the clustered gleaming domes of its churches rising above the shimmering expanse of the Volga.

There has been a settlement at this site since prehistoric times, and it was an important Viking trading post, but the present-day city was founded by Yaroslav the Wise in 1010, when the rulers of Kievan Rus fled their capital in Kiev in the face of the Mongol invasion, and established their new centre of power at Vladimir, close to Moscow.

Yaroslavl is now a UNESCO World Heritage site, known for its beautiful onion-domed churches, its icons and richly glazed ceramic tiles, and riverside panoramas. Unfortunately I was destined to see them all wearing borrowed underwear and an ill-fitting mauve polyester suit.

It was my own fault. A pair of strappy sandals in an airport shop caught my eye – and I missed my flight to Moscow. The rest of my group – I was travelling with four sports teachers on an educational exchange – left without me, but with my checked-in suitcase. (They could, in those days.) It would be waiting for me at Sheremetyevo airport, I was told. Somehow, I managed to rebook myself onto another flight to Moscow, but my suitcase was nowhere to be found. There was nothing for it but to take a taxi to the hotel, where I reconnected with my colleagues.

'No problem. We will find it tomorrow,' said Arkady, our charming and handsome guide, who coached the Yaroslavl football team. He had excellent English, a dazzling smile, and a breezy confidence which I did not share.

How I came to be travelling with a group of Yorkshire sports teachers remains a mystery even to me, but I suspect it had more to do with my knowledge of Russian than with my sporting prowess. The next day, I found myself sitting in a minibus heading east with four hunky guys, a diminutive aerobics teacher from Doncaster called Gail, and no change of underwear.

'Please, can we just call at the airport and ask about the case?' I pleaded with Arkady, as we navigated the suburbs of Moscow. Arkady assured me that this could be done from Yaroslavl.

'I have already telephone,' he replied. 'Have no worry.'

The decrepit road surface made the two-hundred-mile journey seem much longer, but as we left Moscow behind, Arkady pulled out a bottle of some sweet viscous purplish liquor.

'Samagonka,' he said. 'My mother has made it.' Samagonka, I knew, means 'home-distilled', and it could have been made of anything. It certainly helped to ease the bumps.

We passed through countless villages and hamlets of white-washed cottages with sunflowers and hollyhocks in the front gardens, and chickens risking their lives among the potholes. Our first view of Yaroslavl by road from Moscow was disappointing – a dismal jumble of hanging telegraph cables, potholed roads, and bleak housing developments. So was the vast concrete Jubilee Hotel, built during the Soviet era to accommodate Party functionaries on their travels, full of dark wood, worn carpets, dodgy plumbing and mosquitoes, the sombre rooms permeated with the sweat of loveless nights and the smell of oil from the upriver refinery – foreshadowing Yaroslavl's current role as a major industrial centre, producing mainly textiles and petrochemicals.

The fish in the restaurant, fresh from the Volga, which sounded so appealing on the menu, also carried the taint of oil. Before turning in for the night, I borrowed a pair of micro-knickers from Gail, to wear on the days when mine were drying on the unheated towel-rail in the bathroom, and a baggy (on her but not on me) t-shirt to wear as a nightdress, along with a squeeze of toothpaste and a squirt of moisturizer. Fortunately I still had my handbag, the impractical strappy sandals I had bought at the airport, and enough roubles for a shopping spree. All would be resolved by tomorrow, or so I thought.

The next day, while the rest of the group were touring Yaroslavl's sporting facilities, I went shopping. The hotel had a hard-currency shop where travelling Soviet functionaries could stock up on luxuries and buy gifts for their wives, but when I ventured in wearing my travel-crumpled jeans and shirt and asked for toothpaste, the fiercely coiffed shop assistant turned on me and shouted, 'Get out! Don't poke your nose in here!'

'But, I only want...'

'This shop is not for the likes of you!' she declared, and turned her back.

Even by the standards of Soviet-era shop assistants, this was a bit extreme. I retreated into the hotel lobby, wondering where I had gone wrong. Then, with a frisson of satisfaction, I realised that my unkempt appearance and Ukrainian-accented Russian had led her to mistake me for a Ukrainian country bumpkin, not a dollar-rich foreigner.

The woman in the downtown pharmacy where I bought toiletries was more sympathetic, and pointed out a department store across the street where I could buy clothes. Or could I? Although compared with Gail I was a giant, compared with the ladies for whom these clothes had been made, I was a half-starved flat-chested waif. I studied the stiff polyester outfits with growing despondency. I supposed I could remove some of the bows and appliqué embroidery but...

'Oh, you're nothing but a clothes-peg,' sneered the plump middle-aged assistant. 'Try the children's department.'

This would have been fine had I been looking for a school uniform, or a frilly party-frock.

Out on the street, I sat on a bench in the August sunshine and watched the passers-by. Some women were matronly, with generous bosoms to amply fill out the department-store garments, but others were slim and stylish. They were all wearing clothes. Where did they get them?

'How did you get on?' asked Gail when we met up at lunchtime.

'Well, I got the toiletries. The clothes… they weren't quite me.' I turned to Arkady. 'I don't suppose you've heard any more about the suitcase?'

No one had got back to him. He would try again, he said. Meanwhile, he would like to invite us all to dine at his house this evening. His mother was an excellent cook. I mumbled embarrassment about my jeans and increasingly crumpled blouse, but he brushed away my concerns.

The flat where Arkady lived with his mother was tiny, on the second floor of a tall, gloomy block. From the outside it seemed derelict, but inside it was a kaleidoscope of rugs, cushions, curtains, wall hangings, antimacassars, ornaments, icons, family photos, mirrors, flowers in vases, lamps. Every surface was covered in colour. There was one bedroom, where Arkady slept, and a single bed, which doubled up as a settee, covered in a lurid polyester blanket, in the living room, where presumably his mother slept. We ate our dinner sitting in a circle balancing our plates on our knees, because the table was too small for seven of us. After the first bottle of vodka, it didn't seem to matter. The borsch was fabulous, a perfect balance of sweet and sharp, the paprika goulash and dumplings were to die for, and the *vareniky* filled with cherries and laced in sour cream brought tears to my eyes. Well, I was feeling quite weepy by then, anyway. Maybe it was the vodka, or maybe it was Gail's micro-knickers cutting into my belly, making stuffing myself increasingly uncomfortable.

Arkady's formidable, grey-haired mother, who had prepared this feast, did not sit down at all, but circulated constantly, urging us to eat and drink more, filling up our plates and glasses. A guest who left hungry or sober brought shame on the house. When Colin, the outdoor-sports leader from Rotherham, let out a loud involuntary belch, everybody cheered. When Steve, the swimming squad coach from Barnsley, slid off the end of the bed-settee onto the floor, there was laughter all around. I noticed Gail and Arkady squeezed close together, thigh to thigh, on the settee. Arkady beckoned his mother over and whispered something, pointing at me. She seized my free hand and dragged me behind a makeshift curtain that screened off one end of the room. This was her boudoir.

Examining me critically, she tutted and muttered 'Skinny like a clothes-peg' under her breath. Then she topped up my glass with the same sweet purple *samagonka*.

'Special for you, darling. Drink!'

I took an obedient sip, and the world at once seemed happier and brighter. She topped up the glass again.

On the wall behind her, on hooks and hangers, was an assortment of 1950s-style clothes, smelling faintly of mothballs. She riffled through them, and pulled out a couple of dresses for me to try.

'No, please!'

I tried to be firmly polite, but she would have none of it. Soon she had me stripped down to my bra and Gail's micro-knickers – more tutting – and was taking down clothes from the hanger and pulling them over my head. Each time I protested, she tried something else. At last, we came to the mauve polyester two-piece. She buttoned me in, admired me with satisfaction, and gave me three kisses. Then whisking back the curtain, she thrust me stumbling on my strappy sandals into the room. Everyone clapped, apart from Gail, who had fallen asleep, her head lolling on Arkady's arm. The Kiwi rugby coach from Sheffield had joined Steve on the floor, and both were giggling helplessly.

'Beetiful!' exclaimed Arkady. 'Come. Sit. Drink.'

The next day had been scheduled for sightseeing, and Arkady had roped in a history teacher at the high school to be our guide. It wasn't until I got dressed that morning that I realised I had left behind my jeans and shirt at Arkady's flat. There was nothing for it. I would have to wear the mauve two-piece until I could recover them. Gail cried off the tour with a monstrous headache, Steve was indisposed, so there were just three of us. Oksana, our guide, met us in the hotel lobby. She was blonde, willowy and beautiful, wearing a slim-waisted swirling dress in shades of blue and grey.

We set out at a brisk pace towards the Spasso-Preobrazhensky, or Transformation of our Saviour, monastery. This harmonious cluster of white-painted buildings crowned with green copper domes and spires was encircled by massive stone battlements with watchtowers, for the monastery had functioned as both a place of worship and a defensive stronghold throughout Russia's turbulent history. It had originally been built of wood in the 12th century, like the rest of the city, Oksana told us, and had burnt down and been rebuilt a number of times. The monastery cathedral, built in 1516, is the oldest free-standing structure in Yaroslavl. As we climbed the bell tower next to it, forty metres high, the prickly polyester jacket chafed under my armpits in the heat. From the top we could see the whole of the historic city laid out below us, and the broad silvery Volga snaking away through empty plains and undulating birch forests towards the horizon. How I longed to take off the jacket and spread my wings like a bird.

Yaroslavl is famous for its many historic churches, built by wealthy merchants in the 17th and 18th centuries. Among the loveliest is the Church of Saint Elijah the Prophet, so richly painted, hung with icons and steeped in incense that it felt like stepping inside a jewellery box.

'Yaroslavl icon artists are known in Russia for fluid style and gentle expressions,' said Oksana, pointing to a lovely tiny icon of the Virgin, wearing a gold halo above a pink shawl muted with the patina of centuries. 'Typical Yaroslavl icon has pink mauve tone overlaid on dark green sankir base. Have anybody got questions?'

'What you doing tonight, Kosana?' mumbled the Kiwi, his speech still slurred from the night before.

'Where did you buy your dress?' I asked.

She laughed, showing small, perfect teeth. 'I have made it myself. Silk. It was gift. Very expensive. In Yaroslavl is only polyester from petrochemical.' She glanced at my outfit with a pitying expression and said no more.

The following day I had still not recovered my jeans, but Arkady said he would bring them that evening, so the mauve polyester had another outing. The five of us set off by boat down the Volga to visit a children's summer camp. Southeast of Yaroslavl the river is so wide that you can hardly see the other bank as it swirls along at a lively pace towards the Caspian Sea, almost two thousand miles away. In a small clearing between the immense river and the vast birch forest huddled a circle of tents and a collection of canoes and dinghies. Skinny suntanned girls and boys splashed their oars in a shallow inlet under the eyes of a bikini-clad instructor called Darya, who bellowed instructions from a deck chair. On the shady edge of the forest a table was set for lunch, heaped with bread, eggs, fish, salads, mushrooms, cakes, berries, five bottles of vodka and two bottles of a cloudy pinkish liquor. This was *samagonka* made from berries and crab apples, we were told. By then I should have known better, but it was so sweet you couldn't taste the alcohol.

Darya and her three colleagues, Petya, Boris and Masha, who taught in a Moscow high school most of the year, were delighted to see us. In such a remote place, visitors are very welcome, they said. As the shadows lengthened, and the level in the bottles shortened, we started to sing. The Russian songs 'Katyusha', 'Kalinka', and 'Moscow Nights' were wistful and rousing, but we wowed them with a spirited rendition of 'On Ilkley Moor Baht'at'. Then it wasn't far to slip from the wooden benches onto the grassy floor, and sleep a while. I don't know who, if anyone, looked after the children.

Hours later, I was awoken by a little girl with white-blonde pigtails shouting and tugging at my arm. Some other children were trying to rouse Darya and her colleagues. The sky had the mauve hazy tint of early evening, almost the same colour as my outfit. The grass was damp with dew.

'Vodka! Vodka!' the little girl repeated.

'Nyet! Nyet! Spasibo!' I replied drowsily, shaking her off, but she persisted. As I surfaced from my alcoholic stupor, I realised that she was saying not 'vodka' but 'lodka', and gesturing towards the river.

I got up and stumbled towards the wooden jetty just in time to see the silvery wake of a departing motorboat slapping on the shore. Boris and Petya appeared beside me, rubbing their heads.

'Bye-bye!' Petya waved at the boat.

'How will we get back?' I asked.

'Not back. Stay by camp,' said Boris cheerfully. 'Boat is coming Friday.'

There was no telephone, no road, and no way of reaching civilization. As the daylight faded, shadows crept out of the forest and stars blazed in brilliant unfamiliar constellations. The silence beyond our circle of voices was absolute. Spare bunks and blankets were found. More vodka appeared. We slept like the dead.

The next day Steve and the Kiwi ventured out in one of the camp dinghies with the intention of rowing back to Yaroslavl, but after twenty minutes the current deposited them back on the bank a few metres downstream of where they had started. There was nothing for it but to surrender to the river, the forest, and the children, who treated us like captives on whom to practise their English and play tricks. Over the three days that we stayed there, we slept in our clothes, washed and fished in the river, and gathered berries and mushrooms in the forest, all of which left their mark on the mauve polyester. It acquired an antique mossy patina a bit like an icon painting in reverse.

By the time the boat arrived on Friday, we had learned the choruses of several Russian songs and finished all the vodka, vegetables and bread. Darya and Boris accompanied us on the boat to Yaroslavl to stock up. But there was no shortage of the lethal berry liquor. We were each given a bottle to take home with us.

At the hotel, my jeans and shirt were waiting for me, laundered and pressed, and Arkady had more good news. My suitcase had been located and would be at the lost luggage counter at the airport. Embarrassedly I apologised for the stains on the crumpled outfit, but he raised his hands in a charming gesture. 'No, please, is gift from mother.'

At the airport, I wrapped the bottle of cloudy pink *samagonka* inside the grubby mauve suit with its faint odour of mothballs, forest moss, and river mud, and packed them in my errant suitcase along with my memories, for the trip home. In the years since, I have never opened either of them, but sometimes when life seems too dull and predictable, it is good to know that they are there.

Cabbage Soup
Tony Wheeler

Cabbage soup. It's a good job it doesn't come up on restaurant menus too often or I'd regularly become distracted and unable to concentrate on deciding what I really want to eat. It was an early trip – my girlfriend had just turned twenty-one, I was a couple of years older – and it has ever afterwards infused the mere mention of cabbage soup with a curiously erotic flavour.

We'd left London and driven east across Europe, stopping in Prague, a sad city still ground down in the depressing years after the Soviet crushing of the Prague Spring. From Prague we'd turned south to Vienna and then continued further south to Yugoslavia. Back then, with General Tito still in firm control, Yugoslavia was Commie-lite, with beaches and beach life at far lower cost than in Western Europe.

The Prague-Brno-Vienna-Salzburg part of the trip had all been history, culture, museums, and galleries. There'd be more of that later when we travelled across Italy and made our first visit, for both of us, to Venice. In between, Yugoslavia offered beaches and the blue Mediterranean sea. In fact, as we quickly discovered, that stretch of coast interprets the word 'beach' fairly liberally: stones, pebbles and rock seemed to feature more than the traditional sand. But never mind, the water was clear, clean and warm, the food was healthy and hearty, the wine and beer were just fine, the campsites were comfortable and, most important, the costs were low.

One day we turned off the main road to follow a smaller road which seemed to stick close to the coast. It was late afternoon, the road got progressively narrower and rougher, and just when we were beginning to think that we had to find somewhere to set up camp very soon, we arrived simultaneously at the end of the road and a campsite. Perfect. If we hadn't found somewhere in the next half hour or so, we'd have been setting up our tent by our car's headlights.

We pulled into the campsite and everything looked fine. It was a small site, just a scattering of tents and cars between the trees beside the beach. But we quickly discovered there was one small problem – nobody in the campsite had any clothes on.

So we took ours off and set up our tent. Of course we were much younger then and looked much better. Forty years later, I don't want anybody seeing my naked body; I don't even want to see myself in the mirror when I get out of the shower. If I had a cat, I wouldn't even want it looking at me naked.

But back then, and hardly surprisingly, seeing my girlfriend naked all day was very pleasant. Our plan to stay just one night extended to another day and then another. When we did continue on along the coast, it was to another camp, a much larger one, but again one where nobody wore clothes. I can still remember swimming in the bay and surfacing to watch my girlfriend paddling by in a kayak, dressed just like Eve in that biblical campsite. In our well-equipped camp, the dress code even extended to the supermarket. Perhaps the checkout chicks were clothed, I can't remember. Certainly nobody else was.

Yugoslavia became a centre for nude beaches and campsites way back in the 1950s, pushed by the German tourists who were a large percentage of the country's tourist flow. The German enthusiasm for getting their gear off goes right back to the early 1900s and in typical Germanic fashion there is even a multi-part word for it, FKK or Freikörperkultur, which translates, more or less, as Free Body Culture. In the Iron Curtain era, FKK was probably even more popular in East Germany than West. It didn't matter if you'd arrived in a Trabant or a BMW, once you'd set up camp, Ossis and Wessis were pretty much indistinguishable. Along with the Iron Curtain, Yugoslavia has disappeared, or fragmented at least, but to this day the Croatian Adriatic Coast is still dotted with beaches and campsites populated by unclothed people.

We weren't the only ones to inadvertently end up disrobed in Yugoslavia. An English couple we would later become friends with worked in northern Italy back in that era. One day they decided to take a short Adriatic coast break and, like us, ended up unexpectedly naked the next day. They'd barely (in more ways than one) emerged from their tent in the morning when a hesitant representative from the campsite approached our friend, the husband, with a cautious request. The campsite was having a 'Miss Beautiful Campsite' (OK 'Miss Naked Beautiful Campsite') competition and to ensure no national bias crept into the judging, they'd carefully selected an international panel. They'd had no trouble finding representatives from Germany, Switzerland, France, Italy, Austria and assorted other European countries, but our friend seemed to be the only Englishman available. It was a big inconvenience, but would he mind helping judge?

'Well,' our friend mused, 'it was indeed a major imposition, but what could I do? I felt obliged to bring some English fair play to the judging. And anyway, I had nothing else on.'

We left Yugoslavia, all those years ago, and headed back towards London via Venice, a pause which I remember chiefly for being absolutely tortured by mosquitoes at our mainland campsite. Totally unable to keep the damned insects out of our tent, we eventually ended up sleeping in the car.

We never set up in a naked campsite again, although there have been the odd naked moments over the years. I remember some particularly beautiful waterholes in the Kimberley region of western Australia where, once you've carefully ensured there are no resident crocodiles, you can also be fairly certain there's nobody else within a hundred kilometres. And fancy resorts in the Pacific where the number of beaches on the island exceed the number of rooms and you're quietly left alone on your own patch of sand.

I have swum naked, as you are supposed to, at James Joyce's famed forty-foot pool. This natural rock pool gets its name not from its length but, perhaps, from the 42nd Highland Regiment of Foot, which was once based here and used it as a swimming hole. It's at Dun Laoghaire, the Dublin port just a short trip from the centre of Dublin, and like many other Joyce enthusiasts, I went for a bare dawn dip, just like 'stately, plump Buck Mulligan' at the conclusion of the first chapter of Ulysses. The sign proclaimed that 'togs must be worn after 9am'; earlier than that, though, '40-foot gentlemen' and any brave women could still swim nude. Buck Mulligan described its waters as 'the snotgreen sea. The scrotumtightening sea,' and I can confirm that the Irish Sea at dawn is bloody freezing.

Then, of course, there have been traditional Japanese onsen, hot springs where customarily naked communal bathing is required, and Finnish saunas, and numerous stretches of sand where 'clothing optional' signs might appear. On a beach stroll near Noosa in northern Australia one early morning, we were passed by an elderly gentleman who warned us that if we continued in this direction much further we might encounter 'naked people.' Twenty minutes later we did. Him.

But all those years ago, back at that little campsite in Yugoslavia, the couple who ran the place invited us over to have lunch with them. We were joined by the older German couple camping next to us and their teenage daughter, and as we sat around the table a car pulled into the campsite, its occupants, like us a few days previously, looking slightly bewildered and asking directions while trying not to look too directly at any of us. The campsite owner told them where they were, that this was the end of the road and insisted that they were quite welcome to stay right here, properly attired of course. Meanwhile we tucked into our cabbage soup.

Man to Man
Jeff Greenwald

O n a drizzly evening in August 2004, five world-wandering authors sat behind a long table in the Metropolitan Ballroom of San Francisco's Pan Pacific Hotel, discussing our lives and careers as travel writers. The conversation, with Tim Cahill, Jan Morris and Isabel Allende, plus myself and moderator Michael Shapiro, was lively. But I especially enjoyed the Q&A session afterwards—particularly one seemingly innocuous question: What's the most exotic place you've ever been?

I almost tripped over that one. Images of far-flung destinations paraded past my mind's eye: a female lama's remote Himalayan sanctuary; the Great Mosque of Djenné, with its termite-hill towers; an obscure tea bar in Esfahan.

But when it came down to it, there was only one honest answer: The most exotic place I'd ever been was only seven hours from San Francisco, by car.

This story is not about my first time going to Burning Man, although that first time – in 2000 – was memorably traumatic. I was plagued by nightmares a week in advance. Horror stories of the crowds, the dust, the noise and the Porta-Potties tormented my agoraphobic soul. I would be ride-sharing to the Black Rock Desert with a woman I barely knew, and camping next to her Subaru Outback in my lightweight backpacking tent. The sandstorms, I'd been warned, might shred it like Romano cheese....

Arriving at the fringe of the playa, we were met by naked greeters in body paint and clown noses. 'Welcome home,' they declared – a phrase that, wherever one hears it, seems to become a self-fulfilling prophecy.

We parked and set up our small camp within the vast semi-circle of tents and RVs and theme camps surrounding Center Camp's Big Top. Banners snapped in the hot, dry wind. A long promenade led from Center Camp to the iconic Man: a forty-foot-high plywood figure with its arms angled slightly from its sides. On the penultimate night of the festival – five days hence – The Man would raise his arms skyward, and be immolated in a pyrotechnic blaze.

Wandering among the dusty avenues and diverse camps, I came upon a man whose worldly possessions were spread out upon a broad Turkish carpet: a yard sale. There were picture books and cutlery, a jump rope, a vintage toaster, juicers, boots, hula hoops and a beautiful old world globe. I picked up the globe and found Ceylon, East Pakistan, Republic of the Congo and Tibet.

'How much?'

The Burner looked at me in surprise. 'Take it, man. It's yours.'

This was my introduction to the 'gift economy,' one of the signature delights of Burning Man. But even the term economy

is misleading; it's not a barter system. Gifts are given freely,
out of inventive generosity. Payback is rarely expected. Still, it's
good to have something to offer, and I did: fragrant chunks of
frankincense, an exotic tree sap from Yemen.

   Clutching the globe in my arms, I couldn't help but appreciate
the metaphor. It was then, I'm sure, that my 'playa-phobia'
evaporated. During the coming years I would return many
times, in various states of preparedness or disarray, to wander
through this sudden city created in the desert – a place where
it is equally easy to find oneself navigating a river of topless
bicyclists, smoking a hookah amid the rippling folds of a huge
dome tent, or lying alone beneath a carpet of impossible stars.

   The night of the travel panel, when I was asked to recall 'the
most exotic place' I'd ever been, my imagination settled on that
transitory world in the Black Rock desert. My memories were
mostly of offerings and artworks, some so surreal and beautiful
that they were like apparitions out of a dream.

   Like bicycling across the flat, empty expanse of alkaline
desert at two in the morning, riding alone toward the distant
perimeter fence (erected to catch any wind-blown trash). In
the distance I spied a tiny yellow light, and rode toward it.
As I got closer, I saw a shape emerge: The light was hanging
inside the window of a painted step van. Big, colorful throw
cushions were spread on the ground near the truck's side,
with half a dozen people lounging on the pillows and staring
at the stars. I parked my bike and walked up to the truck's
illuminated window. The woman inside was wearing an
apron. 'Would you like a grilled cheese sandwich?' she asked
me. 'And a glass of milk?'

Or an enormous sculpture of a human heart made of iron and steel, above a cauldron of firewood. Some distance away, a gigantic bellows fed into a pipe set beneath the playa. I had to jump into the air to pump the bellows, and as my weight pulled me down, a jet of air blew through the base of the heart, stoking the flames and making it glow like a live volcano.

Or David Best's Temple of Forgiveness, its soaring finials constructed of reclaimed scrap wood left over from die-stamped dinosaur kits. Open to the sky and ornate as jewel boxes, Best's annual Temples are among the most astonishing architectural works I have seen anywhere in my travels – on par with Angkor Wat, the Sagrada Família and the Taj Mahal. Throughout the week, day and night, visitors filter through. They leave talismans of memory, or written testimonies to relationships – with lovers, parents, siblings, pets, partners, children and teachers – that have been cut short. I've seen golden wedding bands hanging from the rafters, thick journals and dog collars, framed photographs and love letters, baby toys, a stethoscope, even an upright piano hauled by a pick-up truck into the open-air atrium.

On the final night of each year's celebration, the Temple—and all it holds—is consumed in a vast conflagration, as thousands of people watch in silence.

But I digress. Probably my most exotic Burning Man memory of all begins early one morning, as I bicycled down one of Black Rock City's alkaline avenues, the fine dust temporarily settled by a water-spray truck, itself chased by half a dozen naked revelers in pursuit of a rare shower. I stopped in front of a large camp where a crowd had gathered. Commanding their attention, the visionary author and poet Rob Brezsny (whose Free Will Astrology is syndicated in more than 125 magazines and newspapers worldwide) was reciting his Prayers for Bigger, Better, More Original Sins. I arrived in time to join the jubilant chorus:

Give me what I want
Exactly when I want it
Forever, now, once upon a time!

Give me what I want
Exactly when I want it
Forever, now, once upon a time!

It was giddy, liberating, and seemed – with every repetition – more certain. And why not? I mean, if you are going to recite a prayer to the Universe, why not ask for everything? For a worried searcher like myself, the chant was simple and empowering. I rode away toward Center Camp reciting the bouncy refrain like a Doublemint Gum jingle.

I stopped at a classic PacBell telephone booth, standing alone on the playa, where one was invited to lift the receiver and 'Talk to God.'

'Hello?'

'Hello. God speaking.'

I looked around, but could see no vantage point from which someone might be monitoring my conversation.

'Okay… What am I wearing?'

'A Tropicana print summer dress, pith helmet, silver goggles and purple shorts.'

'Impressive.'

'You expected less?'

'Of course not… Sorry.'

'No worries. Any questions?'

'Why are there so many contradictions in the Bible?'

'Excuse me. Are you implying that I actually wrote those books?'

'Err…'

'Let's say I wanted to write a book. Don't you think I could write at least as well as Dickens? Or DeLillo? Or Murakami?'

'Yes. Definitely. What was I thinking?'

'Now you've put your finger on it. I may have put you all there, but I never know what you people are thinking.'

I wasn't sure how to say 'goodbye' to God. I settled on 'Thanks for everything.'

'You're very welcome. Enjoy.'

The encounter required some contemplation. Due west was a small camp where a serene-looking woman with flowing gray hair had set up a padded, shaded massage table. I parked my bike, lay down, and allowed her to tune my chakras with a set of seven Tibetan singing bowls. Each emitted a pure, resonating frequency. She placed them in turn on my forehead, throat, solar plexus and groin, and instructed me to breathe deeply.

It would have been a rare spell of utter relaxation, except for the shrieks and moans coming from the adjoining camp, where a raven-haired vixen in a fishnet bustier was pushing her eager victims onto a rack, handcuffing their wrists and ankles, and spanking them with a ping-pong paddle.

'I have to say,' I told my masseuse as the final bowl's vibration faded into silence, 'that you've got a pretty weird neighbor.'

'Isn't it great?' she replied. 'That's my daughter.'

A couple of hours later I materialized near the center of the action, only a few hundred feet from The Man. A hybrid of Steampunk and moai, he rose above the playa with the implacable calm of a Tinkertoy Buddha. Characters of every stripe – including a few striped characters – walked or bicycled by, as well as a group of three self-propelled cupcakes. Farther out on the playa, the Temple spiraled into the sky like a Balinese jigsaw puzzle. The early afternoon sun irradiated the alkaline flats, and eddies of dust spiraled seductively. The low mountains in the distance seemed to ripple in the heat.

I was powerfully thirsty.

I reached behind myself for the bottle of water that, secured in a mesh pocket of my daypack, never leaves my side. Where was it? I groped to no avail, then shrugged off the pack. My fears were confirmed. The bottle had fallen out somewhere, possibly on the bumpy passage from the makeshift 'Roaster Coaster' (riders must sign a lethal harm release form) to the life-size game of Mouse Trap (in which, at the climax, a bicycle is crushed by a falling bank safe).

This was serious. Riding back to my tiny, cluttered camp would take a good half hour, and disrupt my artistic trajectory. And I needed a drink now. My eyes darted left and right; surely another reveler might provide sustenance. But could I trust the liquid in those anonymous jars? It was as likely to be vodka, or some other ecstatic potion, as spring water.

At that moment, inspiration struck. I set my bike on its kickstand, stood with my eyes closed and palms together, and chanted my prayer to the Universe:

Give me what I want
Exactly when I want it
Forever, now, once upon a time!

Give me what I want
Exactly when I want it
Forever, now, once upon a time!

I opened my eyes. It took a minute to reorient myself to
the crystalline light of the high desert. Floaters swirled in my
eyeballs. Bicyclists swerved past me, long scarves streaming.
About ten yards ahead, between me and The Man, I spied
a figure with his back toward me. He was wearing—of all
things—a sandwich sign over a heavy backpack. My eyes
narrowed, then widened, as I read the sign's message:

Ice Cold Horchata!

This was beyond belief. Horchata! The sweet Mexican agua
fresca, usually made with milk, rice, cinnamon and vanilla, is
my favorite drink in the world.

The prayer had worked, just as Brezsny had known it would. I
skipped up to the guy wearing the sign, and tapped him merrily
on the shoulder.

'Some ice cold horchata, please!'

The man – tall, tanned, muscular, and probably in his
early 30s – turned around. He grinned, nodded his head, and
pointed downward.

The backpack beneath his sandwich sign was an insulated
container. A clear plastic hose descended from the tank,
disappeared in his pants, and emerged through the fly—ending
in an enormous blue dildo, at least a foot long. The dildo angled
slyly upward, in coy invitation. The man stood with arms
akimbo, relishing my aghast expression.

'Help yourself,' he said.

My 'Straight Men for Gay Marriage' bumper sticker was
no help to me here. I'd gotten myself into a classic Burning
Man pickle. The horn of a dilemma, so to speak. A lifetime of
unchallenged sexual orientation spun my brain around in its

little pan, as surely as if I'd been stuck on the Roaster Coaster.

I couldn't. I wouldn't. I shouldn't. But I was so thirsty. And horchata is so good... Ice cold horchata...

I felt a tap on my own shoulder, and turned around. A line had formed behind me. A short blonde woman with sparkles on her cheeks and sunflowers painted on her breasts stared up at me impatiently. 'Well?'

Perhaps I'm not the first person to reflect that the Universe works in mysterious ways. And I certainly wasn't the first person to do what I did next – though it was a first for me. I dropped to my knees and, employing a milking technique more familiar to dairy farmers than porn stars, coaxed a steady flow of the ambrosial beverage from its X-rated spout. I drank eagerly – so eagerly that it seemed not a moment had passed before sunflower girl tapped me again, more insistently this time.

'Leave some for the rest of us, please!'

'Sorry...' I stood, sated but unsteady, horchata dribbling down my chin. The old joke about the ice cream-eating penguin and the car mechanic ('Looks like you blew a seal!') circled in my brain. My barista helped me to my feet.

'Well done,' he said. 'Was it good for you, too?'

The Accidental Eco-Tourist

Mary Karr

My bush guide squatted down and clicked on his flashlight, an act that puzzled me. Until now, on the path through the Guatemalan jungle, we'd let the bright disk of the moon do the luminatory work, unless a downed tree or tangle of roots across our path made snakes likely.

We'd been trekking through light bush since 4am to reach the ancient Mayan ruins at Tikal. The air was heavy as gauze. A troop of howler monkeys roared in the trees overhead – harsh, raspy altos that I'd first mistaken for jaguars. Toads croaked. An iguana-shape moved along a rotted log.

Now Nathan's flashlight was blazing in one hand, while his other held a small creature – a lizard, I figured, or some amber-colored cicada husk. Instead, he slid a bright circle onto a tarantula he'd just caught. Right then, my city-dweller's adrenal gland started secreting some strong run-away juice.

Nathan pinched back four of the spider's legs and held it belly up for my study. It didn't waggle a bit. 'You want to touch it?' Nathan asked. His perfect Belizian English had a Caribbean lilt to it. (Spanish and Creole are second and third to English in Belize, with dozens of Mayan dialects sprinkled around.) I demurred.

The tarantula's abdomen held a pair of lacquered brown fangs, which, Nathan pointed out, made its biting you nearly impossible. I suggested that it might easily fall on you from the towering canopy of hardwoods and creeper vines overhead, the way fat drops of moisture had been splatting onto banana and banyan leaves with a sound like fingernails on wooden tables all around us.

Nathan shook his head. There were thousands of species of bird and lizard in those trees, he said, not to mention 250 varieties of snake. So any tarantula without a death wish lives underground. Nathan had fished this one out with a length of straw, maybe to stop my endless, carping fear of spiders (I'd had to shut off the video of *Arachnophobia* halfway through). 'Go on and touch him,' Nathan said.

I'd worked my way up to that Guatemalan tarantula by traveling west across Belize, the Central American country south of Mexico once known as British Honduras. What had first drawn me there was the Mayan mystery – why that civilization's thousand-year-old pyramids and temples had been abandoned to the spider monkeys.

Plus I'm an inveterate sissy in terms of travel, a comfort-seeking missile, and Belize sounded easier to reach and move through than other Latin American countries. It's a three-hour flight from Houston or Miami to low-key Belize City, where (unlike in Mexico City, say) the population is small, literate, vaccinated, and not toting automatic weapons. In a few days of driving west over increasingly rough roads, you could reach bona fide tropical jungle without worrying that screwworm flies (a plague in Costa Rica) would burrow under your skin. Along the way you could drink local water without getting bent over double.

Such are a sissy's concerns. I also hoped to find in Belize the awe my eco-tourist pals have when they wax lyrical about the planet. Before the trip, capital-N Nature had always made me wince. For the first time in my life, my bag held hiking boots instead of hot rollers. The young eco-tourist industry hadn't yet erected any high-rise nightmares that I could see, and some aura of innocence came off the glossless brochures I'd read. Until the peaceful break with Britain in 1981, Belizians didn't even have TV.

The sopping heat outside the Belize City airport put me in mind of the swampy corner of Texas Gulf Coast where I grew up. My linen dress got sweat-stuck to my body in a nanosecond. I'd chosen to stop first in the pampered lap of the Maruba Jungle Spa just outside Belize City. Its proprietor, who was heaving my bags into the back of a Bronco, seemed hyper-thin enough not to sweat. He wore a long-sleeved shirt – doubtless steam-ironed – with nary a damp spot on it.

His name was, miraculously enough, Merickston Nicholson. Whatever miseries the tropical climate held, he'd kept away from. Coconut palms stuttered past his profile while he slid on a reggae CD. When I asked about the gym facilities at Maruba, he said, 'Too much exercise is bad for you.' His surgeon daddy had irrefutable research on the evils of exercise and the benefits of red meat.

We rolled over smooth blacktop past the yellow grass of coastal savannah for about an hour. Then corn fields slid by, and the occasional tin-roofed shack of a farmer.

Merickston and his sister, Franziska, ran the spa with their own brand of health wisdom, which included her line of cosmetic unguents and herbal concoctions. I found a basket of them in my air-conditioned hut, little glass vials of body lotion and moisturizer with eensy cork stoppers you had to bite out with your teeth.

The whole room could have sprung from some Pier One catalogue. A faux zebra skin covered the futon sofa (there are no zebras in Belize). The Pierre Cardin bathrobe on the sleigh bed might have been flayed from some investment banker.

In fact, the only local item was the dead animal skin on the door. More than a hundred nails had been hammered into it, some stab at conceptual art that summed up Maruba's wary take on the natural world. While I am not averse to hunting per se (my sharpshooting sister never misses a duck season), the overkill of the nails grossed me out. I thought of St. Sebastian pierced with 1,000 arrows. Add to that window shades that blocked all sun and a mammoth air-conditioner that'd chill a meat locker, and you had the perfect room for a three-day drunk. I slept like a lotus-eater till sunset.

The sculpted grounds and gardens I toured before dinner were empty. There was something surreal about it: a bubbling hot tub surrounded by dry leaves, a pool with ribbons of steam coiling off its chlorine-blue surface.

I finally stumbled onto a guy in formal pants and cummerbund. He stood at a chicken-wire cage (like those we raised pigeons in as kids) poking something through the mesh. I came closer. An ocelot lay inside, affably mopping off a front paw with an impossibly pink tongue. His fawn-colored fur and white underbelly matched the hide nailed in my room. 'You ever think about busting that padlock off?' I asked the guy. He glanced around before he answered. 'Every day.'

Franziska, the spa's co-owner, showed up for our solitary dinner in gauzy black harem pants, a blinding array of rhinestones and kohl eyeliner out to here. The curly black hair that tumbled to her waist looked as if it had grown her head, rather than the other way around. Franziska perfectly understood my refusal to go diving on the offshore barrier reef reputed to be second only to Australia's. 'Diving doesn't bother me,' she said. 'It's the fish I hate.'

That was the message I took from Maruba – that nature was something to lock up or nail down or inject collagen into. The herbal wrap, facial and massage were all first-rate, but felt narcissistically beside the point in the tropical setting. The ocelot I said goodbye to needed no lip gloss or earrings to jack up its beauty quotient.

An archaeology guide sent by International Expeditions (the darling of the eco-tourist industry there) came to ferry me a little closer to the wilds at Blancaneaux Lodge, the elegant resort that Francis Ford Coppola built in the Mountain Pine Ridge Reserve of western Belize. Raul Valencia met me in a battered Ford LTD wide as a boat, which bucked and shimmied along washboard roads made dusty by the dry season, which runs from April to June. We climbed the winding stone path to the lodge covered in limestone dust like a pair of old ghosts.

Arriving at Blancaneaux was like walking into a high-rent Tarzan episode done in Central American decor. The rugs were Guatemalan. A papier-mâché jaguar arched its back from the glossy mahogany floor.

I followed the curving downward path to my thatched hut. A slatted room divider unfolded onto a breakfast nook – rush bottom chairs and lemon-yellow table. The waterfall I overlooked made a shushing roar and powered the ceiling fan. I plugged in my laptop, pleased when the tiny green eye lit up. On the room's vine-covered screen, a twig-colored chameleon stared in. Despite all the humble resolve I'd taken from Maruba about wanting to get closer to the green world, the wild still spooked me.

Other than that, and the Day-Glo yellow toad that leapt waist-high and made me screech on the way to dinner, Blancaneaux could have been in LA. I ordered oven-fired pizza with goat's cheese and artichoke hearts, followed by a decaf cappuccino. The loud Appalachian folk singers had a clog-dancing doll. Their nasal tunes got amplified through speakers big enough for a Nine Inch Nails concert. Raul rolled his eyes. I longed for a curare dart.

The next morning we set out for the two-hour drive to the Mayan ruin at Caracol. The road had been cut by hardwood loggers in the twenties and gone unrepaired since. After the forest station, the pine trees gave out. Then you hit the lush, psychedelic growth of tropical forest.

We pulled into the site between a pair of unexcavated mounds like giant anthills the jungle has taken back, trees growing sideways out of them. At the foot of one, a flock of wild turkeys were moving – china blue, with iridescent tails that put peacocks to shame. The pyramids we walked up to out of that dense green had an Indiana Jones feel.

At the base of the first structure, I studied stone tablets covered in dense hieroglyphs. While Raul translated, it struck me how disinterested the Maya seemed to be in 'nature' per se. Other than an elaborate astronomy that doubtless determined when they planted corn, the stone records talked about ball court games and conquests.

In fact, the Maya had first despoiled the jungle by hacking down trees to build those pyramids. They too used the jungle as 'motif' – just as decorators at Maruba and Blancaneaux

had. Sure, the rulers had primordial names: Lord Water, Lord
Snake. But the art itself seemed decorative – ornamental rather
than 'natural' – like a Gustav Klimt painting where the pattern
somehow devours the particular shapes it pretends to render.

Any natural power the earth held seemed to come through
human beings, specifically blood. The Maya liked blood.
Cinnabar paint flaked from the walls of burial rooms cool as
caves. Stone reliefs depicted human sacrifices in which captives'
hearts were torn out or heads lopped off. And the priests
impressed the common people partly through blood-letting.
Using stingray spines imported from coastal trade routes or
obsidian blades, a priest would pierce his finger or tongue or
(I found this hard to believe) penis. Blood spilled on Caracol's
ritual temples made them portals to the spirit world.

If you stand atop Caracol's 139-foot pyramid, still the loftiest
structure in Belize, you can imagine how impressive a priest
might look to the 80,000 or so subjects below. He'd be decked
out in regalia weighing upwards of fifty pounds – jade belt and
carved ear flaps, crowned by a vast headdress trailing brilliant
quetzal feathers behind him clear to the ground. Because they ate
better than common folk, priests were nearly a foot taller than
the average five-foot Mayan.

With each step down the impossibly high, steep temple stairs
(far harder on my cardiovascular system than a level-eight
StairMaster), the priest's shell necklaces and jade ornaments
would have jangled. Meanwhile, acolytes with incense torches
would have pumped out enough powerful sweet smoke to turn
the descending figure into something of an apparition.

I took a farewell picture of Raul standing inside the curvy,
gargantuan roots of an ancient hardwood tree. He's grinning
like a Buddha, bird-watching binoculars around his neck. But

the reverence for that tree which shines from his Mayan face is modern, not ancient.

That night he dropped me at Chaa Creek Cottages, a famous eco-tourist spot hacked from raw jungle on the edge of the McCall River by Mick and Lucy Fleming. They greeted me in the oil-lit dining hut with the offhanded elegance of tropical adventurers. She's a long-limbed redhead from the States; he's a rawboned Brit who ran away from public school. They fed me a massive bowl of fragrant chicken stew while they finished a bottle of Bordeaux.

Their tale of a jungle fire that sent snakes swarming into their first house gave me a false courage on the path to my hut, the first without screens. The moon was a smoky circle. Something sweet as magnolia or dogwood hung in the damp air. So I wasn't ready for the wolf spider on the wall of my hut, as big as my head. When it stayed put after I chucked my DEET lid at it, I just turned up my oil lamp and went to sleep – further evidence that some tolerance for the natural world was growing in me.

After breakfast, my new bush guide, Nathan Forbes, took me for a hike around the property. For the first time, jungle that had previously come off as an impressionistic green smear was beginning to take shape. I could actually isolate the strangler fig I'd learned about the day before. It sends out a delicate vine shoot to a host tree and eventually envelops it. You have to picture the scale of this phenomenon to grasp its sci-fi quality – a thirty-foot fig was literally wrapped around another tree's trunk, eating it whole.

A vine snake – like a single strand of neon-green linguini – moved in a muscular 'S' from the fig to a neighboring mango, whose unripe fruit hung big as footballs. A batch of shameless yellow bromeliads were fixed onto the same tree like a Carmen Miranda headdress.

We walked through the property's butterfly farm, where you can watch sticky Blue Morpho butterflies unfold themselves from tight pea-green pods. Afterwards, I stood in a screened enclosure while hundreds fluttered around me like cloisonné flowers, only paper frail. Outside, a whole flock of parrots squawked across the pale blue sky. Down by the river, where we swam off the hottest part of the day, Nathan pointed out three species of owl, turkey vultures with their ghoulishly withered necks and jowls, and toucans like on the Fruit Loops box.

This was all training for Guatemala, which was a culmination of sorts, in several ways. First, the road was the worst yet. Until 1970 you could reach Tikal only by mule-back, and what they'd built offered small improvement. The teeth-shattering bounces I suffered on the way to the border literally left me feeling saddle-sore.

Age and size are the overpowering themes in Tikal. The limestone causeway I walked just before dawn one morning was built circa 300 AD, and the earliest altar dates from 600 years before Christ. If you climb Temple Four to watch the sunrise, you'll be 212 feet in the air looking down on the jungle with a handful of ambitious hikers. (Ambition is required: After the stairs give out, you use a wobbly archaeologist's ladder to reach the final platform.) As the gray mist burns off, you can make out the shapes of howler monkeys bounding in the canopy below. The jungle stretches to a gradually lightening mountain horizon.

While all this unfolded, no one said anything. Tourists from Germany and Israel and Japan squatted on the ancient temple's highest platform, all struck wordless in their separate languages while the sky went pink.

I spent the rest of the day puzzling over the dense code of Mayan glyphs, unable to master them. All travel is about such decipherment. One minute you're lost at a crossroads studying a map's mysterious markings, the next, the world lines up with the map's abstractions, so you can pinpoint where inside that map you're standing. Even where English is spoken, you have to learn new languages, master new forms. On my last afternoon in Tikal, the glyphs got distinct. I could suddenly see on a tablet the ruler's face emerging from the jaguar's mouth, where before there'd been only interwoven circles.

And walking back to the Tikal Inn through a brief patch of jungle, I noticed forms where before I'd seen only tangled disorder. There was a pattern to the wild – complex, but learnable, the way Mozart's busy flurry of notes will suddenly yield up an old theme with new harmonies. Belize taught me – in my lumbering way – to find a place inside that pattern. I'd gone there for its ruins, which my civilized sissy's heart could comfortably get to, but the ease of travel inside that country ultimately let me wander into the jungle.

My own fear was the only obstacle. To get past it, I had to pet that tarantula. Or so Nathan told me. I ran a finger down a hairy leg that was soft, not spiky like you'd guess. The abdomen I went on to stroke felt like a bunny's, nothing you'd be scared of.

Horsing Around France

Jane Smiley

I am very fond of France – whenever I think of going anywhere, I have to say, 'But maybe not France this time.' In France, all Americans are guilty until proven innocent (or perhaps guilty of perennial innocence), but I don't mind, the landscape makes up for it. So in 2007, I signed up for a horse riding perambulation of Aquitaine, a part of France I had never been to – but of course I used L'Occitane Citrus Verbena Shampoo and L'Occitane Shea Butter Verbena Soap and I had seen Katherine Hepburn play Eleanor of Aquitaine in *The Lion in Winter*, so I considered myself fully prepared. It was the end of July. I took my own saddle. My husband, Jack, and I flew Virgin, passed out in Dublin, awoke in Biarritz. Already, the first day, we felt profoundly sophisticated as we strolled around the casino, thinking of Audrey Hepburn and Sean Connery (and it didn't matter that they had made no movies in Biarritz – Monte Carlo was close enough). Jack took a dip in the ocean (colder than Atlantic City) and I took a dip in the language. We smiled.

After four days in Biarritz, we drove east on the A64. It was now August. The fields of maize and sunflowers were perfectly tended and weed-free, but there was no one anywhere nearby – no tractors, no field hands. No litter on the roads, verges neatly mowed. I came up with my first principle of French culture – if you faithfully attend to maintenance for a millennium, you can, indeed, take a month off every year. At Pau, we stopped so that I could pay homage to Marguerite de Navarre, the older sister of Francois I (King of France from 1515-1547) and the author of one of my favorite works, *The Heptameron*. Then we turned north, onto the A65. We were to meet my fellow equestrians outside of Villeneuve-sur-Lot, a 'ville' that was 'neuve' – new – only when it was founded in the 13th century on the site of a town that had been abandoned during the Albigensian crusade. It was evident to me by the time we got there that a horse would be much better for transport in that part of France, because the landscape was simultaneously so beautiful and so particular that it could not be fully appreciated at eighty, or even fifty, kilometers per hour. Five or ten would be much better.

I was an experienced equestrian with far too many horses back home. I had done an equestrian vacation two years earlier, in Queensland, Australia, the home of Seventy-Five Mile Beach and Fraser Island. I had been to France many times. I knew how to say the proper words with a proper enough accent that my interlocutors would smile and talk back to me as if I understood them. Jack planned to drive around the area, never getting too far away, having déjeuner and dîner with us. He did not have to drive on the left side of the road. Our guides spoke English. From a distance, we would eyeball French houses and fantasize about owning one. What could go wrong?

My assigned mount was a tall, slender bay mare. My saddle fit her. A man who spoke no English wrangled the horses, might have been the owner, and drank pastis every day for lunch. A woman who did speak English was in charge of each day's journey; she could not understand either my French or my English. The other participants were good-natured English women. There were six of us altogether.

Aquitaine is shaped by both history and geography. For about three hundred years after Eleanor of Aquitaine married Henry II, the kings of England claimed the region; during the Reformation, French Huguenots took refuge there. The broad, fertile valleys are punctuated by hilltop forts and towns that are reminiscent of those days, and yet the agriculture specific to the region makes it seem uniquely peaceful, not least the sight of the local cattle breed, Blonde d'Aquitaine, grazing peacefully inside of electric fences that look like single strands of ribbon – if the grass is so good, why leave?

My fellow riders were friendly. As we walked, we talked. But I do not remember what we said – what I remember is the beautiful patchy light, the wide trails beside stone walls and under graceful, leafy branches of mature trees. We never watched out for poison oak as we do in California – rather, as we ambled along, we reached out for wild raspberries, perfectly ripe, shared only with the birds. Sometimes we came to fields and trotted or cantered – one of these, I remember, was a large orchard of plum trees fruiting out, almost ripe, and brilliantly fragrant. I was told that France has a whole network of equestrian trails, all linked. I was ready to ship my horses over and buy that house. Our destinations each day were fortified towns – Villeneuve-sur-Lot to Gavaudun to Belvès and onward, northeast. We were not far from the Lascaux caves, maybe fifty kilometers, but we were immersed in a medieval landscape, not a prehistoric one.

We would mount in the morning, ride for a while, stop for déjeuner – the horses would be confined in a temporary pen, also made of what looked like ribbon, set up in a new meadowy spot each day. Then we would mount again and head to the next town. Our pace was leisurely, but there was trotting and cantering, and soon that became my problem, because my agreeable bay mare had something wrong with her left foot. I noticed it the first day, and it kept getting worse. She was off at the trot and reluctant to canter, but since we had to make our day's quota of kilometers, I had to push her. On the third day, after we left the foie gras farm (where we had learned how eager the geese are to do what comes naturally, that is, to gulp down their vast helpings of provisions), we were emerging from a wide, shady path into a sunny valley. My mare stepped on something and then hopped forward, tossing her head and holding her foot in the air. When we walked onto the grass, she seemed to improve, but I could always feel it, walk, trot, slow canter – something was bothering her. I mentioned it to the wrangler. He smiled in a French way, but he did pick her feet. Nothing there.

I explained myself to the English-speaking guide. She did not understand me. We rode along. She seemed to understand the other riders, so I explained myself again, adopting my most non-St. Louis, upper-crust English accent. She understood me. That was a bit of a revelation. After that, whenever I spoke to her, I tried to pretend that I had gone to Oxford. Both she and the wrangler reassured me that everything was fine.

In the meantime, although we covered no more than ten or fifteen kilometers each day, Jack was having difficulty keeping up in the rental car, because in my enthusiasm, I had forgotten to reckon with his dyslexia, bad enough in England, perhaps, but insurmountable in France. Our sylvan trails and his back roads did not run parallel – he had to use signs and maps to meet up with us. Even though each trip was only ten or twenty kilometers, he pretty much had no idea where he was or where he was going. He would look at the map and see the angles of the intersections, then guess from that which road he needed to take. If the names of the towns were short, he could match them – the easiest to find was Domme – but others made no sense. The roads he took were all verdant, woodsy, and clean. The trees were all healthy and old. For a while, he enjoyed himself. At Belvès, he got there before we did. As he was sitting in the town square wondering where we might be, he heard the clip-clop of horses' hooves strolling down the street toward him. That was a first for me, too – riding and window-shopping at the same time. In the evenings, I would read very slowly to Jack from a French guide we had purchased. Perhaps it was Belvès, during the Hundred Years War, that one night sent out a group of marauders to the neighboring town, only to discover that that town had sent marauders, that very night, to Belvès. What each band stole was subsequently returned, and the two towns decided to live in peace.

I made up my mind. After a painful ride the next morning, I approached the wrangler as he was setting up the temporary pen in a pleasant meadow outside the next town. I assembled my rudimentary French, and I spoke very clearly, 'Mon cheval a un mal a pied! Très mal!' I demonstrated by limping around. 'Moi, je ne peux pas monter le cheval.' I assumed that someone would come in a horse trailer to pick the poor animal up and take her back to her stable.

My husband got lost, really lost, unable to deduce by intersection angles, road signs, or landscape where he was going, or even where he had been. Toward evening, he parked the car beside the road and found a pick-up truck full of pipes and other plumbing fixtures. He approached the plumber, showed him the map. The plumber first explained how to go, but that was no use. Finally, the plumber led him to us, to our hostel, himself asking along the way how to get there. It was now evident that our trip was a failure. I believe that for dinner we were served a basket of deep-fried minnows. I shamefully stowed my saddle in the trunk of the rental. The plan was that we would meet the horse troop each evening, and eat with them. What the wrangler and the guide really thought of us, they kept to themselves.

But yes, the car was freeing. Once I was sitting in the passenger seat with the map in my lap, we ranged more widely – a sign directed us to a private botanical garden on an estate that seemed lost in time as well as space. We visited the ruins of a fortress perched on a promontory above the intersection of two medieval roads – a tollbooth of sorts, where carriers of goods had once had to pay up in order not to be robbed. We drove along the Dordogne River – Lalinde to Bergerac, south to Eymet, then up into the hills. Everywhere we stopped, parked, investigated, as you can do so conveniently with a car, but not with a horse.

That afternoon, we arrived in Domme before the horses did. If most of the towns in Aquitaine are hill fortresses, Domme is perhaps the most self-contained and startling one. We entered the gate and walked uphill, past compact buildings of golden stone that demanded our curiosity – who lives here? Can local society be as idyllic as the town itself? Might I set a novel here? Has anyone ever done that? It was a Thursday, and so the market was busy in the town square. The weather was, as it had been all week, bright and warm, but not hot. The breeze was as if ordered up, just enough to lift the spirits. I love markets, so I wandered from stand to stand, until I came to an artist who had arranged his

watercolors around his table. The works were dreamy landscapes –
castles rising through the mist, dark hills in the distance, blue sky
above. We began to chat, a little in French, more in English –
he was well traveled. After a bit, he motioned to me to walk a
few meters toward a fence. And there it was, the valley of the
Dordogne, with the river winding through the green and varied
landscape, as far as the eye could see. Of course he was inspired.
It was one of those perspectives that you might watch day by day,
year by year, perennially noticing some new detail.

When the equestrians arrived, I was not envious, but I was still
abashed, until I asked one of the English ladies about their trip.
Oh, she said, it was lovely. My horse, the slender bay mare, seemed
very happy to wander along with the others, unridden, unsaddled,
unburdened, accompanying her friends through the countryside.
And so it turned out that I had done everyone a favor.

Aquitaine is one of those cherished places I have never
returned to, along with the English Lake District, Queensland,
St. Petersburg, Budapest, Magens Bay on St. Thomas, Crete, and
Kauai – places of such beauty and strangeness that I sometimes
look at the pictures I took, and more often think of special vistas or
moments that I remember as well as I remember the view outside
my own backdoor. Of all these places, though, it is Aquitaine that
taught me this lesson: Every spot on earth is particular, detailed,
and incomprehensibly complex. The speed of a horse is no less right
or wrong than the speed of a car or a bicycle or a hike; a close-up
view of the branches of a plum tree is no less mysterious than a
sweeping perspective over broad landscape; I must live with my
fellow citizens of a small town for decades in order to understand
them, but I cannot resist sampling as many small towns as possible.

Reaching Bliss
Suzanne Joinson

How much does a Kalashnikov weigh? I obsess over this question as I sit in Abdul's house drinking tea. There are four of these guns leaning against the wall and even the youngest teenage son has one strapped over his shoulder. My gun knowledge is limited but the AK-47 is a mythical weapon that crosses from warfare to cultural history, making me think of Soviet-funded vigilantes roaming fairy-tale-sounding cities such as Osh and Dushanbe. Coming as I do from England, I have never seen a gun in real life. I am bursting with questions about them. Do they shoot them? Is it really necessary to carry one around?

We are sitting in the 'family' part of the house in Yemen's capital, Sana'a. This is the formal area for hosting strangers. I came here to meet with a bunch of people to discuss translation. Now the official meetings are finished and Abdul has talked my security guards into letting me visit his home. I am self-conscious because I am wearing a black abaya over the top of my jeans, T-shirt and Converse. I dressed conservatively for this trip, but even so, three minutes on a street where every other woman was covered in black made me feel naked and I was taken to a souq to buy the full rig. The women of Abdul's family smile with their eyes, all I can see of their faces. Even so, I can tell that the girl jigging a black-eyed baby is a devil with a hell of a sense of humour. I'd love to hang out with her and chat, but of course, I'm on best behaviour with the men and the glinting from the metal on the guns is making me both nervous and excited in a way I don't even want to begin to analyse.

Abdul arranges papers on the table. Everything in a house full of guns is unknown. This is my first time in Yemen, but this isn't the only first. It's also the first time I've ever been driven in an armoured vehicle, or covered my body in an unfamiliar long, black, shapeless garment, or seen men walking around the street with huge ceremonial daggers stuffed into their pants. Stepping into Sana'a is like entering a dream. I've certainly been hit with images half-familiar from CNN or Al Jazeera snapshots, the stereotypical instability, heat, and sense of chaos – but it is also like nowhere I have ever been: the buildings, dress and vibe are all totally out of my world.

At Abdul's house we are discussing a book called *Salmon Fishing in the Yemen*. Abdul and his boss, Salah, co-translated it from English to Arabic. I know that in the UK the book was considered a satire on the British Labour Government and the title is a kind of joke, meaning: look, this government puts together foolish initiatives such as attempting to fish for salmon in the Yemen, a place with a catastrophic water shortage problem.

Abdul is very pleasant, wiry and curly-haired, and we discover we share a passion for yoga. For Abdul this is very intense. He is in the middle of translating the Sanskrit text of *The Hatha Yoga Pradipika* into Arabic. We geek out on this and constantly digress but Salah is getting annoyed at our constant digressions into random yoga-tales. We pull ourselves together and concentrate. Salah would like to talk me through his entire translation and I look at the manuscript, guessing it's about four hundred pages. I realise that he has interpreted 'Salmon Fishing in the Yemen' entirely straight, and why wouldn't he? It is no joke to him that there is no water here and there is nothing funny about a Sheikh teaching Westerners how to fish in a desert. I begin to see the point of an abaya. Underneath its folds, my fingers twitch. Abdul's phone rings and he begins a high-voltage discussion, glancing in my direction.

That phone call is about me, I think. Abdul paces, rubs his nose, then turns to me.

'There's a cyclone in Oman. All flights are down.'

'Oh.'

I am meant to leave for Oman tonight. My tour of this region is highly structured with as little time in Yemen as possible. Armed guards and vehicles are expensive and a wandering European woman is a hassle for everyone.

'It is decided: you stay in Yemen, miss out Oman, and then go directly to Riyadh early next week.'

I hadn't figured on a free, long weekend in Sana'a, a place famous for regular kidnappings and for operating entirely outside the sphere of 'Western law'. I recall the British Foreign and Commonwealth's unequivocal website: 'THE FCO ADVISE AGAINST ALL TRAVEL TO YEMEN'. I say to Abdul, half-truthfully, 'Wonderful! I'm so pleased.'

I am not a thrill-seeker or war journalist, or a 'zone of tension' junkie, though I've met a few. In my experience countries or states branded with DANGER or TERRORISM often (though not always) require a visiting traveller to be respectful and thoughtful rather than full of fear. Recently, however, something has happened to travel and me. Our relationship is rocky. Whereas I used to hop onto a plane and think of freedom, now, when I am on the move, what I get is a disturbing sense of dislocation. Travelling is less an experience and more like a postponement, but I can't work out what it is I'm putting off.

We finally reach the end of the session and everyone shakes hands. There is much nodding. I glance around Abdul's home. It is always inside family places that my own feeling of inner-exile becomes most acute, in kitchens and near stoves and fireplaces in particular. I don't want to leave. Now I will be taken back to a hotel where I will spend three days alone in a heavily protected room. The thought makes me hot behind the ears with panic.

'I would really love to walk around Sana'a for a little while, Abdul.' I keep my voice light.

'Of course, I will be your guide.'

It takes him ten minutes to convince the security team waiting outside his house that I am in safe hands and at last I am allowed to walk the dusty, traffic-filled streets like a normal person.

'Life is always better if you take the harder path,' he says, grinning and pointing to a pathway on top of a crumbling rampart.

'Okay.' I follow him.

There is a long drop on one side of us. The houses of Sana'a grow up out of the dust in tall, fairytale towers. They are densely packed together, seven or eight floors high, and their windows are decorated with white gypsum. It is an alphabet city, with signs and letters, graffiti and drawings everywhere. The architecture is blowing my mind, but the dust is getting in my eyes.

'I am a bit Welsh, a bit Irish and a bit English,' I tell him. 'It's possible there is even some Scottish in me. Either way, I come from the land of rain. It's so dry here.'

He laughs, and then sighs as we walk past a row of stalls selling cassettes and CDs of Lebanese and Egyptian pop music.

'There is either no rain, or occasionally too much rain, in Yemen.'

The water shortage, or rather water management, is a deathly problem and I feel an idiot for bringing it up. I realise that the rocky drop to my left leads down to a road where Yemeni men in trucks whiz past, staring and pointing at me, but not in an unfriendly way. They are just looking at an alien wandering in their homeland. I think of my empty flat in London, the thirsty plants. Every time I return from a stint of being on the road, the plants are all dead and I have to buy new ones. It is a stupid system that I need to rectify.

Abdul surprises me, 'You seem sad?'

I am astounded because I believed I was covering my thoughts from this kind stranger.

'I feel a little lost, too much travelling perhaps.' I don't know how to explain the two sensations I live with: loneliness and a permanent state of homesickness, even when at home.

'You don't like it?'

'I do, but lately, it is as if I'm not travelling, I'm running, but I can't find a way to stay still.'

I am frustrated with my inability to say what I mean, and follow him down uneven steps. We are now standing near the famous Bab al Yemen, the main gate to the old city. On relatively even ground again, Abdul looks closely at me and then says, 'Just one minute, please.'

We pause walking and I lean against a dusty wall as he engages in another of his furious-sounding conversations. When he finishes, he smiles but says nothing. We walk past ancient tea houses, through souqs and alleyways where knives, rabbits, doves and copper pots are for sale.

In the anonymous no-man's-land of the hotel lobby, Abdul begins negotiations. The security men shake their heads. If I am kidnapped or something even worse happens to me, these men lose their livelihoods. I drift away and let them talk. There are times when you travel and everything goes to plan, and then there is a shift and you're off the page; after that, anything can happen. I see Abdul coming towards me. He is positively bounding.

'Would you like to see the Yemeni island Socotra?'

'I, I guess so...' In truth, I have never heard of this island. He pats my arm in a brotherly fashion.

'I feel very strongly that you need to see paradise,' he says.

'I would love to,' I say to Abdul, grateful that I won't be eating room service meals alone and convincing myself that everyone ignores FCO advice anyway.

I assess the situation. I am with two men who are strangers to me, sitting in the boiling hot Riyan Mukalla Airport and we are all eating peanuts. Abdul and his cousin Hadi are smiley and have taken time from their own lives to accompany me. They arranged everything; all I had to do was pay for my flight. As I chew the salty peanuts, I try to get a sense of geography and flick through reference points in my head for words relating to Yemeni islands: Sinbad. Incense routes. Southern Arabia. Freya Stark. Yemenia Airlines. (Did their aeroplanes 'fall out of the sky'?)

'Are we flying Yemenia?' I ask breezily.

'Oh, no. Felix.'

'Okay. Great.'

I have never heard of Felix Airways. Another word flutters into my mind: pirates.

'Um, Abdul, is Socotro near Somalia?'

'Oh, yes,' says Abdul, equally breezily as we are called forward towards the fragile-looking craft. He cheerfully recites the facts for me: Socotra is halfway between the coast of Yemen and the coast of Somalia, in the middle of the Gulf of Aden.

'Right, got it.'

I enter the mouth of the plane and inside the cabin the atmosphere is jovial. Each passenger is carrying at least one bag of the much-chewed narcotic, qat. There is a celebratory feel, and every single person smiles and nods at me. When the plane takes off, passengers clap and call out to the pilot. It's impossible not to join in.

I have a window seat. It is a bright, clear day and below Yemen looks like an ocean of brown. Soon we are over the sea. I put my head on the window and have a transient thought: perhaps Abdul is a master trickster, leading me to a cave or a lair? I look over at him, on the other side of the aisle, his toes poking out of his dusty sandals. He has moved on from peanuts to a packet of cashew nuts and giggles when I look at him. He offers me the bag.

Nothing in my entire travelling life has prepared me for the island of Socotra. We are in a Jeep, driven by another of Abdul's relations, and the first thing I see is trees that look like giant mushrooms with bulbous veined branches.

'This is the Dragon's Blood Tree,' Abdul says with a grin as we drive past. He looks different. His shoulders are less hunched, his face less worried. The road drops into a valley and my jaw corresponds by dropping too because it is beyond any scale of normal geography or landscape that I have ever encountered. There are cactus-like plants straight from Star Trek, and the most insane-looking trunks, like a child's drawing: thick, twisted, as if made from Play-Doh, poking from rocks apparently needing no soil to grow. Out of their tops are the strangest blooming pink flowers.

'Desert rose!' Abdul shouts. On the roadside is a dusty sign saying Hadibo in English, the Arabic beneath it. We drive some more and I realise that the road has fizzled and we are driving very slowly over rocky ground. Flittering in and out of otherworldly shrubbery are sparrow-like birds that look nothing like sparrows.

'What's happened to the road?'

'There are no more roads.'

I am at the end of the world, with men I don't know. It is possible that I am a liability, or a ransom, and my heart is beating very fast. I see news headlines: 'English Woman Voluntarily Allowed Herself to be Kidnapped'.

'Now, we can go to Hadibo and find the hotel.' Abdul says. 'Or...'

'Yes?' They are all looking at me with bright laughing eyes. They don't seem the eyes of killers to me, but what do I know? I have a lifetime of conditioned Western thinking.

'Or, we can sleep on the beach, which is, some think, much nicer.'

Camping. I consider myself a traveller, but of late I've gotten a bit used to fancy hotels and drivers. Way back in the dusty parts of my mind I recall campsites, sleeping bags and carefree nights, but now I'm thinking logistics. (Where will I go to the toilet? Where will I get changed?) Or is it a cave?

Abdul's smile wavers, and yet again I give over to trust and instinct. 'I would love to sleep on the beach with you all tonight.'

We all cheer. Hadi opens his bag of qat and begins the long chew. The drive is very bumpy.

'What does it mean, Socotra?' I ask. Abdul is a magician with words. He speaks Socotran, Somalian and several Arabian dialects too.

'Souq is a market. Quta means selling frankincense.'

'Ah.'

'Or maybe,' Abdul says, 'it comes from the Sanskrit: dvīpa meaning "island" and sukhadhara meaning "supporting, or providing bliss".'

Island of bliss.

Evening comes down on our beach camp. Hadi and Abdul have provided me with everything. A sleeping bag. Tea, bread and soup. There is a tent, but we all want to sleep outside. Birds that look like distant relatives of kites and puffins shriek above us. Abdul turns on two lamps and a thousand insects join us, then he jumps up and walks towards the shore.

The beach is the stuff of Robinson Crusoe mythology: a bank of pure white sand, dunes rolling into foliage, the tide lapping. Abdul begins his yoga and I determine in that moment that kidnappers and yoga simply don't go together. I am too shy to join him but it is pleasant to watch the silhouette of his body in triangles and positions of balance.

This island is known as the home of the Phoenix, and as I close my eyes in the evening peace, the myth seems entirely feasible. A feeling comes upon me that at first I barely recognise. Or rather, the familiar feeling that plagues me – of ties to home loosened to a degree that I am permanently untethered – is, at this moment, dislodged. In its place is happiness – a rare, almost impersonal emotion, like a line of moonlight that has accidentally glanced this way, nothing to do with the earth itself. And what I learn is this: there are places in the world where one feels new, young, and alive again. Where plants grow without soil. Rocks exist in formations that make no sense. Trees are made from dragon's blood and their trunks have healing properties. It is possible to feel connected to sand that is a mysterious mustard-yellow colour and to pick a flower that has no name.

Back in Sana'a, the representative at the hotel looks cross. During our time in Socotra there has been an abduction, two foreigners taken by a tribe from the Al-Damashqa area of Marib. I turn to Abdul, trepidation flooding back.

'Don't worry,' he says, brushing it off. 'My friend works at the NGO that deals with kidnappings in Yemen and most of the time the abductions end peacefully.'

I am not reassured by this, but anyway, it is time for me to leave. The traffic to the airport is crazy and the talk in our armoured vehicle is of conflict, kidnappings, trouble. As we drive through the barren-looking land, the driver waves his hand to the yellow hills.

'Look,' he says in English, 'no water, but what little there is they use to grow qat and not food.'

The land outside certainly looks thirsty. I pull my abaya over me for peace and secrecy beneath its black folds. I would like to hug the driver, I would like to hug them all, but it wouldn't be appropriate. At the airport they give me a gift: a copy of *The*

Travels of Ibn Battuta, complete with luxuriously drawn maps. I am touched, and we shake hands.

'I'm not flying Yemenia,' I say. 'Thank goodness for that!'

They laugh and I thank them and then I leave them, to dry gardens and places that Westerners haven't yet invaded, to the dust and the island of bliss, and I wish, very much, that water will find its way to them. As something, not unlike water, found its way to me on the sands of Socotra.

Coming Home
David Baldacci

It was supposed to be a family summer holiday to Italy in 2008, a treat for my wife and our daughter and son, aged fifteen and twelve respectively. We were leasing a villa in Tuscany with two other couples, one of whom had two children the same ages as ours. Months before we flew out, I received an email from the mayor of Barga, a medieval city in the Lucca province in Tuscany. He wrote that he had read I would be coming to Italy to vacation (where he read this I don't know) and he very much wanted me to visit Barga and be his guest for lunch.

Well, I had intended to bring my family to Barga for a very special reason: It was the birthplace of my grandfather Amedeo Giovanni Vittorio Baldacci back in the late 1800s. I had never met him, as he died tragically of pneumonia during a terrible winter storm in Virginia in 1940, a full two decades before I was born. But I'd heard a great deal about the six-foot-four-inch Italian immigrant, who had come through Ellis Island and then headed straight south, getting off the train in Richmond, Virginia (my hometown), where he met my grandmother, a full eighteen inches shorter than he, at the boarding house run by her mother. He owned several successful businesses in Richmond, including a confectionery, a restaurant, a sightseeing business that would take you on a plane over the area, and a coal mine that produced far more water than coal.

Everyone in Richmond called the tall, handsome, Rudolph Valentino look-alike 'Mike,' as apparently Amedeo, Giovanni and Vittorio were too much for Southern tongues to handle. (I won't get into how many tortured versions of 'Baldacci' I heard growing up, but I can tell you that years of therapy have worked wonders for my self-esteem.) My grandfather was said to be beloved by all who knew him, and he and my grandmother produced eight children over a fifteen-year period, with my father being roughly in the middle of the pack.

The year 2008 had particular significance for me in a very sad way. My father had passed away in May. He had never been to Barga. The closest he got was France and later Egypt when he was fighting in World War II. I had planned the trip long before he passed away with the thought that I would bring back all these wonderful stories of the birthplace of his father. While I could no longer do that, I could still go, as his informal representative, to see the land of his ancestors.

Hence, I wrote back to the mayor and said I would certainly travel to Barga and have lunch with him and I would be bringing my family and friends, if that would be all right with him. He graciously assented to the extra baggage, and a time and date were established for the meeting.

In August we flew to Rome and took a train to Florence, where we rented a car and began our journey to the villa on top of a hill that should have been about an hour south of Florence. However, we ran into a snag; our GPS, which we had specifically ordered with the rental, was not properly charging. As we drew close to our destination, an automated voice said warningly, 'Losing power, please feed me or you will be lost here forever.' Well, as it spoke in Italian, my wife and I were just speculating on that. However, as the picture kept going off and the automated voice started to crackle, we knew something was terribly wrong.

We raced like mad down the autostrade, got off at our exit and watched the dire GPS doomsday warnings continue until we were maybe five miles from our destination. Then, with a series of little beeps like a hospital vitals monitor forecasting the end, the GPS went off to the navigation graveyard, leaving us wondering where the hell we were.

The other two couples were traveling separately. We tried to contact them on our cell phones, but those too apparently had gone to the same high-tech cemetery as the GPS. We simply kept getting a lovely voice speaking Italian with the gist being, 'You're screwed.' We eventually reached a village and found a rescue squad team resting under the August sun. In our very poor Italian, we tried to make them understand what we wanted. They were pleasant and kind and had no idea what we were asking.

Finally, one of them seemed to get it. He climbed on his official EMT scooter, turned on his emergency lights and signaled for us to follow. We did so, and then, we began to climb.

And climb we did, on sickening switchbacks and near verticals until I thought our car was going to pull out a gun and shoot itself to stop the agony. The man on the scooter finally stopped and I pulled up next to him.

'Are we there yet?' I asked, hoping and praying that he would simply say 'Si,' or perhaps 'Va bene,' which was about the extent of my friendship with the local language.

Instead he waved us on and said something like, 'Continua ad andare' and then something else that I didn't fully catch but that sounded like the name of a Toyota model, maybe the Avanti. My wife looked at me and said, 'I think he wants us to keep going.'

And we did, while our Italian chum turned and headed back down the mountain astride his all-terrain emergency vehicle with the cool light. To safety.

We kept going, winding our way over gravel roads and then to what seemed like no roads and only barely discernible paths. Along the way we rounded curves where the two-foot-wide 'road' was cut into the mountain's side and the drop down was a couple thousand feet with nothing between death and us except, well, air. I had a quick thought that the helpful EMTs might be the ones to retrieve our bodies from the wreckage. Three times we turned back because, as I patronizingly and stupidly proclaimed, 'It can't be this far up. No one would rent a place that was so damn inaccessible.'

On our third trip back down, we ran into one of the other couples coming from another direction. They had been looking for the villa for about as long as we had. After discussing the matter, we decided to just go for it. I gunned the car. They did the same with their vehicle and we charged headlong up the mountain – the Light Brigade in Tuscany. We passed where we had stopped before and just kept going, gears gnashing, tires trying to gain traction, clouds of gray smoke coating the car; it was like we were attempting a run across the moon's surface in a four-cylinder Peugeot.

And then, when we had virtually given up all hope, and I had managed to damage beyond all repair the comatose GPS by beating it with a large metal object pulled from our luggage – we arrived.

The villa was beautiful, the grounds exquisite, the caretakers beyond gracious and helpful, the wine local and flowing, the food, well, it was Italy after all, and we forgot all about our hellish trip up.

That is until we had to make the hellish trip back down. But Italy is so gorgeous that who really cares about sudden death by toppling off a mountain? And how do you get 'views' unless you're up high? It's actually very logical, even though that logic might have been tied to the forty-odd bottles of wine we three couples polished off in a week and then lined up jauntily on the villa's fireplace mantel.

We swam in the pool, prepared meals together and watched a meteor shower blaze across the night sky. We went to big cities and small villages. As we traveled around, we often saw elderly women in cotton dresses riding bikes up mountain roads, a sight I have yet to see in America.

We ate out a lot, of course. And sampled the local wines, of course, of course. We never had a bad meal or bad wine anywhere we went. People lingered over meals and their glasses of wine. Men were in parks during the day with their children playing chess or tossing bocce balls. Again, not something you see every day in America, where we often work too hard and never stop to smell the roses or even draw a relaxed breath. I have found throughout my travels that people, in certain respects, are very much the same wherever you go. But cultures are very different. And that, for me, is the point of travel. In addition to the food and alcohol, of course.

The caretaker of the villa told us about the wild *cinghiales*, or boars, that roamed the area. We could hear them in the night making their somewhat terrifying grunts and roars.

My prankish son hid in the bushes one night and waited for his buddy – the other couple's younger son – to stroll by before mimicking the call of the *cinghiale* perfectly. His buddy finally stopped running somewhere around Bologna.

Then came the day for us to go to Barga.

We all loaded into two cars and set off. Now, in Italy we found that there is really no easy way to get anywhere, particularly in rural areas. So we left in plenty of time and still ended up being late. We had resorted to paper maps since the navigation systems in the other cars had also died – I think this is a trick Italian rental car shops play on all American travelers to raise blood pressures and get them to drink more wine.

After our third time becoming lost, I just stopped in front of a massive stone wall with a huge gate and turned to my wife.

'Do you think we're here?' I asked in obvious frustration.

She looked out the window and said, 'Well, considering there's a twelve-foot-tall poster of you on the wall over there, I think we found Barga.'

Then I suddenly noticed all these cars and policemen directing traffic. I pulled over to one of them, rolled down the window and asked if he spoke English. He did. I asked him what was going on. He said automatically, as though he'd answered this question many times already, 'It's David Baldacci Day in Barga.' He pointed to an open space to his right. 'Park over there.'

I rolled my window back up and glanced at my wife. She hiked her eyebrows, gave me a scathing look and said, 'David Baldacci Day?'

'I had no idea,' I said.

'Liar,' she shot back. 'And look how we're dressed.'

It was August. We were dressed in shorts, casual shirts and sandals.

We all climbed out of our cars and then the remarkable turned even stranger.

Apparently word of our arrival had spread, because we heard music. And then the mighty Barga gates opened and out came a man wearing both the Italian and American flags. Behind him was a band. Behind them were journalists and videographers. And behind them, apparently, were all the citizens of Barga. I could also see that American flags were flying over the city. I later learned this had not happened since the end of World War II.

The mayor greeted us warmly and then escorted us into the majestic town proper. I have to confess that an image of Dorothy entering the Emerald City did come to mind.

Off we went to lunch, marching Pied Piper-like down the narrow aged streets. And the meal was magnificent, even if I did eat it with 900 new friends. The fried meatballs were especially memorable. And after that we were given four gallons of gelato each. And after that we toured the city, visiting the beautiful Duomo, the Loggia del Podesta, the city hall and the Church of San Francesco, to name a few. I also met a boy, barely two, who, I was told, was a Baldacci, and whose parents had traveled from their home in Switzerland to meet me. All in all there were dozens of family members there, none of whom I had ever met or even known existed.

I did a book signing at the town bookshop, signing both English and Italian versions of my works, and chuckled when I saw my first novel in Italian. Absolute Power was published in Italy in 1996 under a pseudonym. My publisher asked me to change my name because he said Italians didn't think Italians could write. I pointed out that Machiavelli, Dante and Puzo had had pretty good careers. He went on to elaborate that when it came to thrillers Italians wanted to read American writers. When he had phoned me at home and asked me to come up with a really strong American name, I happened to look out the window and saw our Explorer in the driveway. So I suggested the name David Ford. He loved it and David Ford's *Absolute Power* was a bestseller in Italy. I have since reverted to my true name for subsequent books. I guess it was good I didn't own a Ferrari or Lamborghini back then or I wouldn't have sold a single copy in the land of my ancestors.

And then the mayor told me it was time to give my grand speech in the center courtyard of the city.

Grand speech? In khaki shorts, polo shirt and sandals?

We trooped to the center of the city, where the band played one final song to set the mood and then grew silent. Then the mayor started off the ceremony by bestowing gifts upon me. These included a lifetime supply of olive oil, a genealogical map of my family dating back to the thirteenth century (now proudly displayed in my office), T-shirts, a painting, and a journal from the town archives that my ancestor Pietro Baldacci had started writing in back in the sixteenth century. Because paper was so scarce back then, the journal had been handed down to his descendants. The last entry was from the late 1800s. (I have since had the journal restored and preserved by a friend from the Library of Congress.) There were gifts also to my wife and our bambinos. As the crowd parted and my daughter walked up to get her goodies, she gave me a look that every father of a teenage girl knows well: 'You're ruining my life!' My son on the other hand was blowing kisses and absolutely reveling in the attention.

And then I gave my speech, necessarily off the cuff, which was translated by two representatives of the city for its citizens. And as I spoke I realized how truly touched I was by all of this. I'm sure I rambled on, but it was all sincere and heartfelt. As I gazed around at all the faces fixed on me, it began to sink in that my grandfather and his father, and his father's father, and on and on, had walked these streets, had sat in that Duomo, had married, had children, raised families and mourned the passing of loved ones. And the cycle had gone on and on, for centuries.

As my speech concluded and I was making my way through the crowd, one of my friends who had traveled with us came over and directed me to a group of very elderly men who were sitting on a bench, felt caps on, aged hands clasped around the heads of their old walking canes.

'These are all Baldaccis,' my friend told me. One old man whom I had seen before quickly got to his feet and took off his cap and bowed his head as, I guess, a sign of respect. I took his hand, then gave him a hug and told him how happy and proud I was to have explored my roots in such a remarkable way. And though he couldn't speak much English, he understood, I think, what I was saying, and tears crept to both our eyes.

As I walked back down cobblestone streets, the same surfaces that my grandfather had trod as a young man, I could only marvel at the connection I felt to a place that I had been in for only a few hours. But what a remarkable few hours they had been.

Of course, not every place one travels to will conjure these sorts of experiences. But when we do travel to different places, regardless of whether we have a connection to them or not, we add another chunk of clay to ourselves, which changes us in both big and small ways. Although I have not been back to Barga since, I know that I will return there. I have spoken to my late father many times about the place and the trip. And an important part of me believes that he has heard every word.

In the meantime whenever I pick up that old journal and leaf through its pages, I am once more transported back to those cobblestone streets and to that grand city courtyard. In my mind's eye I look around anew at all those family members who had come to me so late in my life. Yet come they had. And I will never forget them, or that extraordinary day. In Barga.

Summer at
the Villa Juju
Anthony Sattin

It was the summer I decided to give up writing. I had a novel and a couple of other books in print, I had contributed to anthologies of fiction and non-fiction. I was reviewing for several publications and writing high profile travel stories for a Sunday paper. I was on a roll but had hit a wall.

I had been working on a novel for a couple of years. I hurried to get a draft finished before Sylvie's pregnancy came to term and, when time was up, I handed it to my agent, saying, 'You keep this. I won't have time to look at it for a while.' My agent did what I hoped he would, and spoke the words that every writer longs to hear, that he had read it and that it was good – very good – and even though it needed work, he was sure he could find an editor and maybe even some money for me to tidy it up.

But he didn't. One senior editor, at one of the more exciting fiction publishers, called me in to discuss the book. Before announcing that he was leaving publishing because the business wasn't what it used to be and everyone else carried calculators into editorial meetings, he advised me to think hard about my future. 'If you can't compete with the likes of Salman Rushdie and Ian McEwan, I suggest you go and do something else with your life.'

The arrival of my first child, toward the end of April that year, focused my thoughts further. I had responsibilities. I had dreams. I had no money. So one night, at a big family dinner, I mentioned that I was going to look for some regular – and regularly paid – work. 'What I am trying to tell you is that I am going to give up writing…'

There was a long silence, broken, I think, by my mother letting out a sob. But there was one more story to write, a commission from the newspaper to write something about Tunisia away from the beaches and package tour hotels. We had already booked flights to Tunis, and rented an apartment, and we left soon after. We, who had travelled the world with minimal baggage, were now packing an unlikely amount of things for this tiny person we were carrying. And I was also carrying the decision that when we returned, I would look for a job.

Sylvie knew Tunis. She had spent long summer days in the language institute chewing over the intricacies of advanced Arabic grammar. But this was my first visit and what I glimpsed, after a flight spent walking up and down the aisle to calm my ten-week-old son, was an uninspiring sprawl of concrete malls and patchy scrubland. Then we reached La Marsa.

The centre of Tunis sits inland from the coast and backs onto a small lake, but its suburbs spread along the Mediterranean shore, from the old pirate port of La Goulette, past the straggling remains of ancient Carthage whose faithful queen, Dido, threw herself on a pyre, around the headland on which perches the blue-and-white hilltop village of Sidi Bou Said, to palm-lined, beach-fronted La Marsa. The apartment we had taken, on the upper floor of a building, looked over an old, single-storey, stone-built villa and its palm-filled garden, and onto the flat blue of the Mediterranean. That night, after we had settled Johnny, we sat on the balcony looking out to sea, both of us excited, me brooding…

I had always been a writer – of bad poems as a teenager, of character portraits and first stories as a university student. After graduation, my friends looked for jobs and I looked for ways to structure some of the stories in my head. I wrote longer pieces, and then a novel. And while it didn't immediately find a publisher, it did get me onto a postgraduate creative writing course and as a result of that, I began to review books, and then to write features for a newspaper and some magazines. I met Sylvie and moved to Cairo. I wrote a book about a year of being in love in a crazy city, and then we left to go travelling around the world.

Wherever I was, I wrote. I remember one memorable week on the Thai island of Ko Pha Ngan when I spent days tapping on my portable typewriter on the ledge outside our beach hut, and nights watching the lights of fishing boats out in the bay and listening to the BBC World Service chart the progress of American and British troops involved in a ground war somewhere to the west. The pages I wrote that year in Thailand, and India, in Aceh, Sumatra, in Kandy, Sri Lanka, in Cafayate, Argentina, and half a dozen other beautiful places, were part of the novel that I finished – and that was rejected – just before Johnny was born. Those pages and that journey stretched behind me now like a cloth of gold, or as part of a dream landscape. A dream from which I awoke in La Marsa, with Sylvie and our beautiful and noisy son, with no more stories in my head, no more words.

Babies teach us many things. Two things I learned from Johnny during those first days in La Marsa were how much can be achieved between dawn and dusk – I watched to see how he learned, the progress he made from morning to night – and that 'later' is not an option. When he needed something, when he was hungry or tired or uncomfortable, he needed it there and then. So we tried to keep one step ahead of him. We, who were not routine people, created a schedule, part of which involved a walk in the morning and at the end of the day, when the light was soft and a breeze took the edge off the heat. Some days, we went together and walked him into the flat, blue sea. Other times I would take him out on my own and have that rare experience of being approached by Tunisian women in the street: freed from public censure, they would stare at his blue eyes, squeeze his cheeks, call him *battuta* (little duck) and smile mischievously at me. The rest of the time, while the baby was brushed by the shadows of a waving palm, we slept, read, talked, worried, tried to plan, and sat on the balcony watching events unfold in the house across the road.

On the front wall of the house there was a plaque – Villa Juju – and beside it a heavy wooden door, painted light blue and decorated with studded nails. This led to a small garden and then to the house with its flat roof and inner courtyard. We could see all this from our balcony, so we knew that an older couple lived there with a young woman, somewhere in her mid-twenties, presumably their daughter. They seemed to be industrious, for they were constantly washing sheets and covers, cleaning and arranging furniture, bringing chairs and beds out into the courtyard, and then taking them back into the house. We nodded at each other if we met in the street, then there were smiles as they would stop us so they could see Johnny. From then on, each time I saw him in the street, the patriarch would nod at me and send salaams. And each day, as more people came to the Villa Juju, he would take furniture out of the house and store it on the roof.

In the soft light of one late afternoon, a battered Mercedes with French plates pulled up and the driver tooted the horn. The people of Villa Juju rushed out to greet a young man. He had dark hair and a moustache, and although he was clearly Tunisian, his clothes were not and there was something foreign about his manner too. We assumed he was part of the wave of Tunisian expats who had gone to Europe in search of work and who return home each summer. There was enough embracing and cheer to suggest that he was the son of the house, although I later realised he was not. He unloaded many packages – gifts – from the car and then drove off.

The following day I left for the hills in search of a story to write for the paper. Wanting the antithesis of the crowded beach life of the big resorts, I had decided to go to the Tell, the western extremity of the Atlas Mountains. Over towards the Algerian border, there were oak woods where Europeans came in the autumn and winter to hunt wild boar. To the east lay the estuary of the Medjerda River. But in high summer it was all about farming and the good road that sloped up into the hills was flanked by corn. No wonder historians liked to call the fertile Tell 'the granary of the Roman Empire'.

It was also peaceful country, as I discovered when I got pulled over driving into a town called Sejnane. The policemen looked bored, and experience had taught me that that meant trouble and usually cost money. While one of the officers checked my papers, I asked the other what I had done wrong. 'Done?' He was surprised. 'You have done nothing wrong, I hope, monsieur. We just want to welcome you to Sejnane.' They were curious and were hoping for a conversation, which they got, and when it was over one of them told me that the next town, a place called Béja, was 'Sweet. Sweet. Much nicer than here.'

Foreigners seldom stopped in Béja, so men at a café in the heart of the souk had many questions that needed answering, including the price of my shoes, the origin of my Arabic accent and my verdict on a hundred and one things in the world. Sweet? Not exactly, but there was something warming about the conversation, as there was about the tall, moustached man wearing a *chechia* (a red felt hat). He was an *oud* (lute) player, and he invited me to hear him play that evening.

'Are you giving a concert?' I asked.

'No,' he replied, 'it is a wedding.'

Other pleasures stopped me crashing that wedding and at the orange hour of dusk I crossed the Medjerda Valley, driving through vineyards planted by French missionaries at the time of the colonies. In the last of the light, a skinny shepherd stopped me on a cross-country track. Disheveled, in baggy tunic and trousers, a bag slung across his chest, he looked like a vision from a distant past. When we finally got beyond extravagant greetings and niceties, he suggested that we drive to his house. 'You are late and the bride is waiting...' It was a great line, but eventually I realised that he had mistaken me for the missing marriage registrar. It took a little longer for him to understand why I would not follow him up to the bride's house on the ridge, overlooking the Roman ruins of Dougga.

Dougga was as satisfying as a ruin could be. It had compact, well-preserved houses, several temples, a large amphitheatre, public baths and even a brothel, all of which helped me create a convincing picture of how the Romans had lived in Africa. Nor was this some empty shell, for I had arrived in time to see a theatre company perform a spectacle in the ancient amphitheatre. The show was interesting and the setting extraordinary, but something even more dramatic was enacted back at the hotel: as I searched for the key to open my room, two women went past, escorting a terrified silver-gowned bride to her husband's bed for the first time.

And so it went on. Forty miles further south, in the Mellègue Valley, I drove down into a cleft of rock and, at the base of a gully, climbed into a cave where a crowd of men and boys were doing what the Romans had done in that place, enjoying a bath in the natural hot spring. We discussed marital status – at last I was able to say I had a son – and soap preferences, the harvest and the prospect of making the haj to Mecca next year. But what brought a smile to their lips was not my jokes, nor their memories, but the ululation of women in the neighbouring bath helping a bride perform her ritual ablutions. In El Kef, the Tell's capital, I watched a couple end their engagement and the woman sit broken, mascara-stained and motionless, apart from her convulsed shoulders, beneath a picture of Mont Blanc. At the hotel in Sbeitla, a couple held their alcohol-free wedding party overlooking a temple dedicated to the Roman gods of olives and wine. When I got back to La Marsa, I had a notebook full of ideas and images, snippets of conversation, details of things that I had thought significant when I saw them. A couple of days later, I sent that last story to the paper.

After it had gone, I felt mixed emotions, including release at having shed something, and a sense of immense loss. Sylvie watched me, as I watched Johnny. The afternoon passed to dusk, the last of the bathers came off the beach and girls came out to parade along rue d'Amérique, as they did each evening, young men following inevitably, bees to nectar. Then a small crowd emerged from the Villa Juju: the parents, their daughter in a flouncy wedding dress and tiara, friends and other members of the family. They walked along the road to an open space where a stage had been put up. There were two gilt thrones at the top of the steps, and coloured lights strung around them and between the trees of the olive grove. More family and friends arrived to greet the enthroned couple and, although we were neither, we were among them, Sylvie and Johnny and me. The patriarch had invited us and insisted that we bring the baby – for the baraka, he had said, for the blessing of a young life. All these years later, with many words, pages and books written since then, with many other journeys made with Johnny, I often think about that moment. The band played, a singer wailed over a whiny PA system, a scent of brine and jasmine washed through the warm grove, a sense of baraka hanging around this young life, and I recognised a truth that has stayed with me ever since then, that I was not finished with writing, that I had many other stories to tell.

The next day was filled with salaams as each guest left the Villa Juju. Later, after the heat of the day, a van came to carry away the wedding presents to the bride's new home. By the end of the week, the roof of the Villa Juju had been cleared and, his labours at an end, the old patriarch slept often and long in his empty courtyard. The sea breeze ruffled the paper on which I was writing all this down, and brought a slight chill, so I put down my pencil and took a blanket to cover Johnny, who was asleep on his back, legs splayed in the palm-shade. Summer was ending.

Saved by a Camel
Amanda Jones

'You are not what I was hoping for,' the terrifying face of my boss was saying. 'I'm not sure you're cut out for the fashion world.' This news was not unsurprising. Shortly after graduating from university with a science degree, I'd somehow talked my way into a middle-management position at a venerable fashion magazine. Though I'd always fancied myself something of an expert when it came to clothing, once I'd arrived I felt more like the country cousin in a Jane Austen tale who marches into society in all the wrong getup. I was thin, but not emaciated. I'd never had a manicure nor spent extravagantly on an outfit. I wore little makeup and my hair was long and unruly and decidedly not sleek. I was a sartorial train wreck.

My boss, the editor-in-chief, was six feet tall and dreadful. Her smile, which was daily more endangered in my presence, was a sneer. She had two obscenely expensive designer suits that she wore every other day with a string of pearls – same suits, same pearls. Without fail she would down an entire bottle of wine at lunchtime alone in her glass office, and following that she would go on the warpath. By 1:30pm, doom crept through the halls like nerve gas.

'I'm willing to give you another chance,' she benevolently told me on this rainy afternoon. 'I have an assignment that you must take. I've asked everyone else. No one wants it.' The assignment was to fly to India – specifically the Thar Desert of western Rajasthan – and take a week-long camel safari. While there, I would shoot scouting photos to see if the location was suitable for voluntarily hungry models to waft around the desert wearing gauzy outfits worth more than the average Indian made in a year.

'And perhaps you could manage to write a travel story while you are there,' she said with that sneer-smile, which faded as soon as it appeared.

This was the eighties; India was still grindingly poor, overpopulated and struggling with such basic commodities as running water, hygiene and electricity. I'd heard of the beggars, the lepers, the smells, the sewage and the inescapability of debilitating illness. I'd never been to the developing world and I wasn't sure I was prepared, but it was either agree or be fired on the spot.

I boarded the long flight for India in a state of fatalistic fear, but as the plane descended into the blue haze above Delhi, I made a decision: I would surrender to whatever I found below the murk. Hitherto, surrendering hadn't been a large part of my life, and I was convinced I'd fail spectacularly.

The drive from the airport was surreal. It was early morning and mist, smoke, pollution and heat stewed to create a shroud through which everything emerged – first as a shadow, then a shape, then reality. Horned cows wove between ancient cars. A man squatted beside me and defecated into the gutter. Bodies lay everywhere, sleeping on sidewalks, median strips, on rooftops and stoops. At stop signs, maimed children appeared at the car window with beautiful, insistent eyes and outstretched palms. It was worse than anything I'd ever seen, but it possessed an honesty and beauty that seduced me instantly. I was in love with India within the first hour.

To reach the camels I was required to catch an overnight train, which meant wrestling a path through the Delhi train station, where it seemed all of humanity had congregated to take a nap with all of their belongings. I fought my way onto the train, and eventually it rattled past murky human humps sleeping trackside and onward into the outreaches of Rajasthan.

I disembarked in a flesh-colored town called Bikaner and was met by Vini, my guide. He was young and plump and spoke in sophisticated and oddly antiquated English with elaborate enthusiasm. It was as if every comment he made was an astonishing edict, even to he himself. 'Now, Ananda,' (he never got my name right), 'you shall present yourself to your camel! You and he shall be stalwart friends for an entire week!'

My camel, Raj, which means princely, didn't look very majestic, only ornery and mangy. Thankfully, I would not be going it alone on Raj. A skinny teenager, introduced to me as Ajay, would sit behind me, prodding Raj with his feet and a stick to keep him under control. Ajay spoke no English. In fact, he appeared to speak not at all. It turned out that Ajay was an extremely tired teenager, and once we hit the trail, he would spend the days draped over Raj's hindquarters sound asleep while I went it alone with my stalwart friend.

Rather than the dread I had expected to feel facing a week on the back of a camel, once we struck out into the hot, flat desert I felt a soaring sense of freedom. I realized that I was unaccountably happy.

This didn't last long. 'Before we reach tonight's destination,' Vini announced 20 minutes into our trip, bringing the camels back to their knees, 'I feel bound to show you a number one surprise!' I would shortly learn that springing 'surprises' was Vini's idea of hilarity. 'Bikaner is the holy home of Karni Mata temple! Guess what animal is worshipped at the Karni Mata?'

'The cobra?' I ventured, hoping not.

'No!' said Vivi, 'There are 20,000 rats living inside this place! They are fed every day by devoted worshippers!'

On the spectrum of adventurous, I rate myself fairly high (a characteristic that also made me a misfit at a fashion magazine). My one great and primal fear, however, is rats. Spiders, snakes, sharks, public speaking, nudity – none of these faze me as much as rats do. Perhaps I had died of plague in a past life.

'You must remove your shoes,' Vini whispered as he ushered me into a marble room, the floor of which heaved with a sea of thousands of rats. It was tempting to yell, 'Hell no!' and run, but I didn't. I surrendered.

Rodent feces crunched under my bare soles. Rats swarmed over bags of grain deposited by supplicant venerators; they climbed walls, they covered a fountain and eventually they dug their terrible claws into my pant legs and climbed upward. And I stood there and allowed them to.

I left the temple feeling pretty chuffed with myself. I had not fled the scene, I'd allowed the creatures I feared most to use me as a jungle gym, and, most satisfyingly, I'd taken earnest temple-rodent photos that I would present as a suggestion for a fashion shoot location. I was so pleased with myself that I didn't even use an antiseptic towelette to wipe my feet before I shoved

them back in my shoes. Oh yes, I was in full-blown love with
India.

'Our dromedaries await!' Vini announced, adding,
unsettlingly, 'You must release all thoughts of creature comfort!
The camel is now your intimate acquaintance and your tent will
be your moving palace!' I wondered if I might be required to
share my tent with Raj.

Accompanying us was a camel-drawn cart fixed with old
airplane tires, enabling it to cross the sands of the desert. On top
of the luggage sat a cook and his assistant. The cook had brought
a harmonium, a hand-pumped organ, and he played lilting
Qawwali music all day as the cart swayed over the empty, sun-
scorched plains. The soaring freedom and the unaccountable
happiness returned, and I sat atop Raj sucking in the purity and
peace of wide-open spaces.

At night we would set up our tents while the cooks prepared
dinner. The only way to wash was with a bucket and a small
amount of water. There was no mirror, it was hot and dusty and
my hair and clothing were stiff with sand. I had never been more
disheveled – and never more content.

Almost daily Vini would bring the camels to their knees and
scream, 'Surprise!' One time the surprise was to climb enormous
sand dunes under the cruel hammer of the midday sun. At
the top of one, he started giggling, yelled 'Surprise!' again and
shoved me off the edge. I tumbled ass over teakettle with my
work camera in hand. It was ruined. There went the venerable
magazine shoot.

Another time we dismounted in a tiny village. Often we would
do this to rest under the shade of the rare tree, so I was atypically
unalarmed. Then several women grabbed me by the arms.
'Surprise!' Vini screamed in my ear. 'These women feel strongly

that you dress like a man! They are going to attempt to make you attractive in a sari!'

'Oh,' was all I could think to say, and I dutifully followed them into the dark hut. I'm not sure if it was conscious spite or an innocent mix-up, but they pulled out an item of clothing that I doubt would have fit me when I was ten years old and that clearly had not been washed in a while. Maybe never. It stank.

The women surrounded me, stripped me of my dusty duds and frantically started stuffing and swathing me into this thing. The choli undershirt was so tight I couldn't breathe. 'I. Can. Not. Breathe,' I told them in English and they stood around laughing and nodding and clapping their hands delightedly. I staggered outside and Vini clapped his hands delightedly. Then I said, breathlessly, 'I. Change. Into. Men's. Clothes. Now.'

The most surprising 'surprise' was when Vini decided we needed to race our camels at full gallop. Unusually, Ajay was awake and he flogged poor Raj into a gangly, awkward and terribly fleet gallop. Bouncing around gracelessly, I determined that posting to the trot was the only method of survival, and so there I sat, posting on a camel like some mad Englishwoman, my laughter trailing behind us, equally mad.

On our last evening, we rode towards camp as the sun was sinking with its usual crescendo of colors. I'd been nursing an idea since day three of the trip, and by this time it had come to full fruition. India had pried open some life lust in me. A dormant part of me had woken hungry and needed satiation. I had, as travelers so often claim, had an epiphany: I wanted to do this forever. Not roam about on camelback with Vini and his surprises forever, but I wanted to explore the further reaches of the world, to stumble about in the unfamiliar, to place myself in trying situations in the remotest of places, to walk among all human conditions, to try to understand the importance of life, to be tested, to be dirty and not care, to get lost and to be in places where mirrors didn't exist or didn't matter.

I had decided to return to the venerable fashion magazine with the broken camera and the photos of a rat temple and quit my miserable job. And this is exactly what I did (in the morning, mind you; I was too chicken to face the fearsome one post-vino).

And that is how I became a travel writer.

Wonder Train
Colleen Kinder

'Nothing I understand haunts me. Only the things I do not
understand have that power over me.'
  – Mary Ruefle, Madness, Rack and Honey

There was one street and one kind of car cruised down it:
pick-up trucks with full-tint windows, norteña music
blaring behind their sealed blackness. Everywhere, men we could
not see were scoping us, and at the same slow float, as though
making sure we knew: nobody wanted us in Batopilas.

A poet from Mexico City and a gringa writing a travel story:
in no way did we belong. I was tackling my first big assignment,
to report on the thirteen-hour rail journey through the canyons
of northern Mexico, a wild backcountry of red rock gorges that
rendered the Grand Canyon a shorty. I'd scanned the map for
towns to decamp and spend the night along the Copper Canyon

rail route, but got easily distracted by a lone dot of a town, off in the mountains, a full day's journey from the train tracks.

Reaching Batopilas required a true detour, horizontal and vertical, cutting through four of the Sierra Madre's major canyons, and plunging, in the process, some 6000 feet.

We could do it, I argued – which was true only if everything that could go wrong went perfectly right.

Everything: if we caught the crack-of-dawn van in Creel; if the van made the five-hour plunge without popping a tire or hitting a cow or dead-ending at a fallen tree. If we had all that luck – and then repeated it, climbing punctually out of the canyon's depths – we could catch the train in Creel in time to make our flight home from Chihuahua.

The poet, my travel-mate, said yes, knowing better than to get in the way of me and forward motion. He'd stood next to me on the train's gangway for hours, watching me stick my head out the window like a dog, pull it back in, fuzzy-haired and beaming. 'You're so hap-py,' Jose Luis kept telling me in English, like he was reading me for the first time, saying happy like 'hoppy,' making me think, bunnies. All his friends were 'suicidal poets,' he kept adding – I was refreshing.

A refreshing bunny: that's how I felt, as the train careened west, pausing ever so briefly at Divisadero, an overlook where the earth cracks right open, glowing every shade of autumn in the late-day light. I'm not that sim-ple, I wanted to crow back, claiming a place among moody poets, but I knew what Jose Luis was seeing on my face: the effects of constant motion.

Aboard the train, there was endless change and beauty ever more remote, snatches of woods and ravines we'd never otherwise see. We sliced through forests, twigs smacking our cheeks, and tunnels that came so fast we flinched as we shot into them, only to go drowsy in the pitch darkness. We bought just-wrapped bean burritos from the hands of Indian women who sold them tippy-toed, track-side; we ate standing up, on clanging platforms, hogging the gangway for ten hours straight. Of course I was dog-wag happy.

The price was straw-hair and sailor legs as we climbed down to sleep the night in Creel, a town perched at about 7500 feet, nearly the apex of the train journey. We made our wobbly way into town to find that Mexico had changed on us completely. There was an alpine nip in the air, the smell of burning wood – or were those leathering chiles? – wrapped around us. Never have I longed harder for hot chocolate between bare hands. By the time we found a hotel, I was so delirious with chill that I bee-lined straight to the lobby's fireplace and knelt down by the crackling fire, ready to crawl in there for a nap. Jose Luis tugged me to my feet, suggested we try the sauna.

Our tangent to Batopilas the next day meant a return to desert heat. All morning, as our van carved down the deep ochre canyons, we watched cacti take back the land. The deeper we went, the more outrageous the saguaro grew, suctioning hungrily up cliff-sides, each lumpy-armed plant a diva, wanting her own lean slice of sun. We peeled off sweaters and regretted socks, feeling back in Mexico, the air we knew. The descent took half a day, our path the epitome of switchback. I kept looking behind us at the ribboning road, confirming what I felt: this was a journey to the bottom of the earth.

Batopilas could hardly have looked quainter, sidling against a shallow river. It was a town of another era; it showed in the height of homes, the distress of porches, bougainvillea crushing through wrought-iron gates. A silver outpost, Batopilas had seen its prime back when ore was paraded out of mountain tunnels, loaded onto donkeys, sent up through these canyons and off to Spain. But though it was covered in dust now, Batopilas was not exactly sleepy.

Men in clean white sombreros looked all too on guard, holding us in long, glassy stares. We walked nowhere without a pick-up truck nudging us off the road, slow as a car set to neutral for a gas station wash. One after another, trucks teased us with the mystery of who was behind the opaque windows and how they afforded a gleaming car in a town where the last silver boom predated WWI.

I could feel Jose Luis's question even before he asked it. All through our train journey, he'd been plying strangers on the gangway to find out, 'De que viven?' – what do people live from? The deeper we traveled, the more mysterious it grew, the question of how people earned enough to eat, given the remoteness and steepness, the bygone-ness of this region tucked so far north into Mexico and still such a ways from the border. We asked anyone who would talk to us, keeping another question private: Why didn't this feel like Mexico?

Warm like Mexico. Generous like Mexico. Not stone-faced, but sunny as we knew Mexico to be. That Jose Luis, a Mexico City native, was baffled by the total change in tone gave me permission to chime in. You could smile right at people in the Sierra and get nothing back, pose a question and watch a stranger ignore it. We kept track of all the differences in canyon country, as though if we added up all the Mexican things missing here – tortillas of corn, tamale baskets, zocalos in the hearts of towns – it might somehow explain how the mood temperature of Mexico had dropped thirty degrees.

But it didn't explain it, and Batopilas only intensified the cold front. I could count on two hands the women moving through town. Quiet cowboys stood idly outside the town's few stores, trying to expel us with their eyes.

Understanding nothing, we went wading across the river, pants hiked up, carrying our shoes like kids. A little boy, a little girl: a platonic adventure with unspoken questions of its own. Was there anything between us? And would we ever? And was ours just the charge of two writers who acted on a whim to travel as deep as they could into Mexico?

Jose Luis fit a type for me – a kind of friend I made in foreign countries: the Knowing Man. Abroad, I was ever hungry to talk culture, to burrow into nuances, to hear it all hashed out, exampled, explained. At a party, I'd find the guy who'd rather profile his country's political parties than spin a girl to salsa music. I had searching eyes, a way of nodding, a way that said, keep talking.

Jose Luis was a poet who made his living selling jewelry. I liked that he was self-made, the son of modest people. So many of my Mexico City friends were pretty boys – impeccable English speakers, Harvard-degreed men who looked nothing like the moon-faced, back-bent laborers in a Rivera mural, and instead like the tall conquistadores at their backs. I'd met Jose Luis on my way out of Mexico, the luster of my year-long journey all but gone. The future was pure blank, and it stirred in me a near-greedy hunger to pull from the people around me all I could about life. Jose Luis was both ready to oblige, and, right as I geared up for one last adventure in Mexico, hungry for one himself.

Ouching across the bed of stones, we forded the Batopilas River, finding on the other bank a stone wall, cascading with the roots of two trees: one the creamiest yellow, the other smoke-grey. The trees knit their tips together in a way so consummate and deliberate and tender it was impossible not to lend them personas. Old lovers had slipped into the tendrils of these riverfront trees, choosing the near-eternity of wood over gravestone marble. I knew Jose Luis was seeing the same thing – anyone would, certainly a poet – and I wished, not for the last time, that I was making this journey with someone I loved.

Had there been any physical gravity between this Knowing Man and his hungry pupil, I'm sure we would have flirted right through the faint friendship line. And it had crossed my mind in Los Mochis, our departure point, where the motel's rules read like a bordello's, prohibiting 'visits,' and again in chilly Creel, where we met in the sauna, our train-sore bodies melting in lazily held towels. But Jose Luis was shorter than me, his confidence more professorial than physical. He liked to poke fun at his looks. 'I look like a gorilla!' he'd say, face scrunched up. Jose Luis didn't look like a gorilla; he looked made for a woman who looked not at all like me.

I followed my travel mate up the banks of the river, past the lover trees, to where an old man sat in the dust, shirt off, hunched over a pile of crushed Tecate beer cans. He was sewing together their scraps to make the garland we'd seen all through town, glinting between roof tips and tree branches. I could almost hear the question in Jose Luis's mind forming – de que viven? – but both the man's posture and scrap work gave away the answer. He was a squatter, living off the past, on the edge of a hacienda that once belonged to Alexander Shepherd.

The last Governor of Washington, DC, Shepherd was an antebellum hero. He fixed the muddy mess that was America's capital, just after the Civil War, commissioning roads and sewers, earning the nickname 'The Boss.' Shepherd might have remained a hero, had he not gotten carried away and spent over ten million dollars more than Congress okayed, prettying up too many of the zones he'd invested in personally. Dismissed, disgraced, Shepherd moved his entire family to Batopilas, and started over, with silver.

Over 350 mines had been plumbed by the time Shepherd reached Batopilas. The Spanish had a two-century head start on The Boss. In 1632, they'd discovered pure silver in the river – it glinted curiously white, polished by the river's stream. White silver in the deepest canyon of a New World: it was the kind of story that inspires men to cross oceans, and this one did. When prospectors declared Batopilas a hotbed of silver, emigration from Spain surged.

There was ebb and there was flow. The flows were called bonanzas, and they called for immediate donkeys. When miners hit upon such a block, they worked like raiders; they attacked it, wrested masses of raw mineral from the walls. Silver in Batopilas grew in the form of crystals and wires and blocks weighing as much as 440 pounds. The bonanzas made overnight fortunes that barons by the name of Pastrana and Bustamante and Esparza struggled to spend. Pastrana failed hardest, laying a pure silver sidewalk in Batopilas to impress a visiting bishop. The bishop, finding the path from his door plated in precious metal, was horrified, and said so.

When Alexander Shepherd unspooled a map in 1880, what he looked down on was a matrix of worked mines. But drawing on lessons from America's Reconstruction, Shepherd surveyed the canyon not like a baron, but a city planner. Rather than focus on one silver pocket, Shepherd bought up hundreds of mining claims; he built the longest tunnel in Mexico; he brought electricity, making Batopilas – one of the most remote towns in Mexico – the second community in the entire country to glow with artificial light.

With electrical power, silver ore could be processed on site, turned to pure bars that mules carried, two at a time, up the gorges and all the way to the train in Chihuahua. The mines were worked at night, illuminated by train headlights that drew townswomen who gaped in wonder, until dynamite blasts shooed them away.

When Shepherd passed away in 1902, he'd overseen underground tunnels of more than 75 miles, a virtual subterranean town deep in the bowels of Mexico. The population of Batopilas had multiplied by a factor of ten. His sons tried to keep the industry alive, but revolution was spreading across Mexico, and Pancho Villa would soon steal $38,000 worth of silver from the Shepherd mines, burying the bars under his patio in Chihuahua, trusting Batopilas silver over Mexican pesos. Still, war meant constant flux in the price of silver.

'It wasn't all beer and skittles,' sighed Shepherd's son Grant in a memoir of the silver days. The turn of the century marked the demise of the Shepherd bonanza. By 1920, Grant and his brother had given up for good. There were a few more attempts to mine but none lucrative enough. The veins weren't tapped completely, but it no longer made sense in a place this remote to keep working them. The population of Batopilas, which had ballooned from 400 to 5000 people, began to shrink back down. There was little left to do at the bottom of the canyons.

De que viven? Hungry for answers, and now food, we brought our questions back across the river to a restaurant called Hanging Bridge, figuring a waiter would have to speak to us.

Only one of us, it turned out.

'Does she want a beer?' the waiter, short as a dwarf, asked Jose Luis.

'One drink and she'll be drunk!' my travel-mate joked back, so desperate for a connection with a local that he threw me under the bus, quickening his Spanish in the hope that I might not catch the ella, hear borracha. I sent him a smoldering look, like a fed-up girlfriend, tiring of our trip dynamic.

The gravity between Jose Luis and me was about knowledge: my lust for it, his urge to transmit. All through the canyons, Jose Luis had held forth, the train's gangway lending the perfect forum. Class divide was a favorite topic of his – the chasm between Mexico's wealthy and poor – and one my mind was constantly mulling. I was leaving Mexico for many reasons: I was tired of goodbye parties for expat friends – a social calendar of constant farewells; tired of dating men who handled me too preciously, maneuvering me always to the sidewalk's outer edge; tired of living in a flat that, lovely as it was, felt flimsy like a tent – a youthful project I'd someday fold up. But my deepest unease was tied up in class – a chasm that no one seemed to question, rich or poor. My most educated friends treated their waiters like lowly boys – waiters twice their age. Mexico felt like a country of masters and servants, a place where I'd always get royal treatment, without a trace of resentment, and for no better reason than I was white and tall.

Jose Luis had the opposite social experience: he got blocked by bouncers at the door of literary parties, and mistaken for the waiter in upper-crust crowds. He wanted to make sure I knew, before leaving his country, that these weren't class divisions; we were talking about a system of caste, divides as deep as the canyons we'd straddled by train all across northern Mexico.

But by the time we got deep into Batopilas, I was tired of being schooled. Jose Luis and I only seemed to talk if I posed questions, and once I noticed that pattern, the pattern pissed me off. So did his insistence on English. His second language was just as sloppy as mine; he just didn't hear the mess. I began jotting down the English words he botched, like I was keeping a secret score.

Service was farcically slow at Hanging Bridge, where no one but us was dining. The waiter brought limes on a plate. He brought water in glasses. He brought a bowl of chipotle salsa. Nothing felt more un-Mexican about the Sierra Madre than its tendency to keep us hungry. Jose Luis wondered whether the waiter was tipsy. Later, I wondered whether he was trying to delay us there, whether the whole point was to keep outsiders from doing what guidebooks suggested: wandering around, hiking the old mines.

By the time the waiter brought dinner, he was drunk and the story of how people lived in Batopilas finally came out. Back in the canyons, in the crevasses and slopes veining all around this lone town, were fields of marijuana, opium crops, airfields just long enough for the planes that ran drugs.

Everything snapped into sense: the ink-black car windows, trucks running back and forth, glassy eyes, unmarked runways we'd found motorcycling through the woodsy surrounds of Creel, public ads urging kids to say no, the sense that we'd crossed some invisible border – changed countries within Mexico. I'd prepped for our journey by reading about the towns along the train tracks, never looking into the state of Chihuahua as a whole, where 30 percent of all drug-related violence was concentrated.

We had arranged to leave in the early morning van and dawn now felt a long way off. I voiced a predictable urge – my usual – to go further, to push ahead. It was the urge that had got us down here in the first place, deep in a wrinkle on the map of Mexico where narcotrafficantes had what now felt like total control.

There was a 'lost church' mentioned in all the guidebooks – a mission that was unaccounted for in history's record, a place that just appeared on the map, without any record of its being built. We could reach it, I claimed, before the light faded.

We couldn't – Jose Luis knew it, and kept saying so as we set out on a zigzagging gravel path, passed by fewer and fewer trucks, the moon showing, lost church eluding. The tension between us was finding new ways to play out, all passive-aggressive. When I spoke Spanish, he replied in English, to which I shot back Spanish, only to hear my own language, bumpily given back.

Traveling with a new friend – alone – means signing up for the full arc of a relationship. One more day together and Jose Luis and I would be chewing with tight jaws. I'd go surly on him, withholding both questions and nods. And as we rounded the canyon's bends, into more darkness and no church, and I heard my travel-mate claim anyone could teach themselves to read French, something in me snapped. I seized on what sounded like self-congratulation and called it that, tired of all this autodidact claimed to know.

Where were his blanks? What was he still figuring out? How could a person our age not be figuring things out? How could a person any age be as certain as this man? Everything in my life was in question, and under the roof of that night sky canopied so high above us in the canyon, I felt my doubt rising up against his certainty.

Suddenly, I wanted to say everything: that I had no idea what my life would become, how to make writing work; that I yearned for a real home soon, friends who lasted; that I was tired of being so politely served by Mexicans who looked nothing like the Mexicans on billboard ads and on television shows and in the bars where I drank. A decade of living in the mode of a student, keeping quiet and absorbent, was coming to an end. I was done with lecture. I'd lived in many more places than most of my teachers. I had no idea where this left me, other than needing to go.

When Jose Luis began telling me what authors I must read – Camus, more Marquez – I revolted. Every couple of steps, I sabotaged his lecture by pointing out the beautiful cacti.

They were stunning – the saguaros – spiky black beasts against the now navy sky. The light was retreating, pulling away everything with it but these lumpen silhouettes.

'That,' I'd plant my feet, making Jose Luis both stop talking and halt, 'is the most beautiful cactus I have ever seen.' A few steps later, I'd give the title away to another saguaro, whose arms reached higher, just to ruin a sentence of this Knowing Man. Besides, the saguaros deserved it, coming alive in the dark, growing into people, suggestive ghosts, just like the trees stitched at the river's edge.

We never did reach the church, and the only things that saved our journey from catastrophe were the stars beading the navy sky. When we turned back, the ground was hardly visible; we needed the glow of dippers and comets to get us to Batopilas. Jose Luis went quiet, but I wasn't done. The cacti gone, inked out by the night, I picked one last battle, pitting English against Spanish, my language against his. For days, I'd been thinking about how the verb 'to wonder' had no good equivalent in Spanish. I'd missed it, all through this journey.

Wondering what, and wondering how, and wondering whether: I didn't know how to travel without these constructions, certainly not at train-speed, through a place as tight-lipped as the Sierra. I was at a loss, groping for its equal, a word that could send the mind pinwheeling off, looking for truth but honoring mystery.

I'd missed it most motorcycling around Creel, clutching at Jose Luis's shoulders as close as a non-lover can. It was late in the day, our gas running low as the light went buttery, and I tried to wonder aloud to him about the magic hour – the slanted sun photographers chase, what makes canyons a mural of the warmest earth tones, aglow in a way that stills you, holds you down deep in one moment.

'If the magic hour were an age,' I mused to his helmet, 'what would it be?'

I was wondering: airing a question, not needing an answer. I'd noticed how beauty blooms – arrestingly – right before it vanishes, and something like that was happening on our journey, on mine. I wanted to ask my travel-mate to help me think through the glow – and whether there's a parallel in life, just before something long ends.

'Que?'

Jose Luis hadn't heard me, so later, I brought my lost verb back up in the dark.

'What about parecer?' Jose Luis tried.

'Nope. Not the same.' I was ready for parecer. Parecer alleged, asserted something. Parecer didn't wonder. No word Jose Luis came up with left room for fruitful doubt.

The next morning, as we carved back up the cliffs, I spent the ride turtling back into my mind, wondering to myself. The radio was on, and what leaked out for hours was news of a policeman's murder, very nearby. I knew the story; I'd been hearing a version of it all year. I couldn't walk by a newsstand in Mexico City without flinching at what looked like cheap Polaroids taken in a morgue. Daily, bodies appeared with the marks of torture and the tags of drug lords. 2009 was coming to a close: the bloodiest year of narco-violence yet. There was no escaping this fact in Mexico, but no comprehending it either. The terminology itself was still getting worked out: if the drug leaders were ex-military, did that make this a civil war?

No answers were to be found, certainly not in the leafy Mexico City barrio where I lived, where baristas cheek-kissed me good morning. It wasn't until Jose Luis and I left Batopilas, crammed into this van where no one said a peep and the latest murder story played on loop, that I felt, finally, like I was listening to local news.

The train snatched us back up in Creel, and as soon as we boarded, I left Jose Luis and wandered off to the dining car. No gangway this time, no happy bunny face out the open window. The homestretch of the Sierra Madre journey is farmland – a flat jaunt. I spent it willfully absorbed in a Xerox copy of a mining history of Batopilas that I'd bought in town. I had just days left in Mexico – a farewell party that night, hasty packing the next morning – and I wanted to spend it tunneling into the canyons at my back. To find something about Mexico that Jose Luis did not know.

I read about mines called Mesquite and Martinez, Todos Santos and Roncesvalles, Descrubridora and Balthazar. I read that men could carry as much as 150 pounds up 500 feet, men whom the sons of DC's fugitive governor called 'peons.' I read about a bonanza pocket that lasted for fourteen years, another vein that collapsed and buried miners alive. I learned that silver grows as coils, in balls, in the shape of ferns. I schooled myself in just how mysterious mining is, how little prospectors actually know when they plunge deep into the earth. I stared at mineral charts and labyrinthine tunnel maps and hardest of all at a sketch of a herringbone crystal that looked exactly like a leafy burst of marijuana. It was all just kindling for wondering, like everything I'd seen from the train. Trains rocket you through the foreign, snatching away street names and strangers on porches as soon as your eyes catch a flash. Trains won't let your gaze settle; they keep your mind chasing; they make the brain a tumbler for questions, ever adding, never resolving.

What do sixty mules look like, saddled with silver, trudging up the sides of the Sierra's deepest canyon? And how about the twinkling floor of a canyon at night, to a person who's never before seen electric light? How many years can a man shoulder silver bullion up ladders, in sweltering mines, before his shoulders ache? Once the mines closed, once all the Shepherds vanished, how did the people of Batopilas live with the knowledge that silver remained, threading under their mountains? Who kept panning for silver in the stream, and who started whispering about another way? What does secrecy do to the pride of men? What happens to a town – its fabric – when the only livelihood left can't be named? Was there shame behind those tinted truck windows, or just men high on the local crop?

I wondered, hardest of all, how to read Mexico's past to decode the present. Why did it feel like this uncanny violence was the upwelling of centuries of repression? Was this the country's poor – the people who'd been carrying silver bullion and serving the rich for centuries – rising up against a status quo? Was there a link between the savagery spreading across this country and the longstanding servility of its majority? Had a sense of injustice – anger I'd heard expressed by no one but Jose Luis – finally, after centuries, erupted? Isn't this how it works, when oppression finds no other release?

Questions I'd never answer, this was the crescendo of a full year's wondering.

The web offered no answers when I later typed in the word 'Batopilas.' There were no news articles exposing the drug trade. A few travel blogs alluded to the pick-up trucks, the silent stares, but most called the silver town 'charming.' No one seemed to stay long.

I eventually wrote my travel story, and it was published. There was no mention of poppy fields, no ode to the interlocking trees, no poet who knew too much. There were two paragraphs – max – devoted to Batopilas. I remember sitting in my childhood home, before I had a next home, with a bulging folder of notes, that faint photocopy of the history of mining in Batopilas in my tensed hands. I was writing my first real feature story – and already, I felt defeated. This was not the container for what I cared about. There was hardly room to capture the mood of the place, and none whatsoever for wondering.

Months after the story was published, I heard from my editor. She'd gotten an email from a reader and wanted me to address it. A man was upset about a mistake in my article. In describing the descent to Batopilas, I said the temperature plummeted. I went straight to the offending sentence and knew what had happened: I'd gotten carried away, narrating the plunge to Batopilas. In my mind, all was drop.

I felt a flush of shame, like I'd been caught – in my sloppiness, but also in posing as a travel writer. When the flush passed, I was annoyed that simple facts were the measure of whether I'd done my job. It took me years to admit this wasn't the job I wanted. All that mattered to me was everything I didn't say about Batopilas. Traveling, I was lost without the power to wonder. The same held true, it turned out, in writing.

To wonder: to observe with ellipses, to imagine from clues, to beckon another mind into your question, to crawl into the blanks of history, to start a file you can never close.

I've carried the 'History of Mining' printout with me to a few cities; it's lived in many a folder. I've decided against throwing it away many times. The space Batopilas takes up in memory is wildly out of proportion to how many hours I spent there. When

I ride down memory's chute into that lone speck on Mexico's map, I go – every time – into the same room.

Over the shallow river, just behind those interlocking trees, Jose Luis and I came upon a hacienda, long abandoned. We could see its orange walls through the fig trees but once we reached the clearing, its height and clay-colored majesty was a shock. There it stood, a castle of terracotta, nothing blocking our entrance through a rusted gate, then the smooth mouth of the hacienda's missing door.

We stood there, made tiny by towering walls. High above us, keyhole windows gaped open, the afternoon sun baking the bougainvillea petals that carpeted the entire ground floor. There was a stairwell, its lumpy clay rising to nowhere – a phantom second floor.

I couldn't move, and Jose Luis froze, too. Ever since I was a little girl, I've thrilled at finding antiques in the raw – the twin tarnish of time and dirt. Never again will I find an antique like the hacienda of Alexander Shepherd.

We stood there, on the blanched petals, like the dry air had cast us into statues. Every hair on my body gave a lift. I still wonder at how close I came to saying, 'Kiss me.' The words didn't just form, they wanted out.

Jose Luis must have felt it, too – the need to do something, anything to match the force of this place, to honor it fast. He reached over – his face screwed up like he was trying to remember the English word for what he was about to do – and squeezed my forearm with two fingers.

A pinch. This was real: a terracotta castle on the floor of the deepest canyon. Like a kid who worries no one will ever believe her ('we found this place...'), I worried I'd never write it. Not with the force that makes you nearly kiss your friend.

Batopilas will never let my mind go, I'm sure. The beauty of that terracotta castle alone is enough to stake its claim in a honeycomb of memory, to say nothing of the magic hour light blooming through my life right then, just before I left Mexico. Never again did I live abroad; I was right in sensing the end of a rare time. But the force this town has for me, I think, has more to do with wondering. It's the places that refuse to answer our questions that hold us always in their air.

Voice Lessons
Anna Vodicka

A few years ago, I was standing in line at a bank in a deserted village in Argentina when a woman behind me sighed and announced in Spanish, 'Don't look… here they come again.' Lifting my gaze, I saw in my peripheral vision the image of two young men – boys, really – walking the dirt road, overdressed in matching blue slacks and white button-downs, name tags pinned to their chests like miniature shields.

It was a familiar sight on the road in Latin America. What remote towns lack in infrastructure and clean water, they make up for in dueling churches vying for converts. But as I waited my turn with the teller, I knew that turning my back on those boys meant turning my back on a part of my past.

My mother's faith was Pentecostalism, that rowdy version of Christianity named for the day of Pentecost, when the Holy Ghost descended upon the disciples in a fiery storm, inciting

them to speak in unknown tongues, and people from every
nation gathered in amazement 'because each one heard them
speaking in his own language.' I was never 'born again.' I was
born into the faith, raised in the art of sensory acrobatics: blind
devotion and superhuman hearing, so we might heed God's call;
speaking in tongues and laying on hands in faith healing. For
years, we watched church on TV (we lived in rural Wisconsin,
where the ratio of humans to lakes, trees and wildlife makes one
reconsider her Creation-story position as dominant subduer
of all the Earth) and my parents portioned tithes toward Jim
Bakker's 'global conquest for souls.' In middle school, I joined an
evangelical church where I was expected to greet the world with
a crusader's spirit – to walk in the footsteps of Joan of Arc, who
strode into battle when she'd never been ten miles from home,
and the apostle Paul, who made a legendary career traversing the
eastern Mediterranean, leaving start-up churches in his wake.

I was taught that a call could come at any moment. But of all
the theological quandaries that charismatic faith presented me,
God's voice was the most perplexing. I knew a girl whose parents
sat her alone in a room while they hid behind a curtain reading
God's commands from the shadows. I knew of parents who
coached kids with Charlton Heston recordings, training young
ears to hear a divine, masculine baritone. My youth pastors gave
me devotional assignments and worksheets, ten-step How-To's
that included keeping a spiritual journal, sitting for hours with
a pen poised over the page, ready for Holy Ghost ink to flow. My
mother taught me the Rule of Three: concordant advice from
three Christians was an indication of God's will.

I meditated in prayer. I buried myself in the Bible. Like a good
Christian kid, I took the Bible itself to be God's Word, believing
the prophets who penned the scriptures were simply diligent

secretaries. That's thousands of pages of direct, complete-sentence dictation. In English.

Still, the Bible never offered much concrete evidence on the subject, and its examples seemed downright contradictory. God's voice is conversational with Cain. It's prophetic with Abraham. It's militant with Jacob. The voice of God 'thunders' from the heavens, but it's a 'still, silent voice.' Sometimes it's tambourines and harps, and then again it's trumpets or a rush of roaring waters.

Outside sources only reinforced the ambiguity. Ralph Waldo Emerson heard a whisper. George Washington Carver could 'tune in' to God on his nature walks. Gandhi called it the 'inner voice': 'When it is the inner voice that speaks,' he said, 'it is unmistakable.'

I had hearing loss as a child, a result of chronic ear infections, and I remember thinking at the time that this disability kept me from hearing God. I practiced sitting with my eyes shut and my mouth shaped in a rounded O, waiting. But even after sounds were restored, even years later, I didn't hear a word from the Lord, my mute maker of Heaven and Earth. If I were going to follow Jesus' charge to 'go and make disciples of all nations,' it would have to be on different terms.

On a winter Sunday in 1997, when I was fifteen, my youth pastors announced that God had called them to expand their ministry abroad. They would be moving from northern Wisconsin to the eastern Czech Republic, indefinitely.

I felt the wind go out of me, as if the congregation's collective gasp deflated the room. Since they'd moved to town, Ben and Amber had revitalized the church, energizing sermons and an entire youth movement with a pop music Praise Band, weeknight games and sports that drew kids from several counties who had nothing to do but go bowling and drink Milwaukee's Best around bonfires in the woods. Ben and Amber were the only adults I confided in about boys and cliques, family and school drama. And they had literally given me a voice.

By the third grade, my hearing loss was so extreme I had to shout to hear myself talk. One day, as I was singing my heart out in music class, a girl turned to face me and howled loud enough to stop the piano: Why do you sing so goddamn loud? Are you stupid or something? In tears at home that night, my mother and I prayed a prayer of forgiveness for that girl. But I was so ashamed of my inability to control or even comprehend my own voice that I never again sang above a whisper unless I was at home with my face pressed against speakers, swallowed by sound.

Ben and Amber built a ministry on music. His smooth Texas twang and her rich soprano blended in harmony every Sunday, and people joined in whether they sounded like an angel or a crow. In the safety of that space, I started to sing again. And the more I sang, the more they encouraged me. They made me lead singer of the Praise Band and enrolled me in Christian vocal competitions. They had led me to myself. And now they were leaving.

'There's one more thing,' they added through tears. 'God has laid it on our hearts to take some of the Youth Group with us ahead of time on a short-term mission to Czech this summer. We ask students to meditate in prayer. If Jesus calls you, please talk to us.'

At home that day, I prayed and listened. I could travel abroad for the first time! I heard, and felt suddenly high. I could make a real difference in people's lives, a more altruistic voice quickly replied. It would be a once-in-a-lifetime experience with the Youth Group and Ben and Amber, I thought. Maybe your last one.

'Absolutely not,' my parents said. Mom and Dad were responsible for my curiosity about the world. They took my five siblings and me out of school for weeks at a time to drive cross-country, 'learning from the road.' But fly internationally? Without family? Unheard of.

For weeks, I pressed them. They couldn't really argue against a mission for Jesus. Eventually, they conceded: If I could raise the money on my own, I could go.

That fulfilled the Rule of Three, as far as I was concerned. I took a job checking groceries for $5.25 an hour. I was heeding the call, whether I heard it or not.

In mid-July, nineteen of my Youth Group friends and I followed Ben and Amber aboard a Continental Airlines flight from central Wisconsin to Newark, and then onto Prague. We'd checked matching black duffel bags, mine packed with floor-length skirts and modest blouses, gifts of local maple syrup for our host families, a Bible, a journal, a cheap camera. We wore identical green polo shirts, scratchy cotton numbers embroidered with our mission slogan, 'Be In The Light: Czech 1997.' Team shirts would help us stick together. If they drew attention from curious travelers, it was a bonus opportunity to share our message.

As I was flying over the ocean for the first time, everything already seemed foreign: the pressed skirts and blouses of airline attendants who looked like they had their hair styled in French salons; the little cups of flan they served for dessert, which I disliked but ate because they seemed European. Listening to in-flight radio, I discovered Astrud Gilberto, her cool alto and smooth samba beats nonplussed through the turbulence. While everyone slept, I wore headphones, timing the radio loop so I could hear that voice every time it surfaced in the queue.

Music helped distract me from my own thoughts. Every week of the last four months had been leading to this day. We had spent Sunday evenings in the church basement preparing icebreakers and skits that could cross language barriers. We read articles on 'Behaving Abroad' and 'Principles for Effective Intercession' and '12 Ways to Ruin a Short Term.' We wrote essays on the Czech Republic: its history of Soviet rule; its recent split, in 1993, from Slovakia; its religious profile. In a country of 10.5 million, forty percent were atheist. Thirty-nine percent were Roman Catholic. The evangelical church made up less than one third of one percent.

'We are ready to reach out of our "comfort zones" and into the mission field,' our donation letters said. 'Your support will be appreciated by all in helping those of us on the team win souls to Jesus Christ.'

But as the plane descended through fog to a sprawling red-roofed city, a gnawing feeling told me no amount of planning could prepare me for what would come next. I prayed for guidance. Then I turned up the volume: 'And when she passes, he smiles, but she doesn't see…'

After a day sleepwalking through rainy Prague, we headed east to Český Těšín, a town of 25,000 on the Czech–Poland border, and a target city of the missionary organization Ben and

Amber were joining. In 1993, inspired by the fall of European communism, a few youth pastors seized on a next-generation movement, partnering with local churches to start youth ministries, English and athletic camps. The Czech Republic, the mission warned, was 'the most atheistic nation on earth.' Even church members – some of our hosts – were unbelievers. I expected Český Těšín to look ominous, a valley of shadows. When we split for homestays, I was afraid.

But I met unexpected scenery: the calm blue Olza River marking the Polish border; a bright yellow town hall presiding over a peaceful square; and in the blue distance, colorful paragliders, like exotic birds, soaring from the rolling green Beskydy mountains.

My friend Jen and I stayed in a Soviet-era apartment building with a girl named Renata and her mom, sister and grandma. That's what they wanted us to call them: Mom, Sister and Grandma. As if we were already part of the family. As if we were daughters.

The apartment was tiny by our standards. The family room, decorated with an upright piano and handmade doilies, doubled as Mom and Renata's bedroom. Sister and Grandma shared a closet-sized room across the hall. They carried our bags to the family room and gestured for us to enter.

'But,' we asked Mom, 'where will you sleep?'

It took a moment to understand that the four of them planned to share the closet.

'No, thank you,' we said. 'It's too much.' But they insisted, and ushered us inside.

The next morning, Mom set breakfast at the far end of our room, serving tea and warm baguettes with butter, liver sausage, ham, peppers and cheese. She and Sister sat across

from us smiling. When we asked them to join us, they said, No. Please. 'Is for you.'

My fellow missionaries experienced similar kindness. Our hosts prepared meals above their means, serving us portions twice as large as their own – double helpings of potato pancakes, dumplings, shredded cucumber, cabbage and cherries. Sister entertained us on piano and guitar, shaking her head modestly at our applause. Before bed on our second night, Mom told us, sincerely, in broken English, that she loved us.

Vodičkova! Czechs cried when they heard my name. Sister pointed to the phone book, and after several pages I understood my surname was the Czech equivalent of Smith. 'Vodicka' translates to 'little water' – in a region where the rivers flow as readily as the beer, its significance is broad – and it was all I knew of my Bohemian roots. But I recognized something familiar in the fair hair, gray-blue eyes, strong features… and something intangible I couldn't name.

This wasn't the welcome I expected from a nation I'd been taught was starving for Christian values after years of Communist oppression, a place of spiritual darkness where we were supposed to shine light.

As a strategy to reach young people in the region, the mission had established English and athletic camps where we would be working throughout our stay. The day before camp started, we crossed the Polish border to Krakow, a medieval hub of arts and intellectualism until 1939, when Nazi Germany converted it to a place of ghettos and terror. Krakow had been the capital of the Third Reich in Poland, and we boarded a tour bus for Auschwitz to witness the remains of that legacy. Barracks and barbed wire shone beneath the brightest sun, and I became mute, silenced by gas chambers, crematoriums, piles of toothbrushes, two tons of hair, and the very steps beneath my feet, eroded by the soles of millions who died on the grounds of purity.

Afterward, we explored Krakow, now reclaimed. The sun shone on the Old Town, lighting the colorful façades of centuries-old buildings, a rainbow of intelligent design. For a while, I stood inside of it, watching people sip beer beneath the bright umbrellas of the main square's outdoor cafes. A flock of pigeons landed at my feet, pecking crumbs. I considered how different my life would be had I been born a Vodičkova in Czech, or a Jew in 1939, or a daughter of Hitler's army. I felt small, like one of those birds. Like a piece of Bohemian glass, which I watched a shopkeeper shape with a masterful hand and a torch of fire.

The next day, we kicked off our first mission in Český Těšín, facilitating a sports and English camp for middle-schoolers. I told myself my nerves were excitement and laughed along with my friends as we drove to the assigned address. We pulled into the concrete gray parking lot of a concrete gray building. The yard, too, was concrete, surrounded by a chain-link fence.

The biggest surprise was not the correctional feel of the facility, but the fact that the facility was empty. Except for a few Czech youth group kids – souls already saved – we had no registered campers. Instead, Ben distributed fliers and sent us into the streets.

I had never doubted Ben, but I took one look at the flier and felt roped into false advertising. I had assumed our Christian angle was part of the promotion, that we were pitching an opportunity to get to know English and God. But the flier didn't mention the God part.

'Hello! Excuse me!' One of my friends approached a pedestrian, a girl about our age. 'Do you like games? Would you like free English lessons?' The girl took a flier but kept walking. I swallowed my doubts, greeting passersby with a smile and an outstretched hand. One man asked where I was from, took my handout, and continued on his way. After an hour, we gave up and went inside.

A few strangers wandered in. Some of the local youth group students brought friends. Mainly, we spent the day playing games and singing with Czechs we'd already befriended. When Ben gave a sermon at the end of the day, some kids slept. Others chatted loudly in their native language, since they couldn't understand ours.

I was relieved when the day was over. We hadn't won souls, but it was too soon to lose faith.

When camp ended a few days later, two girls had accepted Jesus as their personal savior, but we were down multiple Youth Group members. One had twisted his ankle and been rushed to a hospital in Poland; two had contracted the flu; four had laryngitis; the rest of us suffered sore throats. How would we share the Good News if we all lost our voices?

Our host families assured us these were symptoms of jetlag and industrial pollution – nearby Ostrava was 'the steel heart of the republic,' a major producer of black coal and one of the most polluted cities in Europe. But Ben and Amber called a meeting, 'Americans only,' to discuss what was really going on.

'Satan is at work in our group,' Ben announced. He paused to scan our circle, making eye contact with each of us.

'We've been in constant prayer about it,' Amber said. 'But Satan is here. He's had a stronghold on this country, and now we're on his turf. He's battling God over this place and the hearts of the Czech people, and he's trying to keep us from fulfilling our mission.'

I felt their words wash over the group like a cold wave. We looked at one another, our faces guilt-stricken, and then down at the floor – unbearable, the thought of letting Ben and Amber down.

Earlier that day, we had visited the apartment they would be moving into, above the Český Těšín church Fellowship Hall. Reality struck: This was their new home. The Czech kids were our replacements. We had let loose a collective flood of grief in their future living room, holding one another through the deluge, until Ben suggested we walk it off.

Now I waded in the notion that Satan was inside our circle, in one of us. I reflected on my own selfishness. And I hoped, just this once, that Ben and Amber were wrong.

Ben spoke of the challenges ahead. We held hands. We bowed our heads in prayer about staying on the path and conquering evil no matter the obstacles.

Before leaving, Ben turned to us with a hard look and a last word: 'You guys need to remember what you came here to do.'

After a week in Český Těšín, we hugged our host families goodbye and drove a half hour to Frýdlant nad Ostravicí, a resort town that looked like a place in a fairy tale, with wooded green slopes and a blue castle perched in the peaks. I could see why the town was a popular holiday destination, and the mission's chosen headquarters.

The arrangement here felt more like what I'd expected: a spacious mid-mountain facility with dorm rooms, a common area, plenty of outdoor space, organized college-aged English teachers, and eighty-five campers enrolled and waiting on the first day.

Aggie and Michaela were two fast friends. They thought American boys were dreamy, and we laughed together about their respective crushes. And then there was Lenka. She reminded me of my younger sister, who I missed back home – all skinny limbs and spunk, funny and sweet to the core, but not afraid to tackle boys in sports if necessary. She could outrun most of them anyway. We got along instantly.

The days flew in a blur of activity. Hikes. Trips to a nearby convenience store where the grocer laughed at our daily chocolate purchases. Deep conversations spoken in the universal teenage language of flirtation and hysterical laughter. Between English classes, we taught campers our theme song. On a mountain hike after dark, outstretched on the grass and star-gazing, Lenka and I linked arms and sang into the night: Oh Lord, be my light, and be my salvation, all I want is to be in the light.

There was a strategy to our program, a method for efficient conversion. By day, we would cultivate friendships. By night, we would perform skits and songs. Ben would give a closing sermon that would intensify as the week progressed, culminating in a major call to Christ on the final evening. This would be the hard sell. Time to hammer home the reason for our songs and enthusiasm, to meet one-on-one with friends who showed interest. Ideally, we'd pray a prayer of salvation together. God would triumph. Souls would be saved.

We were prepped on this protocol before the trip, but implementing it proved complicated. I was making friends;

it felt strange to treat them like projects come sundown. And while I felt capable of sharing thoughts on faith and love, urging kids to open their hearts so God might speak to them felt like challenging them to a math problem I couldn't solve myself.

On the final evening we sat in a mass of folding chairs, the day's heat spilling over into a packed room, intensifying hyper energy and an acute scent of body odor. My friends and I knew our trip was ending. Aggie, Michaela and several others had accepted Christ, but time was short. We huddled with Ben and Amber for a pep talk and prayer. The lights went down. It was show time.

With blood-flushed cheeks, I stepped alone onstage into the heat of the spotlights to perform in silence, a pantomime.

I stood with my hands outstretched and cupped, as if they held a firefly. Then I pumped my hands, one-two, one-two, as if, instead, I held a beating heart.

My friend Ian, a tall blonde who had Aggie and Michaela swooning, sidled onstage. He put an arm around me and smiled coyly. I smiled back, starry-eyed. He pointed to my pulsing heart and motioned for it. I shook my head, No, but he persisted, gesturing grandly on his knees. Eventually, with hesitation, I offered him my heart.

Now Ian's hands pulsed, one-two, one-two, and we strolled the stage, arms and eyes locked. I was a girl lost in devotion, so I didn't notice, at first, the boy start to toy with my heart. One-two, toss. One-two, toss. I protested, motioning for him to give it back, but he laughed and shrugged me off. One-two, toss. One-two, toss. Higher and higher my heart flew, out of control, until I cried and begged silently for him to stop.

And then, in the heat of the moment, he missed the catch. My invisible heart fell to the floor and shattered, and I fell to my knees with it until the lights onstage went dark.

The audience gave generous applause. We bowed, Ian walked offstage, and my true heart thumped with nerves for what would come next.

Ben and Amber had asked me to deliver the final night's testimony, the prelude to Ben's big talk. I could see Amber smiling at me through the spotlights. Lenka stood at the back of the room, arms folded across her chest. I knew I needed to push aside the nerves and the nagging at my brain and recite the testimony I'd prepared, channeling Amber and Ben and all the great charismatic leaders I'd known.

I took a deep breath. I segued with a line about how the world will break your heart, but God never will. And then I told a story about a little girl who had suffered severe hearing loss, who had felt stupid and ashamed, and how one day, God healed the little girl miraculously, through a faith healer in prayer, and how he could work miracles in your life, too, he could heal your heart, restore your sounds, open your eyes to the light.

Afterward, Ben scooped me in a proud hug as we traded places. Friends high-fived and hugged me as I took my seat among the folding chairs. But when I turned to look for Lenka, she looked the other way.

Perhaps he felt called by God, or mounting pressure as a new hire for a missionary organization, but for the next hour, Ben transformed into a version of himself I had never seen. He paced the stage, agitated and restless. He described the crucifixion in detail. He rebuked us as sinners, and walked us through a Hell he said we deserved, a visualization so gruesome some kids wailed. But he was relentless.

'If you died tomorrow,' Ben asked, scanning the room, 'do you know where your soul would go?'

Back home, Ben's talks had been uplifting and wise, never fire-and-brimstone like this. Now, he was shaking with anger so electric I thought fire might shoot from his fingertips. His face, handsome and kind, had darkened to a purplish red. His voice rose to the point of breaking.

Ben asked if we wanted to live for eternity in paradise and let Jesus shoulder our burdens in the meantime, or if we wanted to die in sin. He told us to close our eyes, bow our heads, and think long and hard about what had happened over the course of the week – the friendships made, the songs sung, and the lessons of this evening. 'If you want to make a change tonight,' he said, 'if you want to be born again in the Spirit and start a new life today, raise your hand and we'll join you in prayer as you become a child of God.'

I could hear my fellow missionaries shuffle through the audience, and opened my eyes to see them praying prayers of conversion with hands in the air. But I could not rise from my chair. I closed my eyes again, trying to center myself inside all of the wrath and doom and promises and images that spun around my head like a haywire halo: Ben's fear, Lenka looking betrayed, my own fifteen-year-old self, alone onstage and preaching.

And there, in the climax of soul saving, from every corner of the fiery room, from inside and outside, from the darkness of my mind and some bright place, clear and emerging: a voice.

There was nothing still and silent about it. This was the booming thunder variety, at once my own and something else entirely, a voice that made my heart pound with a simple word: No.

'No, no, NO.' Again and again, louder and louder, pulsing in time with my heartbeat, No.

It was urgent. It was more than three times. It could have come in any language and I would have understood. It was unmistakable.

The voice shot through me, opening my eyes. I saw Ben, Amber, and my Youth Group friends gripping hands with Czech kids like they might lose them. I saw new friends begging for salvation in Czech and English and something in between. Others looked confused. I turned to look for Lenka. She was gone. When I turned back to the room, I saw myself in it, and I began to weep.

Two friends came to comfort me. They held my hands, and I loved them for it, but I couldn't speak. Someone started singing our theme song. Others chimed in: I wanna be in the light...

I didn't know anymore what that phrase meant. In fact, never before had I been so aware of how much I didn't know.

That was the gift of that journey – the gift of my own ignorance, handed to me in the middle of a mission in the Czech Republic, land of my own lineage, of so-called spiritual darkness, of enlightenment.

I spent the remaining two weeks before my sophomore year of high school locked in my bedroom, crying beneath the covers and wondering what to do next. My journal, which I had kept diligently throughout the trip, stops there. It picks up again six months later, after I quietly left the church.

When I left for college, I received letters from Youth Group friends who worried about my soul. I wrote that my soul was safe, that I still loved them, but didn't need saving; if they still wanted to be my friend, I would be thrilled. I never heard back.

So it was the beginning of the end of my religious life, and the genesis of another. Maybe, then, I was born again after all, the great veil lifted from my eyes, hurtling me free into the world. I haven't stopped traveling since.

Everywhere I go, just as in that deserted village in Argentina, I encounter the fresh, eager faces and earnest smiles of missionaries. Micronesia, where I live now, has one of the highest rates per-capita in the world. Twenty-six countries ban missionary visas, but as long as religion exists, so will they: people like Ben and Amber, who love people, and whose lens for love is Jesus, or Allah, or Jehovah. And people like me, or the girl I was: a foot soldier of the faith, for a time.

It has taken years, but sometimes when I travel I visit a local service just to hear the choir sing, to be inside the sound of voices blending in rapture. But I never stay for the end. It is a language I used to speak, half forgotten now, like a song you've heard before but can't place, a phantom melody, a holy ghost. The world calls me outside, around one bend and another, to a mountaintop, to the sea, and I am lost again, and I am found.

Some of the names in this essay have been changed for the sake of privacy.

Stolen
Lavinia Spalding

The voice was booming, packed with obscenities, and deep – almost supernaturally deep. It was unlike any sound my lungs had ever produced. But there was no time for contemplation. It was 2am in Busan, South Korea, and an intruder was in my living room.

The instant I unlocked my front door and spotted him crouched behind the sofa, the primal, deep-voice response activated. Then, after one suspended moment, he launched himself at me. I sprang back flat against the wall, and he was in front of me. Korean, lanky, wearing a black nylon jacket and baggy pants. I braced for the attack, but he ricocheted against my body, shot into the hall, and tumbled two long flights of steps to the street. I slammed and dead-bolted the door, my hands shaking. Then I heard his feet slapping the pavement outside.

I flipped open my cell phone and stared at it. My *hangul* wasn't fluent enough to explain anything to the police tonight, and it was too late to call my Korean friends. My French boyfriend lived across the world in New Mexico, and we were in a fight anyway – edging toward a breakup. Finally I dialed Marnie. I had put her in a cab ten minutes before, and she lived clear across Busan, near our university; she wouldn't be home yet. I heard her ask the driver to turn around.

'I'll stay the night with you,' she offered.

'Thanks,' I said, finally taking a normal breath. 'But remember I told you my pipes burst? There's no heat in my apartment. It's freezing.'

It was only the second week of January, and already I hated this year.

Two weeks earlier, on the island of Koh Samui in Thailand, I was sharing a *songthaew* – a covered pickup truck with open sides and two long benches in back – with six strangers. It was another sweltering day, and my legs clung to each other like saran wrap.

After two weeks of lounging on Thai islands, I was en route to catch a ferry to lounge on Malaysian islands. I also had loose intentions of visiting the Petronas Twin Towers (then the tallest buildings in the world), staying in historic Melaka, and exploring the Cheong Fatt Tze Mansion in Georgetown. But my only solid plan was to hit the American embassy in Kuala Lumpur and add pages to my passport.

After many years of travel, my little blue book – my most cherished possession – was fat with colorful stamps and visas and memories, and it could take no more. I'd need supplemental pages before crossing any borders that required a full-page visa, and though I had no specific plans, the likelihood of that happening soon was high.

My job in Korea, teaching ESL at a university, was the stuff of expat dreams – a generous salary for working 12 hours a week, a serene mountain campus, students so respectful they bowed from the hip when they saw me at the cafeteria, and five months of paid vacation metered out as a week here, twelve days there, a month, six weeks. I didn't believe in staying home during a paid vacation, so I existed perpetually in four stages: planning, leaving, gone, returning. But Malaysia would be my first solo trip.

When the *songthaew* arrived at the dock and pitched to a stop, I stood up, crouched over, and reached for my purse. I usually wore a money belt, but for this trip I'd opted for a cute travel purse slung over my sunburned shoulder. A cute travel purse containing all my money, credit cards, and plane tickets, as well as my passport. A cute travel purse I must have left in the guesthouse cafe across the island, where I'd just said a teary goodbye to my best friend and her boyfriend.

The *songthaew* driver was waiting for me to pay.

'My bag's gone,' I announced to the truck, looking beseechingly between impassive backpackers and locals. 'Can someone lend me money for the fare?'

A *songthaew*, one of the cheapest transportation options in Thailand, is not where one goes to find magnanimous benefactors. They looked at me sideways.

'Please?' I begged.

Finally a wiry American in a sweat-stained shirt with Thai script fished twenty baht, forty cents, from his pocket. 'Thank you so much,' I gushed – he had seriously saved my life, I said. He rolled his eyes and looked away.

Back at the guesthouse, I found Erin and Drew sipping Singha beers at the table where we'd eaten breakfast an hour before. They were due to leave any minute for Koh Tao, to become dive certified before moving to Canada. Erin paid my tuk-tuk driver while Drew and I searched the cafe in vain. Could I have left it, I wondered, in the *songthaew*, for God's sake? Then their driver arrived.

'We have to go,' Erin said. 'I'm sorry.' She shoved all her baht in my hand, hugged me, and was gone.

That whole week I stayed on Koh Samui. Twice I visited the police chief. Twice he instructed me to stay put. 'You leave, will be difficult,' he said, scribbling a few more indecipherable notes on my police report before handing it back across his desk with a reassuring nod. 'You wait few more day.'

In a fluorescent Internet cafe I researched Bangkok addresses: the American embassy, the Korean embassy, the Korean Air office, the post office where I'd pick up funds my mother would wire. I instant-messaged my French boyfriend in New Mexico who was helpful with research, but increasingly less helpful in the emotion department. A single dad, he'd chosen this week to arrive at the realization that he'd been neglecting his ten-year-old daughter during our intense long-distance love affair. She required more attention, so I got less.

I watched other backpackers arrive and leave, arrive and leave. I walked the island, scribbled in my journal, lay in my hammock, and spent as little of Erin's baht as possible. But mostly I sat by the sea, raking sand through my fingers and wondering how, after all my travels, I had become such an amateur. Wondering how, after all my eagerness to travel alone, I had so quickly come to despise it.

In Busan, I hung up with Marnie and perched on the edge of my mattress, waiting for her footsteps on the stairs. I knew I should search my apartment to see if anything was missing. If I discovered the intruder had stolen something, I'd feel better. I'd know he was just a thief, nothing worse. But I couldn't move.

In five years I had never felt fear in Busan, not even walking home alone in the middle of the night. I hardly ever glanced over my shoulder – guns were illegal in Korea, and violence was scant. I'd never felt anything but safe. Until now.

After one week on Koh Samui, against the police chief's advice, I left.

'I'm sorry you give up,' he said, looking genuinely disappointed in me. I booked a flight to Bangkok (which they miraculously let me board, accepting my police report as identification), and arrived depressed to begin the process of reclaiming my identity.

Khao San Road, the main tourist drag, is a despicable place for someone who doesn't want to be in Bangkok – someone who has logged more than enough time in Bangkok, someone who was this close to her first big solo adventure. Khao San Road is a chaotic vortex of tacky consumerism, dirty hostels, sleazy bars, and soulless cafes. Forget ugly Americans; Khao San Road is where tourists from all great nations converge to get ugly, to haggle over pennies and fall down blitzed in broad daylight. I hated Khao San Road and it was the last place I wanted to be.

'Khao San Road,' I told my tuk-tuk driver.

I would splurge, I'd decided, on a room at the D&D. At ten bucks a night, it cost three times what most other options did, but it was also three times as nice. The rooms had TVs, phones, and private bathrooms. An actual receptionist worked the front desk, actual housekeepers changed beds, and actual walls separated rooms. There was even a rooftop pool, albeit closed for renovation. But I didn't care – perhaps for the first time in my life – about a rooftop pool; all I cared about was securing the necessary documents to get me back out on the road, soon.

My apartment in Busan wasn't merely freezing; without Erin and Drew occupying the second bedroom, it was also quiet and empty. Just last month they'd been showing off kumdo moves in the living room, and after they'd earned their black belts we'd celebrated at a neighborhood expat bar with thumping K-pop and the odd Led Zeppelin song thrown in to keep the Americans drinking. We'd ended up in a back alley at four in the morning ordering *dwaeji guk bap* – spicy stew bubbling in metal vats outside the restaurant, with huge hairy pig parts floating around.

Erin and I had met Drew a year before at a bar in Australia. After ten minutes of chatting with him, I'd motioned Erin over. I'd never been surer of anything: He was my best friend's future husband. I was right; they fell in love, and two months later he moved to Korea, into Erin's room. We occasionally scraped each other's nerves, sharing such close quarters, but now that they were gone and I was alone, shivering in our broken-into apartment, I longed for the murmur of their laughter trickling through my wall.

Day after day, I flagged tuk-tuks to deliver me to the American embassy, the Korean embassy, the Asiana Airlines office. Bamboo-thin women in cherry-red lipstick and snug charcoal suits stood behind desks, clucking their sympathy. I needed a new passport, a new Korean work visa, a new Thai visa, and plane tickets to transport me back to Busan. Once I secured a passport, the rest would be easy. But the American embassy wasn't budging; they could not, they patiently explained, issue me a new passport without identification. I visited daily and begged, unfolding and refolding my police report, which was starting to look ratty. But then, so was I.

Following each unsuccessful embassy visit, I drifted through neighborhoods I never knew existed, stopping in tiny cafés with no English on the menu and eating simple food that tasted more Thai than anything I'd been served on Khao San Road. Each afternoon, I retreated to the comfort of my air-conditioned hotel room.

On day four, I lay in my bed for hours watching a Backstreet Boys marathon on VH1: videos, concerts, exclusive interviews, superfans who screamed and blubbered. I reached for the phone and called my French boyfriend. No answer. I returned to the Backstreet Boys. They were available, and sensitive, and so comforting in their Americanness.

'Show me the meaning of being lonely,' I sang in the shower, when I mustered the will to shower.

The next morning, tired of moping, I toured Wat Arun at sunrise. I'd read enthusiastic reviews of the Temple of the Dawn but had skipped it on past visits to Bangkok, because the guidebooks advised actually arriving at dawn for optimal views and minimal crowds. I was not an 'arrive at dawn' person. But the advice was sound: The site was all but empty, and the colors were dazzling. I strolled by the river, still half-asleep, photographing the white stupa poking the sky, zooming in on enormous statues of kings and Buddhas and a clown-like protector demon with fangs, green skin, and bulging eyes. I climbed the steep steps, ornately tiled with colored glass, porcelain, and seashells, to the top of the central tower, where I photographed the skyline. I'd never seen the Bangkok skyline, and as I beheld the city, with no one to comment to, no one with whom to share the experience, it occurred to me that even as I resented being in Bangkok, I was still doing it, traveling alone for the first time. I'd just expected myself to be better company.

As if on cue, when I climbed back down, a young orange-robed monk began following me, asking questions. I could never remember all the rules pertaining to monks, but I suspected he was breaking them by talking to me. As we walked, he told me about his life, his studies, and his fervent desire to learn English. Then he asked for my email address.

'Sure,' I said, eager to be rid of him. There was something disconcerting about the young monk – a hint of desperation, a hollow that wanted filling. It felt uncomfortably familiar. I scribbled my address, confident I'd never hear from him. But later that afternoon an email arrived asking me to meet him at dusk by the river. He signed it, 'Love me little or love me long let me know.'

I didn't let him know.

I emailed my mom in Arizona. 'Don't you have anything with my photo and name? They won't give me a passport without it, and without a passport I can't get anything else.'

She had excavated her filing cabinets but turned up nothing of use. I'd been away from home thirteen years, and all proof of my identity was now locked in my apartment in Korea, which no one had keys to except my landlord, whose phone number was also locked in my apartment in Korea.

Finally Mom emailed: She'd located my birth certificate and was faxing it to the embassy. I hurried over. The young woman smiled encouragingly. 'Come back tomorrow,' she said. 'I think this can work.'

I returned the next day.

'Sorry,' a different person said. Did I happen to have some photo ID?

The next day, Mom got creative, faxing a copy of her own driver's license alongside a photo of the two of us. I returned to the embassy. The young woman studied the fax, disappeared into the back room for five minutes, then returned and again smiled encouragingly. 'Come back tomorrow,' she said, which of course I did.

'Good news,' the man at the window announced the next afternoon. This would suffice, and – hallelujah! – they would issue me a new passport on Wednesday.

At the Internet cafe on Khao San Road, I wrote my mother: It worked! Then I sent a mass email, informing my entire address book of my trials in Thailand.

Within seconds, a reply came. 'We're in Bangkok, too,' Svetlana's email said. 'On Khao San Road!'

I'd met Svetlana, from Serbia, and her American husband, Mike, in Bangkok four years prior, and we'd kept in touch casually by email. I didn't know them well, but I liked them, and they were here, and I was no longer alone.

It wasn't the first time we'd had an intruder. A few months before, a middle-aged Korean man had staggered into our unlocked apartment in the middle of the night. I'd slept through the entire incident, knocked out on cold medicine. But Erin had woken to see him standing over her bed, peering down at her and Drew, saying, '*Waygukin*?' Foreigner?

Erin screamed, and the man, obviously inebriated, scrambled out of their bedroom. She and Drew followed him to the living room, where they found him trying to drag a sofa cushion out our front door. Drew wrestled the cushion from his hands and ordered him to leave, and he did, but only after taking a few minutes to put on his shoes, which he'd politely removed at the door.

In Bangkok, I met Svetlana and Mike for dinner. Over *pad see ew* and green curry with prawns and one giant Chang beer after the next, we reminisced and philosophized. Mike described a diving trip in Belize, and Svetlana regaled me with her account of recently getting her American citizenship. When we said goodnight, it was late and we were drunk.

At three in the morning my phone rang.

'You have a visitor,' the receptionist said.

'You have the wrong number,' I said, hanging up.

The phone rang again.

'Your friend is here,' the receptionist said.

'I don't have a friend,' I answered.

'Hold, please.'

Svetlana had left Mike. 'We had a terrible fight,' she said, standing in my door, sniffling. 'He raised his hand to me.'

'He hit you?'

'No, but he got so mad he hit the wall in our room.'

Could she sleep on my floor, she asked? Svetlana was supermodel beautiful, leggy and flawless in everything from skin to hair to cheekbones to teeth to eyebrows. But right now she looked a frantic mess – black mascara skid marks beneath swollen eyes, hair disheveled. I gave her a blanket, a T-shirt, and offered her the use of my toothbrush.

She had grabbed only one item leaving her hotel, she told me, sitting on the edge of my bed – her passport.

'Well, that's all you really need, isn't it?' I asked. It was, after all, the thing I wanted most in the world.

'NO!' she said, her eyes filling with tears. 'I can't believe I didn't take my tweezers.'

When Marnie arrived, I was still shaking. 'I can't figure out how he got in,' I said. 'My door was locked.'

'Maybe through the window?'

'Locked. All I can think is that one of the workers who came last month to fix the sink made a key.'

'Get the locks changed,' Marnie said. 'Just in case.'

I nodded, shivered. 'Sorry it's so cold.'

As I recounted the events for her, I tried replicating my freakishly deep voice, but couldn't come close.

'It was like *The Exorcist*,' I said. 'It was not my voice. It was the voice of a pissed-off 250-pound wrestler. And you know, when he heard it, I think he was more scared of me than I was of him.'

'Well,' she said, 'isn't it nice to know you have that big voice inside to protect you?'

Though I'd seen Marnie every week at school, I barely knew her. Living with Erin the past two years, I hadn't needed other friends – not to mention that for months I'd been consumed with my long-distance relationship.

But then I'd returned from Thailand to an empty, heatless apartment in a record-cold winter (during Chusok, the Korean New Year, no less – when the entire country shuts down and no one fixes pipes). Sitting alone and miserable in my unlivable apartment, I'd realized I had to reach out and make friends. Marnie seemed nice, so I'd invited her to go dancing.

Now I looked pitifully at my newest friend. 'Will you sleep in my bed with me?'

In Bangkok, Svetlana and I ran errands. In bustling covered markets we bought pajamas, a toothbrush, underwear, and tweezers. In Internet cafes we updated friends and family; I bemoaned my misfortune while Svetlana informed everyone that she'd left her husband. Mike emailed, apologizing and begging. She ignored him. We picked up money her family wired, at the same post office where I'd retrieved mine. We ate, drank coffee, talked about our men. She taught me to say 'I love you' in Serbian, and I taught her 'hello' in Korean.

On Wednesday Svetlana said she'd accompany me to the embassy to pick up my passport. 'What else do I have to do?' she asked.

After twenty minutes in the lobby, they called my name.

'I'm sorry,' the woman in the window said. 'Unfortunately it's not enough. We cannot issue you a passport without identification.'

I closed my eyes, inhaled and exhaled. 'What am I supposed to do?' I demanded, my voice squeaky, my eyes stinging with tears. 'I'm out of options. I can't stay in Bangkok – I have a job to return to! What else can I do?'

'Well,' she said, pausing, 'there is one other way.'

I have never seen anyone look so proud, so purposeful and dignified and lovely as Svetlana when she handed the clerk her own brand-new passport, then raised her right hand as a United States citizen, and with her left hand on a Bible, swore – in the slightest accent – that I was one, too.

The next day, Svetlana and Mike reconciled and left Bangkok. And since the embassy required several days to issue my new passport, I decided to leave town. I headed to a nearby island, Koh Chang. During the day, I lay in a hammock reading my book; in the evenings, I treated myself to the seafood buffets on the beach. And I finally began enjoying my own company.

Still, when a pair of British honeymooners invited me to join them for dinner my last night on the island, I gratefully accepted – not out of loneliness, but because meeting other travelers felt like part of the experience. The honeymooners seemed perfectly happy and comfortable together, and as we drank and dined and talked late into the night, I began wondering why for months I'd felt so alone, when I was supposed to be in love. The next morning, I joined the bride on the beach. We discussed my relationship, and the fall it seemed to be taking. It was like a slinky tumbling down the stairs, I said, and I was running after it, trying to keep it from hitting the floor.

'You know,' she said, smiling, 'I don't know how to advise you, but I'll tell you what my mother would say. She became a psychiatrist when she was sixty, and it was this big joke among my friends, because she started giving everyone identical advice, no matter what their problem was: She'd just say that each of us has a tiny voice inside us, and all our problems come from ignoring that tiny voice.'

A week after the break-in, my heat restored, my locks changed, my spare room turned into a space for crafts, and my relationship officially over – ended by me and my not-so-tiny voice – I was back at work and planning my next trip. I had started to reach out and widen my circle of friends, and I was studying meditation with a monk who lived in my neighborhood. I was also beginning to relish having my own apartment – the sound of my voice humming into the silence and my own fingers tapping on my keyboard and my own feet walking up the steps.

When a student asked to see my photos from Thailand, I realized I still hadn't developed them. That afternoon I searched the apartment for my camera bag, but it was gone. Stolen. The intruder. And along with my camera, all the film. My mind riffled through photographs: a New Year's Eve full moon party on Koh Pha Ngan, where Erin, Drew, and I danced barefoot on the sand till daybreak. Sunrise at Wat Arun – the mosaics and demons and Buddhas, and a skyline that was all mine. A young monk who would never get his answer. Koh Chang and the British honeymooners. And lovely Serbian-American Svetlana raising her right hand. All gone.

But in a way, this felt right. Because the only souvenir I really needed was my new passport with its clean pages, a fresh picture, and one colorful stamp reminding me that I was never really alone.

A Face You'll Never Forget

Larry Habegger

At a young age my eldest daughter had a fascination with the night sky. When darkness enveloped the world, she'd urge me outside to look for constellations. Her book for beginning astronomers splayed before her, she asked for my help finding Cassiopeia, the Big Dipper, Cancer.

'There, Daddy, look,' she said, pointing up. 'There's Orion.'

I knew Orion. I didn't know many others, especially in the washed-out sky of urban North America, but I knew Orion.

Long before my daughter was born, I had stood at midnight by railroad tracks on the tropical island of Sri Lanka, looking at a sky full of stars. The moon was long gone, the darkness so complete I could barely discern the outlines of the surrounding forest. Above, pinpricks of light so filled the

275

sky that I began to believe I could see in three dimensions, looking into the depth of the cosmos at layer upon layer of stars, rather than the usual flat expanse of sprinkled light. It seemed I was viewing the universe for the first time. A trickle of sweat meandered down my spine and I wondered if it was caused by the tropical heat or the sudden awareness of my utter insignificance.

The scrape of a shoe on stone startled me.

'Train coming soon,' a lilting voice announced, and I turned to see the outline of the stationmaster silhouetted against the faint light of the shed-like train station. In this rural outpost, in the middle of the night, he was my only company and I his only customer.

'Do you see the faces?' he asked.

'Faces?'

'Yes, the constellations. I have always thought that they look like faces. For, once you recognize them, they become faces you never forget.'

I let the thought drift in the night and looked again at the sky. We were silent together, both seeing our own visions in the stars, until he spoke again.

'Do you see the three bright stars very high in the sky? Look high, very bright, do you see?'

I did see, but there were so many, so bright.

'That's Orion,' he said.

'There are so many stars here,' I said, 'more than I see where I live. It's hard to recognize them.'

'But once you look closely, really see them, you never forget.'

I wasn't so sure about that, but I looked closer, did my best to memorize the alignment of stars so I could find Orion again another time.

Just then, a faint clatter grew to a rumble, and the train made its slow approach, its beam of light spearing the night. As it drew closer, hissing steam, I shouldered my pack and turned to the stationmaster, whose face I could now see, glistening with sweat from the humidity.

He smiled. 'Now you have seen Orion, and you will remember. When you see it again, I hope you will think of Sri Lanka. It is a face you will never forget.'

I thanked him and boarded, headed for Mannar on the coast, and the overnight boat to India.

The stationmaster's words stayed with me as I settled in for a few fitful hours of sleep. I had already seen a face I would never forget, that of a twelve-year-old girl in the Tamil village of Kalkudah, midway between Batticaloa and Trincomalee on the eastern coast. She was one among many children living in the compound where I had paid a few rupees to sleep a few nights before. She had a remarkable maturity in her face, a beauty and wisdom beyond her years that shone through her dark eyes and open, gentle smile.

She and her friends had pranced around me as I walked up the dusty beach road, laughing and beckoning me to follow them. No doubt they knew that a foreigner with a backpack would be looking for a place to eat and sleep, and their parents were in the habit of taking in vagabonds like me. It was the sweetest experience with touts one could ever hope to have, these playful girls who asked for nothing but for me to follow them to see their home.

I did, and arrived at their collection of simple bamboo huts with a central dirt courtyard, which I soon realized was both their playground and joint living room. Their parents welcomed me with smiles and rudimentary English, enough to determine that they had a place for me at an agreeable price. I settled in, and soon after the girls surrounded me, delivering a plate of papaya, and a fresh coconut for me to drink. When they saw that I was content, they ran off and played games in the courtyard, drawing pictures in the dirt with sticks and palm fronds, and dancing around them.

The place felt like paradise. The warm sea washed gently onto the beach just a hundred yards away. Fruit hung from the trees for the picking. The people seemed content, the children happy.

On a walk later that day, I noticed that many of the palm trees were spindly sticks with no fronds. A cyclone had blown through a few years ago, I was told, and snapped them off. Now they'd bear no fruit. Down a nearby lane I came across the ruins of a bamboo hut similar to the one I was staying in, scorched and blackened as if it had burned down just yesterday. Other backpackers I met that day said they'd heard rumors that a backpacker like us had burned it down because he felt cheated by the villagers.

I couldn't fathom that. If that had happened, I wouldn't have been so warmly welcomed.

There were other rumors, that social strife between the majority Sinhalese and minority Tamils was simmering out of control. Could this have been the cause of the arson?

Back in my compound, I had no answers, but I had the evidence of joy and delight before me. That evening the girls danced while the adults played makeshift percussion with sticks and coconut husks. We had a simple dinner of rice and fish, then settled in for the night.

Before I left the next day, I took out my camera, hoping to get a few portraits of the villagers. They complied, and posed, and the girls hammed it up for the camera. But one image stood out from the rest. All the girls posed together, some looking away, some teasing each other, some laughing, but one looking directly into the camera, the smile in her eyes just about melting the lens. I would have had that picture for a lifetime even if I hadn't released the shutter.

We arrived at Mannar in darkness, boarded the boat with the faintest hint of pink light adorning the eastern sky, and began the slow crossing to India. For a long time I'd dreamed of reaching this fabled land, but I'd never expected to arrive by sea, to make the journey up the subcontinent from the southern tip. At dawn we anchored off Rameswaram and the crowds pushed to the gangway to try to get aboard the first lighter to the pier. It could take hours for all the passengers to disembark, I'd been told. But soon I was on land, and a few hours later I had reached Madurai, home of the Meenakshi Amman temple complex devoted to Parvati and Shiva, its stupendous towers adorned with thousands of multicolored stone figures.

Later that day I passed under the gateway tower and entered the temple, swept into the dark interior by a flood of women in iridescent saris and men in simple dhotis, the white diaper-like wrap worn by men all over southern India. I felt like I'd stepped into a kaleidoscope, a frenzied rush of colors and people wherever I turned: statues smeared with so much colored wax their features were indistinguishable, garlands of marigolds draped around their necks, chants echoing off the stone walls, candles casting light off the ceilings, and the scent of sandalwood wafting on incense smoke.

There, huge in the stone chamber, stood an elephant, its head adorned in jewels and glitter, accepting alms from penitents with its trunk and then patting them on the shoulder. To me in my addled state, and in the smoky half-light, that bejeweled elephant seemed to mirror the cosmos, the deep night sky I'd seen the previous night at the train station in Sri Lanka. Dazed, I watched as the crowd swirled around me, a stone in the current, feeling farther away from the world I knew than I'd ever been, yet oddly feeling at home.

Just a year later, after I returned to the US, the news from Sri Lanka grew worse by the day. The social strife erupted into full-blown civil war. Massacres were reported in places I knew: Trincomalee, Batticaloa, unnamed villages all across the east and north.

I didn't have to see the name Kalkudah in the news to deduce what had happened. All I had to do was step outside and look at the night sky. When I saw Orion, I felt I knew.

The stationmaster had hoped I would think of Sri Lanka when I saw that constellation. I do, but what I see in Orion is the face of that girl, the stunning beauty at age twelve, who danced and sang for me with her friends in that faraway place. Although I had no hard evidence, when I saw Orion a sense of certainty drifted down from the stars, telling me that she didn't make it to adulthood.

My eldest daughter is now past age twelve, as is her younger sister, both well on their way to adulthood. When we step outside at night, we find different meanings in the stars. My girls see an incomprehensible vastness of wonder and magic and mystery. I see the place we all came from and will return to. I also see the silhouette of the stationmaster, the innocence of those Kalkudah children, and a moment when I encountered a place that felt like paradise. But mostly I see her face, the one I'll never forget.

War Story
Jim Benning

I'd always assumed my father had killed people. He'd never talked about it. To be fair, I'd never asked him. I'd never had the nerve.

But today was different. We were away from home, and through the paradigm-shifting power of travel, I felt emboldened. I was driving our rented Opel station wagon through the Belgian countryside, past fields dotted with wildflowers and fat cows. I was 30. He was 76, a gentle man with short, gray hair and big glasses.

I kept my eyes on the road and took a deep breath.

'Dad, in all of the time you've talked about the war, you've never talked about having to shoot people.'

It wasn't exactly a question – more of an observation. It was the best I could do.

My dad grew quiet and looked out the window.

'Who wants to talk about something like that?' he said.

He had a point. The afternoon sunlight reflected off the Opel's silver hood. I wondered whether to press on or drop the subject forever.

Father-son relationships are rarely easy, but my dad is one of the 'Greatest Generation' – men who grew up during the Depression, fought in WWII and, upon returning home, were often frustratingly quiet and inscrutable. My dad was 46 when I was born. The older I got, the more aware I became of the gulf between us – not just the decades or our differing diction (my dad was old enough to call companies 'outfits'), but our openness with each other, or lack thereof. He was a good man – always supportive – but he could be remote, and even, I thought at times, unknowable.

I longed to bridge the divide, and I was just young enough to think I could. Like many sons of veterans, I thought my father's years at war might hold a key to understanding him – that somewhere in the bloom of youth and the trauma of combat, the kernel of the man I knew was formed. What's more, I believed in the power of travel to work magic: Blend enough time and movement in a foreign place and a kind of alchemy can occur. Things can happen – good things – that might not occur back home. So I asked my dad to travel with me to Western Europe, to show me some of the places where he'd fought. If I were lucky, I'd return home feeling closer to him, and maybe a little more at peace with myself, too.

We landed in Paris on a cool spring afternoon and wasted no time in hitting the road, exploring small towns where he'd been. One afternoon, we headed for Bastogne in Belgium. In December of 1944, the German army attacked Allied troops here, igniting the Battle of the Bulge. At the time, my father was a paratrooper with the 82nd Airborne Division. He was soon embroiled in combat, and would be for days.

We wandered into a museum and watched a short documentary about the Battle of the Bulge. Black-and-white footage showed American soldiers marching through snow. Explosions flashed on the screen, along with photos of corpses. My father was sitting beside me, and I heard his breathing change. He wiped his eyes.

Afterward, we drove past towering evergreens. He was quiet.

'How did you feel watching the movie, Dad?'

'Emotional.'

'Sad?'

My father was capable of wide-ranging political conversations. I hated asking a question that sounded better suited for a child, but in this case, I thought conversational baby steps might be the best approach.

'Yeah.'

'How so?'

'Just seeing all that. It was such an awful war.'

As we drove on, I thought about my dad's teen years. He'd grown up in St. Louis. When the US entered the war, he and his three brothers enlisted. My father was just 17 at the time – still a kid, really. He took part in some of the war's worst fighting, including the Battle of the Hürtgen Forest, in which tens of thousands of Americans were killed. I wondered how much of my dad's reticence was innate, and how much was shaped by those battles. I thought about how we can never really know the toll war takes on survivors, nor the extent of the effects passed from fathers to sons, and mothers to daughters – a kind of lingering post-traumatic stress that trickles down, however

Jim Benning

subtly, through generations. I thought about the grief my father seemed to carry at times, and wondered if it was the same grief I sometimes felt, seemingly inexplicably.

I didn't mention any of this. In fact, I was so quiet my dad grew concerned.

'How are you doing?' he said.

Maybe this was an opening.

'Okay, I guess. You don't always have much to say. It can be hard sometimes.'

'You think that's unusual?'

'Just a generational difference between us, I think.'

He grew quiet. We passed a creek.

'Pretty river,' he said.

When we pulled into downtown Bastogne in the afternoon, I had a hard time finding a parking place. I spotted a tight spot along the road and backed in, accidentally tapping the bumper of the car parked behind us. A big, gray-haired man got out. He waved his hand at his bumper, shouting something in French I couldn't understand.

I got out and raised my hands apologetically.

'Pardon, monsieur,' I said.

He rattled off something angrily.

I shook my head. 'Non parlez français,' I said.

He furrowed his brow and looked puzzled. 'Non?'

My dad was standing next to me now. I gestured toward him. 'American,' I said.

He studied my dad's gray hair and slim frame.

'American?' he said.

My dad and I nodded.

The man's expression softened. He bowed toward us, as if to show deference.

'Très bien,' he said.

Then he got back into his car and drove off.

I couldn't believe it. Never in all of my overseas travels had being an American actually been an asset.

'I bet he lived through the war,' my dad said, smiling.

That, I thought, was a little magic.

A couple of days later, we drove toward Stavelot, another Belgian town that played a role in the Battle of the Bulge. I asked my dad about his time there and he recalled a bridge in the area being blown up, and having to march while carrying 30-calibre machine-gun canisters. He recalled mortar rounds raining down. He and others attacked a farmhouse occupied by German soldiers.

Which brings us back to the moment I'd been waiting for. The moment I chose to ask whether he'd ever killed anyone. I didn't want to force my dad to discuss the question if he didn't want to. I mean, I assumed that to survive the kind of fighting he did, he'd had to kill. But if I'm honest, I wanted to push him into uncomfortable territory. I wanted him to open up, to talk to me, to tell me things. I wanted to connect.

My first attempt rebuffed, I tried a slightly different approach.

'You must have had to fire at people just to defend yourself.'

After this, I would drop the subject. My dad could reply if he felt up to it, or he could simply leave the statement hanging there, like a dangling question mark.

A moment passed. He was quiet.

'I shot people,' he said, finally.

I glanced at him. He was looking out the window.

'You become callous to it in combat,' he said. 'You fire at a guy, see him drop, then fire at someone else. You don't dwell on it.'

'You're probably just too concerned with staying alive,' I said, eager to express understanding.

'Definitely. In spite of what some guys say, I was scared to death. I never got over that. I don't think you can come away from that unscarred.'

'How could anyone?'

'I've always been a private person, perhaps to a fault,' he said. 'The war probably exacerbated that.'

This wasn't a great revelation. But I was touched that my dad opened up about it. For him, and for me, that was no small thing.

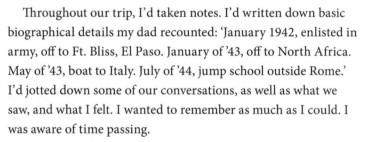

Throughout our trip, I'd taken notes. I'd written down basic biographical details my dad recounted: 'January 1942, enlisted in army, off to Ft. Bliss, El Paso. January of '43, off to North Africa. May of '43, boat to Italy. July of '44, jump school outside Rome.' I'd jotted down some of our conversations, as well as what we saw, and what I felt. I wanted to remember as much as I could. I was aware of time passing.

Not long after we returned home to California, my father began complaining that words were escaping him. Over the subsequent years, his memory faded. As I write this, he is 90, with advanced dementia. He has trouble speaking. He remembers very little – at least little he is able to communicate. I'm left with my notes, and with some of the images and moments from our journey that I can remember.

One memory is still vivid: The day after we got home from Europe, my dad sat at the dinner table with my mom and opened up a map, tracing his finger along the roads we'd driven. He told a few war stories, and recalled stories from our trip. His eyes were glowing. He was as happy and as alive as I'd ever seen him.

Ironically, he couldn't stop talking. At one point, he looked up at me and said, 'You're a great travel companion, Jim. I'd travel with you anywhere.'

Of course, we won't be traveling again. The time for that has passed. My dad is more remote than ever. But we did make this trip together, and for a few precious moments, the gulf between us shrank. I felt closer to my dad, and I think he felt closer to me. This is the story I tell myself – now more than ever.

Forty-Five
Cheryl Strayed

O ne winter day I received a glorious proposition. Would I agree to travel anywhere in the world on 24 hours' notice? My only obligation would be to spend six days in that place, doing whatever I liked, and then write about it. I would not have the faintest clue what my destination would be until the day before I departed, when my electronic plane ticket would be emailed to me. Only countries deemed war zones were off the table. Everything else was a possibility. It could be Iceland or China. Tanzania or Peru. I said yes, but I had a condition of my own: I had to depart for my trip on September 18, the day after my forty-fifth birthday.

It was a birthday that had special significance to me. My mother had died at forty-five and I'd been thinking for quite some time about how to commemorate that crossing. In the twenty-three years since she'd been dead, the idea of this birthday had loomed painfully in the distance. A sore spot of impossibility. How could I outlive my mother? Would I? For many years I thought not. But here it was and I wanted to honor the juncture where my mother's life ended and mine continued. The surprise trip into the unknown seemed the perfect way to do that. Though my mother hadn't traveled much – with three kids to raise single-handedly and very little money – she'd always wanted to. It was the thing she was going to do next, before cancer put an end to it all. I don't believe in heaven or an afterlife, but I've felt my mother's presence within me every day since she died and I hear her voice too, and always it says only one word. It's what she wanted for me and what she didn't get for herself: Go.

So go I would.

When, on my birthday, I received the email that announced Andorra as my destination, I immediately hit Reply and wrote, 'YAY!' But in truth, I was thinking, 'HUH?!' I'm a world traveler with a lifelong map obsession, but somehow I'd missed Andorra. I dimly recalled a Pete Seeger song by that name. It sounded like a material you could knit a sweater from. My best guess about what continent it might be on was South America. That was dead wrong.

I soon learned that I was going to a tiny landlocked country that's sandwiched between Spain and France in the eastern Pyrenees. Officially called the Principality of Andorra, the country measures 181 square miles, has a population of 85,000, and is so mountainous there are no airports. To get there I'd have to fly to either Barcelona or Toulouse, then travel three hours by road. After reading that it is known primarily for its stellar ski slopes and abundant tax-free shopping – the latter of no interest

to me and the former irrelevant because of the season –
I had to dig deep to hold onto the enthusiasm that had inspired
my initial all-caps, exclamation-point-punctuated email.

It wasn't the easiest thing to do. Andorra is all but ignored
by travel guidebooks and it has none of its own. One telling
fact: When I typed the word 'Andorra' into a search engine, the
first item that came up was a bra. Sources that do mention the
country outside of its appeal as a skiing destination often sum it
up as a hub of ugly consumerism worth a stop only if you want
cheap cigarettes. My inquiries on social media were likewise
discouraging, met mostly with suggestions that I go to Spain or
France instead.

Yet a day and a half later at the Barcelona airport, when I
boarded an overly-air-conditioned, Andorra-bound mini-bus, I
felt more optimistic than doomed. In the course of my mad-dash
research, it had dawned on me that a country known for its great
downhill skiing was most likely my kind of place in the off-
season, and a quick Internet search confirmed my hunch: When
all that snow melted away, there were hiking trails galore in one
of the most beautiful mountain ranges in the world.

In a jet-lagged daze, I gazed out the window as the arid
Spanish landscape gave way to tree-covered peaks rising against
the sunny blue afternoon sky in every direction as we wended
our way through the narrow valley that leads to the capital city
of Andorra la Vella. After the bus driver let me off in the town
center, I dragged my rolling suitcase past stores selling all matter
of things – shoes, perfume, china, fancy scarves, knives, cell
phones, leather jackets, and tchotchke shops featuring plastic
statuettes of Our Lady of Meritxell (the patron saint of Andorra)
– and went straight to the tourist office, a glassed-in room in a
building on the Plaça de Rotunda.

Though I'd come by then to know that the official language of the country was Catalan, I had to rely on my awful Spanish to inquire about hiking trails. The man behind the counter stared at me blankly, so I repeated my request in English and then followed that up with a pantomime, which at long last compelled him to pull out a map.

'Many hikes!' he boomed, setting the map before me only to whisk it away a moment later, proclaiming that it was impossible to hike now. 'You could be shot,' he stated when I asked him why, his voice almost elegant in its certainty. In a confusing mix of Catalan, Spanish, English, and pantomime, we worked out the unfortunate fact that I'd arrived during the single week in the entire year that was hunting season in Andorra. The animal in question was a Pyrenean chamois, a goat-like antelope that's more commonly referred to by Andorrans as the izard.

'You wait a week and then you hike,' he said. When I explained that I had to hike now because now was the only time I had in Andorra, he shrugged and said, 'You only live once. Why risk?'

Disheartened, starving, and smelling like a goat-like antelope myself beneath the clothes I'd been wearing since I'd left home, I dragged my suitcase out of the tourist office and across the way, to a statue by Salvador Dalí called 'Nobility of Time,' which he'd gifted to the city. I hadn't slept since I'd been in my own bed in Portland, Oregon, some twenty hours before, and nearly hallucinating from exhaustion, I found the melting clock to be a perfect reflection of how distorted and faded I felt. I ambled across the street to a hotel that looked promising and inquired about a room.

As the woman working the desk ran my credit card, I told her about my conundrum. 'Do you think I'll be shot if I go hiking?' I asked, silently willing her to say no, but instead she nodded and advised me not to go.

An hour later I asked the waiter at a nearby café the same question and he nodded in the solemn manner the woman at the hotel had. 'Yes,' he said. 'It is likely you could be shot.' After he brought me a glass of wine, I sat at my sidewalk table overlooking the Gran Valira, the concrete-lined river that runs through the city, feeling grim and alone. It was six o'clock – far too early for Andorrans to eat dinner – so all the tables surrounding me were empty, the waiter emerging from the café only occasionally to bring me the dishes I'd ordered. As I worked my way through the sort of unexpectedly bizarre salad one gets from time to time in a foreign country and a pizza that came with a bottle of oil, I tried not to brood, though I didn't entirely succeed. What would I do now that the thing I most wanted to do in this country of skiing and shopping was the very thing I could not do during the short window that I was here? I asked myself over and over again, in silent annoyance, regretting I'd come.

But a solo seat at a riverside sidewalk table has a way of settling things, even if the river is lined in concrete. As the sun sank behind the mountains, a magic light spread over the city. I drank another glass of wine and watched the people who passed by. Children toting backpacks from school. Women carrying bags of groceries for dinner. Couples linked hand-to-hand. Before long, I realized that I was charmed by Andorra la Vella, my mood and the disparaging descriptions I'd read in guidebooks be damned.

Besides: What else is there ever to do in life and in travel but make the best of it?

If I could not walk in the wilderness, I would walk in the city. So the next morning I set out rambling up and down the streets, marveling at the sheer number of stores in spite of my aversion to them, buttoning and then unbuttoning my sweater as the late summer sun duked it out with the cool edge of ever-present mountain air – Andorra la Vella is the highest capital in Europe, at 3,356 feet above sea level. I bought a watch for my husband and a copy of my own book in Catalan, which I spied, to my surprise and delight, in a bookstore window. As far as places to shop go, I found Andorra la Vella to be a rather pleasant one – far nicer than any American mall – and the city's historic district is downright lovely, full of cobbled streets and enchanting old buildings, some of which date back to the 11th century. Tiny boutiques and mysterious commemorative plaques spill onto an esplanade that features a long row of basketball hoops lined with flower boxes.

The next day, on my wanderings, I found my way to the enormous Caldea Thermal Spa, which sits like a space age glass church on the edge of the city center. Without knowing precisely what I was signing on for when I handed over my credit card, I was led to a section of the building called Inuu – the fancier, inner sanctum sister spa of Caldea, it turned out – where I stripped off my clothes, donned the robe I'd been given, and immediately became lost among a maze of futuristic doors and hallways. Fearing at every turn that I'd either wander into the men's dressing room or be abducted by health-conscious Martians, I finally happened into a sauna room of sorts where I interrupted an old German couple engaged in a passionate make-out session. They were kind enough to overcome our mutual mortification and guide me to an enormous thermal pool. I swam in its strangely cool waters before a member of the staff shuffled me off to a room where I was slathered in mud by a Russian woman and scrubbed with sugar then massaged to within an inch of my life while wearing a horribly unflattering one-size-fits-all disposable thong.

Afterwards, I sat on a bench at a playground near the spa, feeling tense and lonely rather than relaxed and blissed out. Watching the children on the swings, slides, and monkey bars made me miss my own kids – my daughter and son, who were then seven and nine. As I listened to the incomprehensible chatter of the parents and the universally recognizable laughter of the children, I got the feeling I sometimes get when traveling alone. Like I didn't know where I was or why I was there or what I'd been thinking to ever leave home. Like the only thing that would set me right was to keep moving. Like I really truly needed to go for a hike.

Even if the country was teeming with people set on shooting izards.

By mid-afternoon the next day I was in the village of Arinsal, seven miles and a world away from the capital city. I'd been drawn to Arinsal for its vast array of hiking possibilities, but especially for its proximity to Andorra's highest peak, Coma Pedrosa, a pyramid-shaped mountain that tops out at 9,665 feet. I got a room at a hotel near the gondola lift in the center of town, and chatted with the British expat who manages the place.

'Do you think I'll be shot if I go hiking?' I asked, and to my great relief she only looked at me quizzically and chuckled.

An hour later I walked a stony lane that ascends behind the hotel and leads to a grassy footpath that soon becomes the Cami de Percanela. I followed the trail without a map, but with a deep sense of wonder as I climbed above the village, watching the sun slant toward the high mountains that surrounded me. I walked for more than an hour, listening for gunshots. Hearing none.

Instead what I heard was myself. Here I was. Forty-five. Alive. Alone. Out there, I could feel those facts as if for the first time, each one slightly shocking. I'd outlived my mom. It made me feel old and young. I could feel my own life moving beyond hers and I could also feel how very much was ahead. I'd been traveling the world for work almost constantly for the previous few years, but out there on the trail I realized I hadn't really traveled at all. I'd gone places, but the purpose of going had been set for me – to do this or that and then rush home to my children as soon as possible, steeped in mom-guilt and murmuring apologies about having been away. In accepting the mystery birthday trip – in saying yes to Go – I'd let myself travel in a way I hadn't for years. In Andorra, at the very cusp of moving beyond my mother, I'd also returned to the woman who used to be a daughter.

I set out the next morning for Coma Pedrosa, again walking straight from my hotel along the road to the hiking trail. Within a half hour I'd entered the Comapedrosa Valley National Park, a place so beautiful it's impossible to overstate it. The alpine landscape of trees and meadows and lakes against the endless blue sky was so breathtaking I couldn't help but stop to look around every fifteen minutes – never mind I also needed to actually catch my breath because of the rigor of the trail. Up and up and up it went without mercy, at turns rocky and steep and at others winding beneath shady forests and over bubbling streams. An hour into the hike, my half-hearted and overly-optimistic goal of reaching the top and getting back before sunset – a nine-hour round-trip – faded into the pleasant challenge of hiking to the Refugi de Coma Pedrosa, a rustic stone lodge that offers meals and shelter to hikers and sits midway up the mountain near the picturesque Trout Lake.

When I limped into it in the late afternoon, weary but elated from my hike, the lodge was buzzing with a group of perhaps twenty hikers speaking French, each of them devouring the plates of thick bread slathered in olive oil and slices of cured meat that the staff set before them. In the usual Catalan/Spanish/English accompanied by pantomime that had become my own personal Andorran language, I asked the gray-haired woman who worked at the hut to bring me the same, along with a lemon Fanta.

There's really no better meal than one earned after hiking a hard trail. I sat alone eating in a mild ecstasy while eavesdropping on the French hikers. Though I hardly understood a word they were saying, we exchanged smiles and nods, all of us happy to be in this place together doing the same glorious thing as summer turned to autumn. After lunch, I retraced my steps, making the long hike back down the steep trail and into town, arriving tired and hungry and weather-beaten, grateful I'd not been mistaken for an izard, and even more grateful that I'd risked the chance that I might've been.

As the man in the tourist office had told me, you only live once, after all.

Rebirth
in Rome

Stanley Stewart

The first time I visited Rome I stayed in a rickety budget hotel just off the Piazza del Popolo. There were tall shuttered windows with a couple of cracked panes, a door with a decorative pediment that I am sure included cupids, a bathroom of sorts several floors down, a beautiful receptionist, and the sound of a saxophone drifting up from the corner of Via Angelo Brunetti in the evenings.

At night, when the saxophonist had gone home and the traffic finally ceased, I lay awake listening to the sound of the fountains in the piazza, thrilled to be in Rome. It was my first serious sojourn abroad, and the first foreign city that I would come to know well. Now, thirty years on, I have returned to Rome, just in time for one of life's great transitions.

On that first visit I sallied forth every morning on an old scooter someone had lent me to explore the city. I careened between ancient ruins and baroque sculptures and delicious meals, between Roman triumphal arches, the soft thighs of Bernini's Proserpina in the Galleria Borghese and divine croissants in a bar in Via Ripetta. I discovered – in those days everything was a discovery – Santa Maria in Trastevere, barnacled with age, its gold-hued interior freighted with incense and prayer. I made a pilgrimage to Velasquez's portrait of Innocent X in the Palazzo Doria Pamphilj and another to Sant'Anselmo on the Aventine Hill where Benedictine monks filled the Roman dusk with Gregorian chants. I climbed the steps of the Capitoline Hill at night to Michelangelo's exquisite piazza and the equestrian statue of Marcus Aurelius bathed in moonlight. I gazed down on the ruins of the Forum from the spot where Gibbon had conceived the idea of writing The Decline and Fall of the Roman Empire and where John Wilkes and his mistress, Gertrude Corradini, overcome by desire, disappeared behind some ruins while their guide distracted Gertrude's mother.

How long did I stay that first time – four or five months, I think, from a wintry November through to spring. I remember the chestnuts roasting on the corners of Piazza di Spagna and the Abruzzese shepherds in their fleece waistcoats in the streets at Christmas playing their bagpipes for coins. I remember the divine stationers, Vertecchi in Via Condotti, a temple for anyone who has ever put pen to paper. I remember mass at St Peter's on Christmas Eve, the massed ranks of choirs, the red cardinals, the elaborate flummery, the Pope, a distant figure like a tiny white puppet beneath Bernini's colossal *baldacchino*. I remember the plane trees overhanging the river, coming into leaf with fat sappy buds while their old roots cracked and lifted the pavements along the Lungotevere like buried bones rising to the surface. At night in my spartan room, listening to the sibilant sound of the fountains from the piazza, I read Moravia's Woman of Rome, a subject of new and fascinating interest.

At one point I managed to get arrested, always a great option for getting under the skin of a place. It was while I was musing on Marcus Aurelius and Gibbon on the empty Capitoline in the middle of the night. Rome still suffered from anxieties about the Red Brigade who some years earlier had kidnapped and murdered Aldo Moro.

I seemed to fit the profile of the foreign revolutionary – tattered maps of Rome, a notebook full of illegible scribblings, a jacket with a hole at the elbow. To an Italian, anyone so shabbily dressed had to be guilty of something; while I waited for the questioning down at the station, I could hear a couple of the policemen in the adjoining room bemoaning my terrible trousers. In the end there was no need of the thumbscrews; a brief interrogation, followed by a trip in a police car to the shabby residence off the Piazza del Popolo to retrieve my passport for purposes of identification, convinced the Carabinieri that I was a hapless innocent.

The run-in with the police rather scuppered any chances I might have had with the beautiful receptionist. Until that time, I had managed to exchange only five words with her – 'La mia chiave, per favore' – 'My key, please.' Her attitude hardened towards me; admittedly, it had only ever been warm in my imagination. She waited now every day for the happy news that I was checking out.

One of the lessons of Rome is the easy pleasure that Romans take in beauty. It helps of course that there is beauty at every turn, from a gorgeous archway in a side alley to the morning cappuccino, as handsome as it is delicious, from the paintings of Raphael to the colourful cashmere scarves – bright yellow, pale blues, rose pinks – that were the male fashion accessory of the season. In cafes and on streets corners, the phrase most commonly overheard from snippets of other conversations is not 'thank you' or 'excuse me' or 'I am sorry'. The most common phrase in Rome is 'che bella' – how beautiful – repeated so often it acts as a kind of Roman mantra.

In the years since that first visit, my travels have been promiscuous, and there have been many cities with which I have fallen in love. But the attachment to Rome survived. I had friends in the city, and life had a curious way of prodding me back towards the Tiber, so that Rome became a persistent presence, a touchstone. I was never long away from her.

Now, thirty years after that first visit, I had returned to Rome to live with my Italian partner. And I found myself again in the Piazza del Popolo, not as a visitor, but as a new resident. Again it is late at night, and the only sound in the square is the one I remember so clearly from that first visit – the whisper of water on stone, the sound of the fountains.

I had left the car near the Ponte Margherita and descended on foot into the wide bowl of the piazza. It was one of those delicious moments when the turning world seems to pause, when time is stilled. I sat on the rim of the central fountain where four lions spout thin fans of water like imperfect panes of glass. Above me was the obelisk quarried in Aswan on the banks of the Upper Nile, just over three thousand years ago.

I had just come from the birth of my daughter, my first child, born just over six hours ago. I would have liked to have been on hand to greet her arrival but in Rome the vexed issue of parking takes precedence over all else. While I ushered Irene into the clinic to a posse of waiting nurses, a queue of cars leant on their horns in the street. Half an hour later I was still looking for a parking space. Romans would have long since abandoned their cars in the middle of the street. But I had not been in Rome long enough, and still had naive concerns about bringing the district of Prati to a halt for several hours. Sometime, perhaps on my twentieth fruitless circuit of the Piazza dei Quiriti, Sophia arrived in the world.

When I finally made it back to the clinic, she was already in il nido, the nest, or nursery. Someone pointed me to a cot by the window. Looking down at her for the first time, I felt the world shudder to a halt.

In that first moment her face was like a misericord, not new but something very old, arcane, polished by centuries, as if she had arrived meaning to conform to her city, to Rome. She lay there bare-chested, the stub of her umbilicus pegged shut, her clenched fists hanging onto invisible ropes as she lowered herself into the world. While nurses padded to and fro across the room, oblivious to this miracle, I laid my hand over her scalp. Her head was warm, slightly flushed, her hair as fine as a spider's web. I bent my head, and laid my ear on her tiny chest to hear the sound of her heart, beating like a promise. I thought of birds, fallen to earth, their bones as light as air, the soft pulse in their breasts.

Sophia arrived like a revelation, capsizing all about her. I thought that I had not known a thing about love, about the helplessness of it, until this sudden moment. Sunlight streamed through the windows of the nursery onto my arms, onto her face.

When my parents died, I felt I bore them with me into decades they would never see. I remember emerging from the catharsis of my father's memorial service into an unreasonably bright afternoon, into a quiet street where cars slid past unperturbed, where people stopped to talk on corners of other things, feeling that I was holding his whole life in my arms, the whole intricate thing, that he handed it to me suddenly without a word before disappearing. And I did not know what to do with it, where to put it, until now.

Later, with Sophia and her mother asleep, I stole home in the middle of the night, to get some fresh clothes. And so I came back to Piazza del Popolo in the hollow of the night, the hour when they say souls escape, the hour when my mother had died, dreaming as always of Ireland, the hour when the sound of water seems to be the only sound in Rome. As I sat by the fountain, I was overcome by tears thinking of the new life across the city, the stranger asleep in her cot, her brow furrowed with her first dreams, her feet drawn up, treading air. Tears, especially tears of joy, are often inexplicable. These, perhaps, were prompted by the way this vivid present dredged so profoundly at some of the deepest currents of the past.

'The past is never dead,' William Faulkner said. 'It is not even past.' That the past persists so powerfully in our many presents is another of Rome's lessons. The city shows us time's fluidity – how porous is the frontier between past and present. At any moment, we are deep in other moments, other times. All the clutter of my own past was here with me on the rim of this fountain in the middle of the night in Rome.

In that moment my life changed, but Rome changed too. The city was suddenly central to my personal geography. It was the city of my daughter. She would grow up here. Rome was acquiring new meanings, and its old meanings acquired a new resonance. I splashed my face in the spray of water from one of the lion's mouths, a christening in the waters of the Acqua Vergine which had been pouring into Rome's fountains for two thousand years.

The following morning, back at the clinic, I bundled my sainted treasure with her little determined fists and her flushed cheeks in swaddling blankets and took her out into the Roman streets, into the world for the first time. In the corner cafe, strangers abandoned their coffees for a glimpse of her face so intent and so strangely thoughtful on this, the first morning of her life.

Their fluttering and complex hand gestures seemed to say many things – about the wonder of birth, about the heart-stopping recognition of life's renewal and persistence.

But each voice said only one thing. 'Che bella,' they said. 'Che bellissima.'

A Strange Place Called Home

Torre DeRoche

Australia looks browner and flatter than I remembered; it's a straw-coloured rug of grass dotted with hardy scrubs and unremarkable buildings. The lighting is violently harsh, as though it's beaming down through a giant magnifying glass that belongs to a freckled kid with buck-teeth and a fetish for frying small beings. Between the airport and the car, the air has sucked the moisture from my skin and eyeballs, and I find myself longing for the humidity and verdant foliage of the tropics.

My friend's voice rattles away in the driver's seat and I 'Ah-huh' and 'Oh really?' on cue to appear interested in her string of gossip about acquaintances whose faces I have long forgotten, whose stories I've stopped caring about. My excitement from the plane has staled, replaced by a dread in the pit of my gut over one sinking realisation: I don't belong here anymore.

'Something wrong?' my friend asks, taking her eyes off the road to study my expression with her all-knowing eyes.

I could never hide the truth from her, but still I attempt a lie. 'Just tired,' I say, not knowing how to articulate the grief of this homecoming without insulting her.

She accepts my lie with an unconvinced shrug and then turns her gaze back to the road, which cuts through tightly clustered housing estates featuring identical stucco walls and terracotta roofs. I keep blinking, hoping to bring back into focus images from the shanty towns of Asia: steam curling off boiling pots, woven baskets spilling with strange fruits, pregnant woman pegging sarongs to clotheslines, giant hogs foraging in the dirt alongside naked toddlers. 'Sabadee!' the kids would yell out to us, greeting us with fearless smiles and enthusiastic waves of their tiny hands.

I giggle at the thought.

'Something funny?' my friend asks.

'Oh, just a memory, ' I say. 'The little kids in Laos were so friendly. When we'd pass them in the street, they'd yell at the top of their lungs, "Sabadee! Sabadee!" which means "Hello! Hello!" If school had just gotten out, there'd be a chorus of greetings all around and our arms would get sore from waving back to all the kids. It was just so incredible to be welcomed like that by children.'

'Cool,' she says, and then – 'Hey, guess what? I had my bathroom renovated!'

'Wow,' I say. 'Tell me more.'

And then she does, sparing no details, and I 'Ah-huh' and 'Oh really?' on cue. Renovations, kids, full-time jobs, mortgages: these are the standard conversation topics of thirty-something women. In the years since I left, my friends have matured into responsible adults, but I'm stuck in another place entirely, more cozy in a chicken bus teetering on the edge of a Himalayan mountain than inside a conversation about renovations. If they are all grown-ups now, then what does that make me?

Beside the freeway, billboards advertise insurance for every possible pitfall, pushing their policies with messages so undermining that I'm shocked to have never noticed it before. Everything here is so orderly and sanitised. So clean. The air lacks the complex blend of offensive and delicious smells that I'm used to: that soupy perfume of rotting fruit, cooking spices, exhaust fumes, and raw sewage. The smell of Asia is something you want to crawl away from and into at the same time. Am I really nostalgic for the smell of raw sewage?

They say that travel changes you, but I never anticipated it would be like this.

I close my eyes and return to the sensation of the plane's turbulence that has lodged in my cell memory, longing for the excitement of being propelled at 565 miles per hour to somewhere foreign and untamed. But I must find a way to stay this time. My dad has been diagnosed with a terminal illness and so here I am, back in reality, back to my roots, even though this fact is now a dull concept that I have to keep repeating in my head like I'm learning phrases in a foreign language.

This is where I'm from.

This is what I've been craving to get back to all this time.

This is my home.

This is where I belong.

Dusk settles over Melbourne. A crisp breeze quenches the midsummer heat that's been trapped between skyscrapers and

Victorian townhouses all day. I sit by the French doors of a cafe, sipping a foamy cappuccino and observing the city, as day becomes night. Honking taxis, the shuffle of expensive shoes on pavement, a miasma of colognes...

The chaos of the city centre, where various cultures merge into an eclectic blend, is my comfort zone. During the months that have passed since the shock of returning, I've found peace with the fact that I'll probably never again have the same sense of belonging to one place that I used to. That's okay, though. I belong everywhere now.

Overhead, in the purpling sky, I see a plane hovering, waiting for its chance to land. I see myself from above, in this cafe, a tiny ant among skyscrapers. Anyone who has spent a significant amount of time travelling will have observed the bizarre aerial perspective of our civilisation. It's an alarming sight, because you realise that from above, lights flow through night streets in a hauntingly similar fashion to cells pumping through arteries. Rivers, too, pump blue water like fine branching capillary vessels.

Once you see that, you can't un-see it. You can't un-learn that we're just microscopic organisms within a huge energy system, always coming and going. Always moving. Nothing ever remains in one place. Belonging is an illusion.

I sip my coffee and smile at a pregnant Ethiopian woman who waddles past. I find myself lost in thoughts about her home, if she's happy here, whether or not she feels she belongs anywhere. One day, I decide, I'll go to her country so that I might know a little piece of her story. She catches my eye and smiles back.

Authors

Alexander McCall Smith is the author of the beloved, bestselling *No. 1 Ladies' Detective Agency* series, the *Isabel Dalhousie* series, the *Portuguese Irregular Verbs* series, the *44 Scotland Street* series, and the *Corduroy Mansions* series. He is also the author of numerous children's books. He is professor emeritus of medical law at the University of Edinburgh and has served with many national and international organizations concerned with bioethics. He was born in what is now known as Zimbabwe and taught law at the University of Botswana. He lives in Scotland. Visit his website at www.alexandermccallsmith.com.

Amanda Jones is an itinerant soul lucky enough to have ended up as a travel writer. She writes for magazines and newspapers globally. She is a New Zealander by birth, but now lives in the San Francisco Bay Area.

Amy Gigi Alexander is a writer of fiction, memoir and travel tales. She has won several awards for her travel writing. She's been to many places, but she's missed most of the important sights, since she prefers to spend her time in villages, slums, and huts. She lives in Northern California with her cat, who sits on her lap as she writes.

Ann Patchett is the author of six novels, *The Patron Saint of Liars, Taft, The Magician's Assistant, Bel Canto, Run*, and *State of Wonder*. She was the editor of *Best American Short Stories, 2006*, and has written three books of nonfiction, *Truth & Beauty, What Now?* and *This is the Story of a Happy Marriage*. She has been the recipient of numerous awards and fellowships, and her work has been translated into more than thirty languages. She is the co-owner of Parnassus Books in Nashville, Tennessee, where she lives with her husband, Karl VanDevender, and their dog, Sparky.

Anna Vodicka's essays have appeared in *Brevity*, *Guernica*, *The Iowa Review*, *Michigan Quarterly Review*, *Ninth Letter*, *Shenandoah*, and other literary magazines. In 2013, she won *The Missouri Review* audio contest for prose and her writing was shortlisted for Best American Essays and the Pushcart Prize. While her heart resides squarely in the lakes region of northern Wisconsin, she has lived on the East Coast and the West, in South America and Spain, and most recently, the island nation of Palau, in western Micronesia, where she is at work on her first book. You can find her at www.annavodicka.com.

Anthony Sattin is a journalist, broadcaster and the author of several highly acclaimed books of history and travel. He has been described as 'a cross between Indiana Jones and a John Buchan hero' and one of the key influences on travel writing today. Anthony's books include *The Gates of Africa*, the story of the 18th century search for Timbuktu, and *Lifting the Veil*, a history of travellers in Egypt from 1768 to 1956. *The Pharaoh's Shadow* looks at Egypt's surviving ancient culture, while *A Winter on the Nile* tells of parallel Nile journeys made by Florence Nightingale and Gustave Flaubert, and was chosen as a Book of the Year by the *Financial Times*, *Telegraph*, *Independent* and other publications. His latest book, *Young Lawrence*, looks at the five years T.E. Lawrence spent in the Middle East before World War I. His award-winning journalism on travel and books has appeared regularly in the *Sunday Times*, *Condé Nast Traveller* and publications around the world. He is a fellow of the Royal Geographical Society, contributing editor on *Condé Nast Traveller* and editorial advisor on *Geographical Magazine*.

Candace Rose Rardon is a writer and artist whose stories and sketches have appeared on sites such as BBC Travel, AOL Travel, World Hum, Gadling, and National Geographic's Intelligent Travel blog. A serendipitous invitation to move to London after her college graduation sparked a six-year love affair with the world – one that has taken her from a black pearl farm in the South Pacific, to a 2000-mile rickshaw run across India, to a remote village of nomadic sea gypsies in Thailand. Originally from the state of Virginia, Candace has also lived in England, New Zealand, and most recently, a cozy yurt on a rural island in Canada.

Cheryl Strayed is the author of the memoir *Wild*, the novel *Torch* and the essay collection *Tiny Beautiful Things*. Her writing has appeared in *The Best American Essays*, the *New York Times Magazine*, *Vogue*, *Salon*, the *Sun*, and elsewhere. Her books have been translated into more than thirty languages around the world. She lives in Portland, Oregon.

Colleen Kinder has written essays and articles for the *New Republic*, *Salon*, *National Geographic Traveler*, the *New York Times*, Gadling, the Atlantic.com, the *Wall Street Journal*, *Ninth Letter*, *A Public Space*, the *New York Times Magazine* and *Creative Nonfiction*. She is the author of *Delaying the Real World*, and the founder of *Off Assignment*. She currently teaches travel writing at Yale.

Dave Eggers is the author of several books, including most recently *The Circle* and *A Hologram for the King*. He is the founder of McSweeney's, an independent publishing company based in San Francisco that produces books, a quarterly journal of new writing (*McSweeney's Quarterly Concern*), and a monthly magazine, *The Believer*. McSweeney's also publishes *Voice of Witness*, a nonprofit book series that uses oral history to illuminate human rights crises around the world. Eggers is the co-founder of 826 National, a network of eight tutoring centers around the country. 'Song' will be included in Eggers' forthcoming book, a travel collection called *Visitants*; a version of the essay was first published in *Nowhere* magazine (nowheremag.com).

David Baldacci published his first novel, *Absolute Power*, in 1996. A film adaptation followed, with Clint Eastwood as its director and star. In total, David has written twenty-eight novels, all of which have been national and international bestsellers; several have been adapted for film and television. His novels have been translated into more than forty-five languages and sold in more than eighty countries; over 110 million copies are in print worldwide. David has also published four novels for children. As a passionate advocate for literacy, David's greatest philanthropic efforts are dedicated to his family's Wish You Well Foundation®. Established by David and his wife, Michelle, the Wish You Well Foundation supports family and adult literacy in the United States by fostering and promoting the development and expansion of literacy and educational programs; it has funded programs in more than forty-five states. In 2008 the Foundation partnered with Feeding America to launch Feeding Body & Mind, a program to address the connection between literacy, poverty and hunger. Through Feeding Body & Mind, more than one million new and gently used books have been collected and distributed through food banks to families in need. David and his family live in Virginia.

A native San Franciscan, *David Downie* has also lived in New York City, Providence, Rome and Milan. He moved to Paris in the mid-1980s and now divides his time between France and Italy. His travel, food and arts features have appeared in over fifty leading print publications worldwide. Downie is co-owner, with Alison Harris, of Paris, Paris Tours, which offers custom walking tours of Paris, Burgundy, Rome and the Italian Riviera. The author of two thrillers, including *Paris City of Night*, Downie has also written a dozen nonfiction books, among them the classic, critically acclaimed collection of travel essays *Paris, Paris: Journey into* the City of Light, and the bestselling Paris to the Pyrenees: A Skeptic Pilgrim Walks the Way of Saint James. His new book, to be published in spring 2015, is A Passion for Paris: Romanticism and Romance in the City of Light. Downie's Paris Timeline and Food Wine Rome travel apps are available from iTunes. His websites and blogs can be found at www.davidddownie.com, www.parisparistours.com, http://wanderingliguria.com, and http://wanderingfrance.com/blog/paris.

Fiona Kidman lives in Wellington, New Zealand. Her house is on a high cliff overlooking Cook Strait, the sea that divides the North and South Islands. She is the author of some thirty books, mostly fiction, poetry, and memoir. Her most recent novel, The Infinite Air, was based on the life of the aviator Jean Batten. The recipient of several literary prizes, she has also been honoured with a damehood and the OBE in New Zealand, and with the Légion d'Honneur and the Chevalier dans l'Ordre des Arts et des Lettres in France.

Jan Morris' latest (and, she says, last) book is Ciao, Carpaccio!, a short caprice about the art of the 15th-century Venetian painter Vittore Carpaccio. She is Welsh and lives in Wales, and her previous books have included 40-odd works of travel, history, memoir, biography, and invention.

Jane Smiley has been a member of the American Academy of Arts and Letters since 1987. Her novel A Thousand Acres won the Pulitzer Prize and the National Book Critics Circle Award in 1992; her novel The All True Travels and Adventures of Lidie Newton won the 1999 Spur Award for Best Novel of the West. Her novel Horse Heaven was short-listed for the Orange Prize in 2002, and her novel Private Life was chosen as one of the best books of 2010 by The Atlantic, The New Yorker, and The Washington Post. She has written several works of non-fiction, including Thirteen Ways of Looking at the Novel and The Man Who Invented the Computer. She has also published five volumes of a horse series for young adults, *The Horses of Oak Valley Ranch*. Her new novel is *Some Luck*.

Oakland-based *Jeff Greenwald* is the author of six books, including *The Size of the World* (for which he created the first travel blog), *Scratching the Surface* and *Snake Lake*, a memoir set in Nepal during the 1990 democracy revolution. The 25th anniversary edition of his *Shopping for Buddhas* was released earlier this year. Jeff also serves as Executive Director of EthicalTraveler.org, a global alliance of travelers dedicated to human rights and environmental protection. His improvised solo show, Strange Travel Suggestions, premiered in San Francisco in 2003 and continues to draw critical acclaim.

Jenna Scatena is an adventure junkie. When she's not climbing the tallest volcano in Bali or road-tripping through Mexico, she disguises herself as a magazine writer and editor in San Francisco. Her work has appeared in *AFAR*, *Travel + Leisure*, *Sunset*, *Via*, *AlterNet.com*, *The Best Women's Travel Writing*, and *San Francisco* magazine, where she was formerly an editor. She leads journalism workshops for college students at UC Berkeley, UCLA, and Stanford, through the Center for American Progress, and received her B.A. in Nonfiction Writing from Ithaca College. When not surveying distant corners of the globe, she can be found exploring the nooks and crannies of San Francisco on her red scooter. Her website is jennascatena.com.

Jim Benning co-founded the online travel magazine World Hum. His writing has appeared in *Outside*, *Men's Journal*, the *Washington Post* and the *Los Angeles Times*. He lives in Los Angeles, California.

John Berendt is the author of *Midnight in the Garden of Good and Evil*, a finalist for the 1995 Pulitzer Prize in General Nonfiction. He met Fiora Gandolfi while living in Venice from 1996-2003, researching his second book, *The City of Falling Angels*. In prior years he was the editor of *New York* magazine, an editor and columnist for *Esquire*, and a writer-producer for Dick Cavett and David Frost. A graduate of Harvard, he was an editor of the *Harvard Lampoon*.

Kerre McIvor (née Woodham) has been the nighttime talk host on New Zealand's NewsTalk ZB for 17 years. She is a newspaper and magazine columnist, a books ambassador for the Paper Plus franchise and has written three books of her own. She is married to Tom, is the mother of Kate and is a most reluctant marathon runner.

Larry Habegger is a writer, editor, journalist, and teacher who has been covering the world since his international travels began in the 1970s. As a freelance writer for three decades and syndicated columnist since 1985, his work has appeared in many major newspapers and magazines, including the *Los Angeles Times, Chicago Tribune, Travel & Leisure*, and *Outside*. In 1993 he co-founded the award-winning Travelers' Tales Books with James and Tim O'Reilly, where he has helped develop the company's publishing program and worked on all of its 100-plus books. Larry is an inspiring writing teacher and coach, emphasizing the craft and art of the personal essay, and he is a mainstay at the annual Book Passage Travel Writers and Photographers Conference in Marin County, California. He is also the founder and leader of the writers' group Townsend 11; a founder of The Prose Doctors, an editors' consortium; editor of the annual magazine *The Travel Guide to California*; editor-in-chief of Triporati.com, a destination discovery site; and executive editor of Tales To Go, a subscription publication of travel narratives for mobile devices.

Lavinia Spalding is series editor of *The Best Women's Travel Writing* and author of two books: *Writing Away: A Creative Guide to Awakening the Journal-Writing Traveler*, and *With a Measure of Grace: The Story and Recipes of a Small Town Restaurant*. She also wrote the introduction to the reissued e-book edition of Edith Wharton's classic travelogue, *A Motor-Flight Through France*. Lavinia's work has appeared in many print and online publications, including *Yoga Journal*, *Sunset*, the *San Francisco Chronicle*, *San Francisco*, *The Guardian*, *Tin House*, *Post Road*, *Gadling*, *Overnight Buses*, and *The Best Travel Writing*. She lives in San Francisco, where she's a resident of the Writers' Grotto and co-founder of the award-winning monthly travel reading series *Weekday Wanderlust*.

Lloyd Jones is the author of *Biografi* and the novels *Mr Pip*, winner of the Commonwealth Writers' Prize and short-listed for the Man Booker Prize; *Hand Me Down World*, short-listed for the Berlin International Prize; and *The Book of Fame*. His most recent title, *A History of Silence*, is a memoir. He lives in New Zealand.

Marina Lewycka was born of Ukrainian parents in a refugee camp in Kiel, Germany, after World War II, and grew up in England in Sussex, Doncaster, Gainsborough, and Witney. She now lives in Sheffield. Her first novel, *A Short History of Tractors in Ukrainian*, was published in 2005 when she was 58 years old, and went on to sell a million copies in thirty-five languages. It was short-listed for the 2005 Orange Prize for Fiction, long-listed for the Man Booker prize, and won the Saga Award for Wit and the Bollinger Everyman Wodehouse Prize for Comic Fiction. Her second novel, *Two Caravans* (2007) (published in the US as *Strawberry Fields*), was short-listed for the George Orwell prize for political writing. *We Are All Made of Glue* was published in 2009. Her most recent novel, *Various Pets Alive and Dead*, published in 2012, brings together hippies, hamsters, and the financial crisis. Her short stories have been broadcast on BBC radio, and her articles have appeared in *the Guardian, Independent, Sunday Telegraph* and *Financial Times*. She is now working on her fifth novel.

Mary Karr writes poetry and nonfiction. Her three memoirs, *The Liars' Club*, *Cherry*, and *Lit*, were all New York Times bestsellers. She's the Peck Professor of Literature at Syracuse University.

Pico Iyer began his traveling life at birth – as the son of Indian parents in Oxford, England – and continued it when he began flying over the North Pole to go to school, three times a year, from the age of nine. Since the boyhood misadventures recounted in this piece, he's returned often to Brazil and Bolivia and Colombia and the other landmarks of his teens, his blunders growing more experienced every time. Accounts of his travels have appeared in such books as *Video Night in Kathmandu*, *The Lady and the Monk*, *The Global Soul* and, most recently, *The Man Within My Head*.

Richard Ford is the author of 11 books of fiction, most notably *Canada*, which won the Prix Femina Etrangere in 2013, and *Independence Day*, which won the Pulitzer Prize in 1996. He's the author of many, widely-anthologized stories and essays, and writes frequently for newspapers in Europe, including the *Frankfurter Algemeine Zeitung*, *La Nouvelle Observateur* and *La Reppublica*. He lives in Boothbay, Maine, with his wife, Kristina Ford.

Simon Winchester began his career as a geologist in East Africa after leaving Oxford in 1966, but soon migrated to writing – first as a journalist and foreign correspondent for the *Guardian* and the *Sunday Times*, and later as a full-time non-fiction author. He has so far written twenty-seven books about a wide variety of topics, from Victorian lexicography to plate tectonics, and from Alice in Wonderland to the history of Chinese science. All of his books since he left Hong Kong in 1997 have been *New York Times* bestsellers. He was awarded an OBE by HM The Queen in 2006. He became an American citizen in 2011 and lives on a small apple farm in the Berkshire Hills of western Massachusetts, with a bolt-hole in Manhattan. With his wife, Setsuko, he raises bees and chickens and makes cider. He likes woodworking, railway trains and stamp collecting, and in 2010 founded the local village newspaper.

Sloane Crosley is the *New York Times* bestselling author of
I Was Told There'd Be Cake, *How Did You Get This Number*
and the e-book, *Up the Down Volcano*. She edited *The Best
American Travel Writing 2011* and is a frequent contributor to
NPR, *The New York Times* and *GQ* magazine. Her first novel, *The
Clasp*, will be out in 2015.

Stanley Stewart is the author of three highly acclaimed travel
books, *Old Serpent Nile*, *Frontiers of Heaven* and *In the Empire
of Genghis Khan*. The last two were both winners of the Thomas
Cook Travel Book Award, making Stewart the only writer to have
twice won this prestigious award. He is a contributing editor of
Condé Nast Traveller, and a long-standing contributor to both
the travel and book pages of the *Sunday Times*. He has also
written for the *Guardian*, the *Daily Telegraph* and the *Financial
Times* in the UK, as well as for *National Geographic Traveler*
in the US. His travel stories have frequently been included in
anthologies on both sides of the Atlantic. When not travelling,
he divides his time between Rome and Dorset in the UK.

Suzanne Joinson's debut novel, *A Lady Cyclist's Guide to
Kashgar*, was published in 2012 by Bloomsbury. It was long-
listed for the International IMPAC Dublin Literary Award and
translated into 16 languages. Suzanne won the New Writing
Ventures award for Creative Non-Fiction in 2008, and writes
regularly for a range of publications. She is currently working on
her second novel.

Tim Cahill is a founding editor of *Outside* magazine. He is the
author of nine books and co-author of three documentary IMAX
films, two of which were nominated for Academy Awards. He
lives in Montana.

A trek across Asia on the 'hippie trail' of the early 1970s led
Tony Wheeler to write the very first Lonely Planet guide and
the *New York Times* to describe him as 'the trailblazing patron

saint of the world's backpackers and adventure travelers.' The co-founder of Lonely Planet with his wife, Maureen, Tony worked on numerous Lonely Planet titles, including the award-winning India guide, the best-selling Australia guide and the pictorial essays *Chasing Rickshaws* and *Rice Trails*. His most recent book, *Dark Lands*, is an eight-country follow-up to *Bad Lands*, his journey through George W Bush's 'Axis of Evil' and assorted other troubled countries.

Torre DeRoche is an Australian native and self-proclaimed fearful adventurer, who, despite her many phobias, has explored the Pacific on a sailboat, toured Thailand by motorbike, hiked in the Himalayas and lived a year in a beachside Thai bungalow. Her travel writing has appeared in the *Atlantic*, the *Guardian*, *Open Skies* and the *Sydney Morning Herald*, and her first book, *Love with a Chance of Drowning*, is currently being adapted into a film. When she's not at home in Melbourne, Torre is at large in the world hunting down experiences and stories worth telling. Her words and pictures can be found on her blog www.fearfuladventurer.com.

Virginia Abbott has been on the move since she was a young child. By the time she was seven years old, she had lived in Uruguay, New Zealand and Puerto Rico. She and her family eventually settled in San Francisco, where she was raised. Her early exposure to travel instilled in her a restless desire to discover the world, which, as an adult, has driven her to places as remote as Mozambique, Easter Island and the Puna of northwest Argentina. In her professional life, Virginia has worked as a lawyer, in immigration and criminal law in the United States and international judicial reform in Colombia and the Republic of Georgia. In her free time, she is an avid writer, photographer and croissant-baker.

Also from Lonely Planet

Tony Wheeler's Dark Lands
Tony Wheeler goes deeper into the world's darkest corners to explore a rogue's gallery of troubled nations. Join him to find out if there's a happy-ever after in these tales from the dark side.

Lights, Camera... Travel!
Editor Andrew McCarthy asks some of the most widely travelled people in the film industry to share their own personal, inspiring and funny stories from their time on the road.

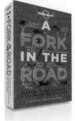

A Fork in the Road
Award-winning editor James Oseland invites you to a 34-course banquet of original stories from food-obsessed writers and chefs in this James Beard Awards-nominated collection.

Better Than Fiction
A collection of original travel stories told by some of the world's best novelists, including Isabel Allende, Peter Matthiessen, Alexander McCall Smith and DBC Pierre.

shop.lonelyplanet.com